When Islam and Democracy Meet:
Muslims in Europe and in the United States

When Islam and Democracy Meet: Muslims in Europe and in the United States

Jocelyne Cesari

palgrave
macmillan

First published in 2004 by
PALGRAVE MACMILLAN™
175 Fifth Avenue, New York, N.Y. 10010 and
Houndmills, Basingstoke, Hampshire, England RG21 6XS
Companies and representatives throughout the world.

PALGRAVE MACMILLAN is the global academic imprint of the Palgrave Macmillan division of St. Martin's Press, LLC and of Palgrave Macmillan Ltd. Macmillan® is a registered trademark in the United States, United Kingdom and other countries. Palgrave is a registered trademark in the European Union and other countries.

ISBN 0-312-29401-8

Library of Congress Cataloging-in-Publication Data

Cesari, Jocelyne.
    When Islam and democracy meet : Muslims in Europe and in the United States / Jocelyne Cesari.
        p. cm.
    Includes bibliographical references and index.
    ISBN 0-312-29401-8
        1. Muslims—Europe. 2. Islam—Europe. 3. Muslims—United States.
    4. Islam—United States. 5. Europe—Relations—Islamic countries.
    6. Islamic countries—Relations—Europe. 7. United States—Relations—
    Islamic countries. 8. Islamic countries—Relations—United States.
    I. Title.

D1056.2.M87C47 2004
305.6'97'0944—dc22   2004044763

A catalogue record for this book is available from the British Library.

Design by Newgen Imaging Systems (P) Ltd., Chennai, India.

First edition: December 2004

10 9 8 7 6 5 4 3 2 1

Printed in the United States of America.

To Jeffrey and Izzy

Contents

viii • Contents

Acknowledgments

Many people have contributed to the research for this book. I would like to thank all the Muslim leaders and intellectuals in Europe and the U.S. that have made this study possible by giving me their expertise, time, passion, and feelings to help me understand what is to be a Muslim in the West. I am particularly grateful to Fouad Allaoui, Abdellatif Cristillo, Talal Eid, Abdelwahab El-Affendi, Hakim El Gissassi, Hassan Hathout, Dilwar Hussein, Ahmed Jaballah, Sherman Jackson, Larbi Kechat, Ural and Altay Manço, Salam Al-Marayati, Precious Mohammed, Ingrid Mattson, Mohamed Nimer, Suleyman Nyang, Fathi Osman, Tariq Ramadan, Louay Safi, Muzammil H. Siddiqi, and Amina Wadud. I am also grateful to all the Muslim men and women who shared their faith and spiritual life with me during these years.

In Europe, I am particularly grateful to CNRS, and especially to the GSRL Institute and their successive directors, Jean Bauberot and Jean-Paul Willaime, for their continuous support. Thanks also to my colleagues from the Network of Comparative Research on Islam and Muslims in Europe for all the meetings and exchanges we had on our common research interests. I am also grateful to my French mentors: Bertrand Badie, Jean Leca and Remy Leveau.

In America, I would like to thank Connie Buchanan at the Ford Foundation, and Lisa Anderson at the School of International and Public Affairs, and the Middle East Institute at Columbia University for allowing me to be part of their research program on Muslims in New York City. I am particularly grateful to Cemal Kafadar and Leila Parsons, Director and Associate Director at the Center for Middle Eastern Studies at Harvard University who has hosted me for so many years and given me the opportunity to expand my knowledge on Islam in America by organizing the "Islam in the West" seminar. I would also like to thank my friend

Susan Miller, former Associate Director of the Center for Middle Eastern Studies, who has made many things possible in my life. I am also deeply grateful to Bill Graham, Dean of the Divinity School, for his constant support and intellectual guidance for the project "Islam in the West" during these many years. Many thanks also to Peter Hall, Director of the Center for European Studies, for having agreed to help with the seminar from the beginning and for being open to the idea of a comparison between Europe and the United States. Thanks are also due to Frank Vogel and Peri Bearman of the Islamic Legal Studies Program at the Law School for their help in preparing this seminar.

I am also grateful to all my other mentors and models at Harvard, who gave me continuous support and feedback on the project "Islam in the West" in its different stages, and from whom I learned so much: Leila Ahmed, Ali Asani, Steven Caton, Diana Eck, Stanley Hoffmann, Roy Mottahedeh, Nathan Glazer, Roger Owen, Laurence Sullivan, and Werner Sollors. All of them, particularly Ali Asani, Steven Caton, and Roy Mottahedeh, provided generous and effective help in developing the program for Islam in the West.

I am also grateful to my friends and colleagues from other institutions: Jose Casanova, Josh Dewind, John Esposito, Yvonne Haddad, Martin Heisler, Glenda Rosenthal, Jane Smith, Martin Schain, and Ari Zolberg.

I express my special gratitude to all my research assistants during all these years, in and particular to: Andrea Balan, Maryam Hassimi, Louis Hourmant, and Hussein Rashid.

Special thanks to Erica Weitzman for help in editing and for translation into English.

INTRODUCTION

From Clash to Encounter

I t's graduation day at Harvard University, or "Commencement," as they call it here. The mood of the day—which marks the end of an era for each student and the beginning of a new one—is always one of great solemnity. On this particular sunny day of July 6, 2002, the families of the graduates have gathered in the Yard, that mythical square bit of greenery that makes up the heart of the University.

Zayed Yasin, a major in Biology and Pre-med, stands and walks toward the large tent to deliver one of the commencement speeches, a privilege reserved for only a few. The message he proposes to deliver to the assembled crowd: "Faith and Citizenship: My American Jihad." In spite of protests, a petition signed by 1,300 people, and pressure exerted on the ceremony's organizing committee to read the speech in advance, Zayed is there. The word *jihad* has been struck from the title, but the content of the speech has been neither toned down nor censored. The words are ones of reconciliation and appeasement, and their meaning is clear: it is possible to be both an active Muslim and an American citizen without experiencing a conflict of values.

Later, I take the airplane at Logan airport—under heightened security since September 11. My passport is checked by a young woman wearing *hijab*, alone in the middle of her other colleagues, clean-shaven men and women without veils.

In Paris, Woissila and Ilham organized a demonstration on December 21, 2003, to protest a bill that proposed to outlaw all "ostentatious" forms of religious expression in the public schools. More than 3,000 people participated in the demonstration. On January 17, another rally, this time organized by the French Muslim Party, attracted over 11,000 protesters. "We must politically terrorize those who insult us," goes the slogan of Mohamed Latrèche, president of the party.

These are the contrasting images of Islam on the two sides of the Atlantic: one, American, conciliatory even in the damaged environment of post–September 11; the other, European, more conflictual and hostile. These two images reflect not only a difference in the styles and attitudes of Muslims in the various countries, but, also and especially, a difference in the societies that are in the process of integrating them. Of course, difficulties certainly exist on the North American continent as well. Who could deny the atmosphere of extreme suspicion brought on by the "War on Terror," which has resulted in an explosion of discriminatory acts against the daily observance of Islam? And in Europe, positive signs are beginning to emerge with the ascent of new Muslim political and intellectual leaders on both the local and the national levels. What is common to both continents is the influence of international politics on the domestic conditions of Muslim minorities. In other words, there is a widespread tendency to conflate Islam as an international political force with the ordinary Muslims living as a minority population in the countries of the West. This conflation has consequences not only for the minority condition of Muslims themselves, but also for current scholarship on the European and American manifestations of Islam.

Western Perceptions of Islam: The Logic of War

The simultaneous visibility of Islam on both sides of the Atlantic encounters equal hostility from the societies that host it, albeit for different demographic and historical reasons. Islam is seen as both the enemy outside and the enemy within. Long before the destruction of the World Trade Center towers and the attack on the Pentagon of September 11, 2001, political Islam above all else was feared from Muslim society.

The media presents a one-sided view of Islam that exploits the ambiguities of images and terminology, encouraging the stereotypical connections between Islam, violence, and fanaticism. These stereotypes obscure all other aspects of the Muslim world, and the ordinary citizen whose knowledge is limited to the 6 o'clock news has only a dim understanding of events in Algeria, Egypt, Iran, or Afghanistan. In thinking of Islam and the Islamic world, this citizen feels only fear, particularly insofar as the different shades of religious and political belief are treated as one homogenous entity. It is hardly surprising, then, that when these same citizens are asked—as they were in the United States in 1994—if they consider Islamic resurgence to be a danger, 61 percent say yes. For the greater part of the general American public, Islamic revivalism is, quite simply, a synonym for global terrorism. In Europe, the fear of Islam takes similar forms: in a 1991 survey, 51 percent of people in France stated that the greatest danger for France came from the Global South. Iraq, Iran, Libya, and Algeria were cited as the four countries most feared, specifically due to their Muslim character.[1]

Certainly, a series of events over the past 20 years, each one more "explosive" than the last, have provided indelible images of all the militant versions of Islam: the Iranian Revolution and the taking of hostages at the American Embassy, the assassination of Anwar al-Sadat, the Lebanese hostages, the Rushdie affair, the crisis in Algeria, the conflict in Afghanistan. Islam, now perceived as a significant risk factor in international relations, has taken the place of Communism as the most pressing global threat. In the language used not only by the Pentagon, but also by NATO, certain countries or regions "of an Islamic character"—whether this refers to Iran or the Sudan—find themselves at the top of the list of those labeled as "terrorist" by the American administration.

Confronted with this situation, scholarly research on Islam (particularly in Europe) has not always been successful in escaping the trap of presenting Islam and Muslims as a special case. The crucial question for scholars of Islam, which recent events have done nothing to change, is that of Muslim integration in European societies. Integration here means not only socioeconomic adaptation, but also acculturation to mainstream culture and to secularization. That is, is Muslim integration comparable to the process other immigrants have undergone, or does the fact of being Muslim indeed constitute some kind of extraordinary situation?[2]

This question, which underlies almost all European research on Islam, has been exaggerated and to a certain degree biased by various political agendas. In Europe, political interest in Islamic integration has existed since the 1980s. This interest is due to the influence of certain Islamic political movements in neighboring Islamic countries—such as the Islamic Salvation Front (FIS), based in Algeria, or the AKP (Justice and Development Party) in Turkey (a reincarnation of the Refah Party, banned in 1998)—not to mention the close ties between certain European countries and Islamic nations such as Algeria, Morocco, and Turkey, as a result of colonial and postcolonial history. We should note that the term "Islamophobia" emerged as early as 1997, during the discussions in Britain on the topic of anti-Muslim discrimination.[3] This fact should indicate that the process of victimization, which affects all European Muslims, was already well underway long before September 11, 2001.[4] The practical consequence of this is that most of the works on Islam published in Europe merely attempt to deconstruct the misrepresentations and false notions that rule over the discriminatory practices against Islam and Muslims.

In the United States, on the other hand, political and media interest in Islam is almost entirely an after-effect of September 11—which, if the European precedent is any indication, will undoubtedly influence American research on Islam in the decade to come. Although religion is not necessarily a taboo subject for American scholarship, American research on Muslims has, thus far, primarily taken an ethnographic approach. The broad ethnic diversity of American Muslims has essentially favored the production of works focusing on local ethnic communities, with some—such as Black Muslims or the Arab community of Detroit—more frequently studied than others. Despite several pioneering works,[5] a thorough examination of the diversity of Islamic religious practices and methods of adaptation to American society, via the systematic comparison of different ethnic groups, remains to be written.

Nevertheless, the extremely tense political climate that has surrounded the question of Islam since September 11, 2001, has in fact brought European and American research closer together. Islamophobia continues to remain strong in Europe, and is expressed in public with increasing frequency. During the 1990s in France, anti-Islamic statements were almost exclusively the prerogative of the far right. Today, however, intellectuals, journalists, writers, and artists unashamedly express their aversion to Islam.[6] In an interview in the September 2001 issue of the magazine *Lire*, the writer Michel Houellebecq stated,: "Islam is definitely the most f. . .p of all the religions." Oriana Fallaci's *La rage et l'orgueil* (*Rage and Pride*),[7] which sold more than a million copies in Italy and France, is a collection of insults aimed at Islam and Muslims that resulted in the author being prosecuted for inciting racial hatred in October 2003. That same year, on October 24, the founder of the newspaper *Le Point* declared himself an Islamolophobe, calling the Islamic religion an "inanity of various archaicisms."[8] Similarly, in the United States, insults against Muslims or against Islam continue to pour forth, even if the term "Islamophobia" is itself never spoken. On April 23, 2004, a Boston radio announcer even called for all Muslims to be killed. Since September 11, 2001, Evangelical leaders have produced scores of pronouncements and publications attacking the idea of any coexistence with either Islam or Muslims. This same aversion can be found at the highest levels of government, in statements by the attorney general and by high-ranking military officers.[9]

Avoiding the Essentialist Trap

Such anti-Islamic discourse has the additional affect of hiding the complexities of change and acculturation that bear not only on Muslims but also on the cultural and political institutions of Europe and the United States. It utterly fails to take into account the fluid and contradictory reality of Islam's integration into Western societies.

Existing European and American scholarship on Muslims often amounts to little more than a description of Muslims' modes of adaptation to their new context,[10] accompanied by a critique of the general atmosphere of Islamophobia.[11] Certainly, a critique of domination is an important step in explaining the condition of Muslims in the West. But such an approach is insufficient; one must also examine the instances and places of reciprocal influence between the cultural constructs of the European and Muslim worlds. This mutual influence creates a transcultural space in which theories of opposition can give way to a more subtle analysis. As Salvatore and Hofert have pointed out,[12] both Western religion and the Western conception of modernity have been deeply influenced by the transcultural space between Europe and the Middle East, even during eras in which the Western powers ruled over the Muslim world. The idea of Western culture that emerged with the birth of modernity corresponds to a specific political and cultural situation, in which the West came to define itself in opposition to the Ottoman Empire. The crystallizing of this identity *vis-à-vis* the Muslim Other is frequently found in literature from the sixteenth century onward, for example, in the writings of the Renaissance Orientalist Guillaume Postel, often considered the originator of the dialogue between Islam and Christianity.

This book attempts to examine Muslim immigration to Europe and North America as the foundational moment of a new transcultural space, which still remains to be analyzed. This transcultural moment takes place within the context of globalization, this particular period characterized by the mobility of cultures and religions. Any understanding of the Muslim minority in the West must, therefore, take the phenomenon of global Islam into account as well. Once again, the risk is of taking Islam out of context, reducing it to a series of essentialized symbols and principles. In order to break through the iron cage of stereotypical Islamic images and representations, then, one must consider discursive practices of religion in general, and of Islam in particular. No religion or culture can be taken as a given. Instead of trying to discover what constitutes the essential quality of Islam, one must examine the social and historical contexts within which Muslims create their discourse on what is important or unimportant in Islam, in *their* Islam.

As Talal Asad notes, tradition is the conglomeration of discursive practices that allow believers to determine what is correct and meaningful for a given time.[13] Avoiding essentializing descriptions means not to assume that meaning is constructed as a unified system, from the international to the national and local level. Islam, then, should be considered as a conglomeration of discursive practices, situated within the democracies of the West. These discursive practices are not only debates about the content of Islamic observance, but also about what it means to observe Islam in the first place. The act of going to the mosque to pray, the choice of whether to eat *halal* or drink wine, to wear the *hijab* or a miniskirt, all have to do with Islamic discourse every bit as much as the discussions taking place in books, in conferences, and on websites. It is necessary to examine how the production of meaning and cultural symbols intersect among different levels of communication and action—in local, national, and international contexts—and to refuse to define these levels *a priori*.

In order to avoid the trap of essentializing either Islam or Muslims, several considerations must be taken into account. First, this study avoids any sort of unilateral approach that confines itself only to the examination of religious or cultural changes among Muslims. Instead, this study explores the *mutual* transformation that is currently changing both Islam and the Western societies with which it interacts. To this end, Part I of this book examines how the nationalism and secularism of Western societies are transformed by Muslim presence, at the same time as these new political and cultural circumstances are transforming Muslims' Islamic practice into a individualized and less public act of faith (chapters 2 and 3). The secularization of Islam is seen in the transformation of individual religious observance, as well as the acceptance—by the vast silent majority—of the separation between public and private space respective to each society. In some European countries, this secularization also manifests itself in the creation of Islamic organizations—often associated with or even established by the government, as in Belgium and France—designed to represent Islam in the public arena (chapter 4).

Through their words as well as their actions, Muslims in the West contribute to the imaginary of contemporary Islam. As Arjun Appadurai has pointed out, the imagination is now itself a social and cultural force.[14] Participation in the Islamic imaginary is given concrete expression in a variety of disparate religious practices and mobilizations, which are examined in detail in Part II of this book ("The Imagined Community"). The most visible of these practices have to do with participation in radical or proselytizing transnational movements such as Salafi or Wahhabi Islam. These groups promote a defensive or reactive identity, sometimes giving rise to a veritable theology of hate (see chapter 5, "The Absolutized Community"). On the opposite end of the spectrum are practices such as the production/ consumption of Islam on the Internet, practices that signal an acceptance of modernity and which are sometimes, though not always, accompanied by real innovations and new syncretic forms of religion. Part III of this study examines how the encounter with democratic and secularized culture has brought certain long-standing crises within the Muslim world, particularly the crisis of religious authority, into sharp relief, at the same time encouraging the development of religious innovations (see chapter 7, "Bureaucratic and Parochial Leaders"). The Muslims of the diaspora are also in the process of revisiting certain concepts such as democracy, secularization, and human rights, and are questioning many interpretations of Islamic tradition. The third section discusses this phenomenon in terms of Islam's discourse on women, non-Muslims, and apostasy (see chapter 9, "The Reformation of Islamic Thought").

The research for this study comes from several different sources. First, from surveys that we conducted in Europe and the United States during the years 1999–2003. Second, from interviews with Muslim men and women of various cultures and ethnicities, heads of religious and secular organizations, and religious leaders who allowed us to record their development, their struggles, and their hopes in cities such as Paris, Brussels, London, New York, Los Angeles, and Chicago. We have also been able to observe the daily life of Muslim communities in Marseille, New York, and Boston. Finally, this study has drawn on existing research on different aspects of the lives of Muslim communities in Europe and the United States, including scholarly research, official government, or administrative reports, and studies conducted by Islamic organizations, particularly in the United States.

The situation of contemporary Muslims who live as minorities in democratic and secular societies constitutes a kind of putting into practice—a "case study"—of all the theoretical and conceptual debates about democracy that have troubled the Muslim world for centuries. Moreover, the new context in which Muslims find themselves has resulted in an unprecedented and dramatic series of changes within Islam, in terms of both ritual practice and intellectual reflection. Finally, the situation of Muslims in Europe and the United States should be studied because, this evolution does not happen in isolation. It also has dramatic consequences for the ideas and concepts currently circulating in the Muslim world. The Muslim world's reaction, in 2004, to the French proposal to outlaw religious symbols, is a perfect example of the phenomenon of global Islam. In short, our study hopes to demonstrate how the Americanization/Europeanization of Islam cannot be dissociated from the space-time of global Islam, and the political crises that go along with it.

CHAPTER 1

The Numbers Debate

Muslims are the largest religious minority in Western Europe. Today there are more than 11/12 million Muslims living in the major countries of the European Union, and Muslims constitute almost 3 percent of the total population in Europe.[1]

Six countries stand out in particular for the high number of Muslims who call them home: France, Germany, Great Britain, the Netherlands, and Greece. In each of these countries, anywhere from 4 to 7 percent of the current population is Muslim. With the exception of Greece, these countries experienced massive influxes of immigrant manual laborers during the 1960s. In Sweden, Denmark, and Norway, Muslims constitute about 1 percent of the total population. And in the south, Italy and Spain—which currently have more or less the same ratio of Muslims to Europeans—are quickly becoming the new destination of choice for Muslim immigrants.

The ethnic diversity of European Muslims is striking. Arabs constitute the most numerous ethnic group, with some 3.5 million, 45 percent of which are of Moroccan origin, living in Western Europe. The second largest ethnic group is the Turkish, with more than 2.5 million individuals scattered throughout Europe. The third largest group, with more than 800,000 people, is immigrants from the Indian subcontinent: India, Pakistan, Afghanistan, and Bangladesh.

It is difficult to obtain accurate statistics on Muslims since, in most European countries, religious affiliation is not a question on population censuses. Only place of birth and country of origin give any hint of religious allegiance. France's 1999 census showed 1.3 million immigrants out of a total of 4.3 million, from North Africa. The census also indicated a growing number of immigrants from Turkey (200,000).[2] In terms of calculating the number of

Muslims living in France, children born in France to immigrant parents, as well as immigrants who took French citizenship in earlier periods, should also be added to these statistics. This brings the estimated number of France's Muslim population to more than 4 million. France is thus one of the most important European countries in terms of the issue of Muslim minority populations.[3] In Germany, the most up-to-date statistics show almost 3 million Muslims, with the overwhelming majority coming from Turkey (70 percent), even though, due to the recent upheavals in Eastern Europe and the Balkans, the number of Bosnian and Kosovar Muslims is also on the rise. This is also the case in Austria and the Netherlands, which have been similarly affected by the recent conflicts in the Balkans. They have also experienced the consequences of the more distant conflicts that have occurred in Somalia, Iran, and Iraq. After war broke out in Bosnia-Herzegovina, Germany took in more than 300,000 Bosnian refugees, while Austria took in 70,000. In its 2001 census, Great Britain, making an exception to its policy of not asking individuals to state their religion or their ethnicity, for the first time included a question on religious and ethnic affiliation. According to the results of this census, 1.591 million Muslims are living in Great Britain, most of Pakistani and Bangladeshi origin (658,000 and 260,000 respectively).[4] The younger generations increasingly claim British citizenship, due to the fact that a large proportion of children are born on British soil, and today more than 450,000 Muslim children are educated in the British school system.

A further problem in estimating the number of Muslims in Europe is a result of the difficulty in getting an accurate number of conversions from country to country. The number in each country also tends to vary depending on who is doing the reporting.[5] According to a study conducted by Telhine at the Mosque of Paris, 1,689 conversions were recorded in France between 1965 and 1989.[6] In the Netherlands, the number has been estimated at 2,000,[7] and from 3,000 to 5,000 in Germany. The phenomenon of conversion affects certain countries more than others. In Spain, for example, the number of Muslims is anywhere from 300,000 to 500,000, of which 3,000–5,000 are converts. A nostalgia for the Andalusia of Muslim Spain, brought back to life by the presence of immigrants from North Africa and the Middle East, has contributed to the attraction of Islam in the Iberian peninsula.[8] It is in the United States, however, that the phenomenon of conversion has had the greatest impact by far.

As in Europe, censuses in the United States do not include questions of religious affiliation: nonetheless, the most current estimates put the number of Muslims in the United States at approximately 6 million. The numbers debate is even more contentious in the United States, particularly since September 11.

In October of 2001, a scholar at the University of Chicago published his independent findings indicating that only 1 percent of the population in the United States (i.e., 1.9–2.8 million people) was Muslim.[9] In the tense climate after September 11, these findings became the subject of much public debate and polemic. The debate reached its peak after they were republished by the American Jewish Committee, a Jewish lobbying group, with the implication that they were attempting to minimize the importance of Islam in America. From there, a battle of numbers began between the representatives of several prominent American Jewish and Muslim organizations.[10] This discrepancy in estimated figures illustrates the ideological stakes involved in the official definition of the Muslim community, stakes that have incidentally risen after September 2001. The difficulty of conducting an accurate census also shows the extent to which the gathering of data is influenced by ideology, particularly as it is Muslims who generally produce the most information on American Islam. A counterexample serves to illustrate this situation. In the pages of the *New York Times* during the month of October 2003, several Islamic organizations expressed their indignation that one of the most important post–September 11 surveys on Arabs and Muslims in the Detroit area was conducted by a research team from the University of Michigan, and not by a Muslim organization.[11] For lack of better options, our study follows the most common estimate of 4–5 million Muslims, including Muslims of all origins and ethnicities, currently living in the United States.

What is particular to the American situation is that almost half of all Muslims in the United States (46 percent according to a 1994 estimate[12]) are converts. Even more significant, *vis-à-vis* the situation in Europe, is that the majority of these converts come from within the Afro-American community. Thirty percent of these African American Muslims adopted Islam while serving prison terms in, following the model of such figures as Malcolm X or Imam Jamil Abdullah Al-Amin, the former Black Panther once known as H. Rap Brown. Another 56 percent of Muslims in the United States, as in Europe, come from a variety of countries and ethnic origins. Unlike in Europe, however, Arabs are not at all the dominant minority (12.45 percent of all U.S. Muslims), and are far outnumbered by ethnic groups from the Asian subcontinent (24.4 percent). After that come immigrants from Africa (6.2 percent), Iran (3.6 percent) and Turkey (2.4 percent).[13]

The Three Phases of Muslim Minority Presence in Europe

Islam's status on the two continents displays both similarities and differences. One difference stems from the long history between Europe and the Muslim world. In essence, European Muslims constitute a postcolonial minority culture, in that they come primarily from countries formerly colonized or dominated by the most influential European countries. Thus it is that in France, the statistical dominance of North African (Maghrebi) Muslims is entirely a product of France's former colonial empire. Indeed, Muslim presence has been a factor in the French political and social life since the beginning of the twentieth century, when Algeria was still part of France. The influence of colonial history is also seen in the resilience, and even the expansion, of the Harki community, the group of Algerians who fought alongside the French army during Algeria's war of independence, and who emigrated to France with their families in 1962.

The beginnings of the Islamic presence in Great Britain are similarly linked to British colonial expansion in India.[14] During the latter part of the eighteenth century, the British East India Company hired manual laborers for their ships from Indian ports. Some of these hired hands were Muslims. Islamic presence grew still further after the opening of the Suez Canal in 1869. Large numbers of Yemenis and Somalis also emigrated to England by way of the Port of Aden. These Yemeni communities established themselves in Great Britain, creating *zawia* (Sufi brotherhoods) and even importing a sheikh to oversee them.[15] It was only after the 1960s and 1970s, however, that mass immigration from Pakistan and India truly began. By the 1970s and 1980s, Bangladeshis made up the plurality of Muslim immigrants.

Even the history of Islam in Germany is linked to the imperialist projects of the Kaiser: who, toward the end of the nineteenth century, looked to strengthen the fledgling German state by means of special economic and diplomatic relations with the Ottoman Empire.[16] The result was a significant presence of Muslims in Berlin in the years leading up to World War I. Obviously, Germany cannot boast of having had a colonial empire; nevertheless, the close relations between Germany and the Ottoman Empire go a good way toward explaining the Turkish mass immigration to Germany. In the Netherlands as well, though the Muslim population there is much more diverse (mainly from Tunisia, Morocco, and Turkey), colonial history played a role with the hiring of Surinamese laborers.

These colonial, later postcolonial, origins of Muslim presence in Europe has a direct bearing on the perception of Islam in European culture. In particular, it explains the "delay effect" in European understanding: that is, how long it took Europeans to recognize that Islam has become a permanent fixture in the religious landscape. How else to explain the fact that Muslims have been present in the main countries of Europe for half a century, and yet it is only in the past three decades that Islam has emerged as a cultural and religious phenomenon? Three migratory movements have contributed to the creation of the Muslim minority in Europe. The first spans the period from the end of World War II to the beginning of the 1970s, and corresponds to the arrival en masse of workers from the Third World and Eastern Europe, in response to the reconstruction of the European economy and the need for manual labor in the postwar period. The arrival of these Muslims was thus the result of a conscious policy of immigration, drawn up between industry and the most powerful European states. Several agreements regarding the importation of workers were signed between the governments of Muslim and European countries: France signed an agreement with Algeria in 1968 in addition to agreements with Morocco and Tunisia in 1963; Germany signed agreements with Turkey (1961), Morocco (1963), and Tunisia (1965). Islam was thus incarnated, in this period, by the anonymous and silent mass of unskilled laborers working in industry and the tertiary sector. Largely on the fringes of society, living in groups with their own, separate, social spaces, their primary goal was to earn as much money as possible and then return home. As long as they could, they held off the arrival of their wives and children. Thus their own denial of the social and religious consequences of their migration dovetailed with the prevailing view—in the host countries as much as the countries of origin—that this migration was only a temporary one. One should also keep in mind just how much the ideologies of the time emphasized ideas of nationalism, anti-imperialism, or socialism, but not at all Islam, as a means of mobilizing and giving voice to migrant workers.

The oil crisis of 1974 signaled the end of this period of reconstruction and European economic prosperity. The process of Muslim immigration, however, continued, entering a second phase in which families formerly split apart by migration were reunited. In the 1980s throughout Europe, the doors slammed shut for the masses of unskilled immigrant workers. At the same time, however, the number of women and children coming from Muslim countries increased dramatically. The reuniting of families on European soil marked a decisive change in the nature of the relations between Muslims and Europeans. For the Muslim, this resulted in the increase of opportunities for interaction outside the workplace. The movement of Muslims from the segregated environment of the workers' dormitory to the integrated (i.e., not completely Muslim) public housing project, has the effect of opening up the migrant worker's world. Immigrant workers now found themselves coming into contact with representatives of the school system, members of the bureaucracy, and social workers. It was no longer possible to think of oneself as a worker in transit: the signs of permanency were numerous and irreversible. Educational, consumer, and of course religious needs were added to economic concerns. The creation of prayer rooms in the 1970s was the first visible sign of this change in Muslims' conditions and mind-set. After having been all but nonexistent in the preceding decades, prayer rooms began to pop up like mushrooms in Paris, Marseille, London, Bradford, and Berlin. By the end of the 1990s, there were more than 6,000 mosques in Western Europe.[17] The 1980s were thus a crucial decade for the advent of Islam as a new religion in the heart of European cities.

These aforementioned prayer rooms would become central in the development of the various forms of Islamic social and religious life. Marriage, burial, circumcision, Qu'ranic teaching, pilgrimages, religious festivals: everything begins in the mosque, or at least in contact with the mosque. In the 1990s, a new phase in immigrant society began with the increased visibility of mosques and their demand to be recognized as public buildings, equal in status to temples, churches, and synagogues. These demands have elicited a general debate on the institutionalization and self-representation of Islam in Europe. Numerous coalitions, councils, federations, and committees of all kinds are currently being established whose aims are to establish a line of dialogue with the representatives of public authority, and to define, bit by bit, what shape the different varieties of native European Islam might take.

For the European, Islam's progress in establishing itself as a permanent feature of European culture has been and continues to be a difficult phenomenon to accept. For many decades, Muslims were exclusively perceived as temporary guests relegated to the fringes of society. Their evolution—from foreigner to permanent resident to citizen—has been a troubled one, particularly as it signals the definitive end of Europe's universalist and imperialist pretensions, and puts colonized and colonizer on equal footing. Thus the initial reaction of many Europeans to Islam's establishment in Western culture, even at the institutional level, was resistance, if not outright rejection. It should be recalled that many European countries initiated, without much success, several programs to return immigrants to their countries of origin. In France, the Stoléru Law of 1979, also known as the Law of One Million (since the law offered 1 million French centimes, or about $1,733, to every immigrant who decided to return to his country of origin), failed in its goal of encouraging Algerian immigrants to repatriate.[18] On November 28, 1983, the German government passed a similar law, with a financial incentive of 10,500 DM per adult (about $6,600) and 1,500 DM per child ($953). Between 1983 and the first half of 1984, approximately 250,000 foreigners, most of them Turks, left Germany. In the United Kingdom, the turning point for immigration policy was the Commonwealth Immigration Act of 1961, which imposed the first restrictions on immigrants from the former empire who wished to set up residence in British territory. In 1964, the Minister of Labour put an end to the right to work that so many unskilled workers on British soil had previously benefited from. The consequence was that many immigrant husbands and fathers had to send their families back to the country of origin, forcing the families to change their entire way of life.

The third phase in the history of Muslim immigration to Europe begins with the waves of refugees and asylum-seekers in the 1980s. The severe restrictions placed on legal immigration to Western Europe, as well as the upheavals in the dying Soviet Union, are the two most important causes of this third wave of immigrants in general, and of Muslim immigrants in particular. Germany was particularly affected in this third phase. Between 1980 and 1990, 60,000 Afghanis, 110,000 Iranians, and 55,000 Lebanese came to live in Germany as refugees. After Turks, refugees from Bosnia-Herzegovina comprised the second largest group of Muslim immigrants (340,000). Immigrants continued to pour into Germany even after the German government changed Article 16 of the Constitution to stipulate that immigrants entering the country via a third country considered safe (such as Bulgaria, Gambia, Poland, Romania, the Czech Republic, and Hungary, but also, and notably, Turkey) were not eligible to claim refugee status.

Close to 70,000 Bosnian Muslims also headed for Austria. Italy and Spain were also affected by the waves of refugees, and by the end of the 1980s had themselves become established countries of Muslim immigration. If it remains the case that Italy lays claim to one of the smallest immigrant populations in Europe, it is also true that it has the highest percentage of non-Europeans—as well as, it seems, of illegal immigrants. Out of the more than 1,600,000 foreigners who were living in Italy in 2001, 600,000 (37%) came from Muslim countries.[19] In Spain, the arrival (or perhaps the return) of Islam has been due to an influx of illegal immigrants from North and Sub-Saharan Africa. These waves of mostly poor and young immigrants have become a point of tension in Spanish–Moroccan relations, and has resulted in tragedies like the boats filled with illegals that regularly sink in the waters of the Strait of Gibraltar.

This dawning of European Islam has occurred just as Islam is emerging as a social movement and a political force both in the Muslim world and on the international stage. Significantly, the 1980s was also the decade in which conflict broke out between Saudi Arabia, India, Pakistan, and Iran for the domination of the Muslim world. In this intense battle, Europe became a target of missionary and proselytizing efforts, as the massive increase in the distribution of petrodollars to Europe for the creation of mosques, Islamic schools, and university chairs attests to. This activity should nonetheless be seen in the context of the diversity of branches and movements that divide up Islam in both Europe and North America. While the influence of Saudi doctrine is an established fact, it is nonetheless just one of the many options offered to European and American Muslims, and is very far from holding uncontested sway in the Muslim community. The real question is to determine just how, and how much, sectarian literature—in the form of books, brochures, free Qu'rans, and so on—contributes to the shaping of Islamic behavior in Europe. (See parts II and III for a discussion of this topic.)

Islam in North America: "Deferred Visibility"

The Islamic revival taking place in Muslim countries has also had consequences for the visibility of Islam in the United States. On the other side of the Atlantic, however, this visibility takes a different shape than in Europe. In the 1970s, immigrants from the middle classes and the intelligentsia of Muslim countries began to arrive en masse. Though there had been a Muslim presence in the United States at least since the eighteenth century with the arrival of African slaves, Islam's history in America really begins with the voluntary migrations of the nineteenth century. From 1875 to 1912, Muslim migration was essentially made up of families or individuals fleeing economic or political hardship in their country of origin, principally in the rural areas of Syria, Jordan, Palestine, and Lebanon. These immigrants settled in mid-sized towns, finding employment in the mines and factories or making a living as itinerant merchants.

The second wave of immigrants occurred between 1918 and 1922, and the third over the course of the 1930s. These groups of immigrants were largely made up of people fleeing the economic depression and the political crises that followed World War I and the disintegration of the Ottoman Empire in the countries of the Middle East. A fourth wave occurred after World War II, and concerned not only countries in the Middle East but also India, Pakistan, Turkey, and the Balkans. In contrast to the previous waves of immigrants, these new arrivals, better-educated and more well-off than their predecessors, came primarily from the urban centers of Muslim countries. This difference in socioeconomic status meant that they were better equipped, both intellectually and culturally, to resist the assimilationist forces that had made all but invisible the preceding generations of immigrants.

The fifth wave of immigration began in 1965 during the Johnson administration. In this period, the United States relaxed its quota policy, and immigration was no longer held to a strict standard of quotas and limits by country. This easing of restrictions allowed highly qualified Muslims from Africa and Asia to enter the country in large numbers. This trend in immigration continued to go strong, and conservative estimates before September 11 put the number of immigrants arriving from the Middle East and Africa at 35,000 per year. Each major crisis in the Muslim world has translated into the relocation of populations to the United States: the Six Days War of 1967, the Iranian revolution of 1979, the problems in Lebanon and Pakistan—and, closer to home, the conflicts in Afghanistan, Bosnia, and Kosovo.

Despite the long-standing presence of Muslims in the United States, Islam's visibility in American society is a relatively recent phenomenon, a result of the religious dynamism of the two most recent waves of immigrants. The Muslim immigrants of the first part of the twentieth century were more concerned with defending various secular ideologies than with promoting Islam. In this period, the Arab-Muslim world was fighting for its independence from the West by borrowing the West's dominant ideologies: nationalism and socialism. Since the 1970s, however, the new arrivals, particularly those from the Indian subcontinent, have thrown themselves into religious activities of every kind: the building of mosques and madrasas, publishing religious literature, and engaging in lobbying efforts. In the 1990s, more than 2,300 Islamic institutions were counted in the United States, of which 1,500 were mosques or Islamic centers. American society is undergoing a definitive and visible process of Islamicization, and an assessment of the situation of Muslim minorities in a non-Muslim society is indeed beginning to take shape.

This rise of Islam after 1965 encountered neither hostility nor real surprise on the part of American society, since from the outset it established itself within the normal context of U.S. inclusiveness toward new groups, within the framework of American civil religion. Islam did become an object of international attention after the 1980 hostage crisis at the American Embassy in Teheran, but there was nonetheless a distinction made between Muslims in the United States and Muslims abroad, a distinction that had a positive effect on the identity construction of the Islamic minority. Even the antiterrorist law of 1996 did little to halt this development. This dissociation of domestic and international political agendas was profoundly altered, however, by the events of September 11. From that moment on, Muslims living on American soil have been the victims of surveillance and suspicion as part of the "War on Terror." As noted above, the Muslims of Europe were already quite familiar with this perception of domestic Islam as a kind of fifth column, long before September 11. The idea of collusion between the enemy outside and an enemy within is perfectly illustrated by the creation of the

"Vigipirate" plan after the Paris subway bombings of 1995, attributed to the Algerian Armed Islamic Group (GIA). The cultural corollary to this security measure is the general suspicion of all forms of Islamic religiosity, particularly when it comes from the youth of the poor suburbs.

Understanding the condition of Muslims in the West means taking into account the particular political and cultural contexts of the respective Western countries, and to show how these contexts act upon the identities, practices, and collective actions of Muslims. Thus, the different forms of nationalism and secularism in Europe and the United States are also crucial factors in the evolution of Muslim culture.

PART I

Islam and the West:
Mutual Transformation

CHAPTER 2

Islam as Stigma

Dominant social and cultural environments exert a decisive influence over the formation of Muslim identities and behaviors. Any analysis of Muslim religious practice has to take into account a particular challenge for Western Muslims: namely, the meta-narrative on Islam. The importance of public opinion and its impact on identity-formation in general hardly needs to be proven. More than any other religious group, however Muslims seem not to be the masters of their own identity in their adopted countries. An essentializing discourse on Islam, existing on every level of society, is imposed on them from the micro-local to the international level. This narrative, which is largely based on the idea of a conflict between Islam and the West, portraying Islam as a problem or an obstacle to modernization, has forced all Muslims, from the most secularized to the most devout, to examine their beliefs and think about what it means to be Muslim.

Emphasizing the relations of domination and power in relation to Western Muslims, however, should not imply that the potential ways of being and acting in the name of Islam are always predetermined. The purpose of this emphasis, rather, is to show the gap between the racialization of national discourses, the meta-narrative of Islam as enemy, and the diversity/fluidity of individual Muslims' attitudes. Studying the modes of Muslim practice in response to an imposed frame of reference based on power relations should not imply that Muslims are all prisoners of their culture, or that they model themselves on some pre-assigned identity.

One of the difficulties faced by both European and American Muslims in the post–September 11 context is the constant conflation of an Islam perceived as an international political threat and the individual Muslims living in Western societies, as demonstrated by the outbreak of hostility toward Muslims following the World Trade Center attacks. The fact that American and European Muslims are now inevitably defined in terms of the international political situation demonstrates the persistence of the essentialist approach to Islam and to Muslims, which has developed over centuries of confrontation between the European and Muslim worlds.[1] No ethnic or religious group, of course, escapes stereotyping when it comes in contact with other groups. But what seems specific to the case of Islam, in our opinion, is: (a) a historical moment in which the set of representations operates from the micro-local to the international level; and (b) the reinforcement of stereotypes by the specific scholarly tradition that has developed around Islam.

The essentialist approach so famously described and criticized by Edward Said[2] is far from dead. It is instructive to consider how the descriptions of Islam as a risk factor in international relations that have circulated since the 1980s are supported by representations of Islam built up over centuries and which would be familiar to any eighteenth-century gentleman. The same reifying ideas are continually brought back and readjusted to fit changes in the international and domestic situation. It would seem that the attacks of September 11, 2001 have only served to strengthen an interpretation that considers Islam to be an inherent risk factor.

This meta-narrative on Islam did not emerge with the events of September 11, however. What is more, it does not take the same form in Europe as it does in the United States. The automatic association of ethnicity, Islam, and poverty was widespread in Europe long before September 11, just as was the resurgence of xenophobic and race-oriented nationalism. The attacks of September 11 merely initiated a third stage in the meta-narrative on Islam as enemy, which has reached its peak in the case of American Muslims.

Ethnicity, Islam, and Poverty

The conflation of categories of race, class, and religion works to the detriment, above all, of the most vulnerable Muslim communities in both Europe and the United States, reinforcing their ethnic segregation even to the point of isolationism or separatism. In every country in Europe, the rate of Muslim unemployment is higher than that among European nationals. In 1995, a report from France's National Institute for Demographic Studies showed that, with an equivalent diploma, unemployment is twice as high among young Muslims than among non-Muslim immigrant youth. A report by the Economic and Social Council, published May 29, 2002, shows that discriminatory hiring practices continue to aggravate problems of social and economic marginality.[3] In general, Muslim immigrants are forced into the less-skilled employment categories of primary or secondary production, which are usually unstable and badly paid.[4]

The connection between race/religion and poverty is a socially dangerous equation whose destabilizing effects are everywhere visible. In England, for example, it is particularly in the northern cities, hit hard by the end of the industrial economy, that the conflation of race, Islam, and social poverty is at its strongest. Bangladeshis and Pakistanis make up part of the very poorest ethnic groups, gathered in the heart of England's larger cities: London, Bradford, Manchester, and Birmingham. Statistics show that the rate of unemployment among Muslims in England is three times higher than among other ethnic or religious groups. Moreover, Muslims born or educated in the United Kingdom face the many of the same disadvantages as first-generation immigrants. In 1991, the rate of unemployment among people of Pakistani origin between 16 and 24 years was almost 36 percent, whereas for "whites" it was below 15 percent. And while in 1998 the unemployment rate fell to only 21 percent among Pakistanis, this number still remained considerably higher than the "white" unemployment rate of the same year (estimated at 5 percent). Today, the rate of unemployment among young Muslims continues to be twice as high as that of young "whites."[5] This discrepancy also extends to more prestigious professions, such as medicine or teaching.

Social discrimination also affects conditions of education and housing and the way of life in general: Muslims tend to live in overcrowded and underserviced apartment buildings in crime-ridden urban areas. This socioeconomic vulnerability brings with it the further risk of political destabilization, as the frequent riots in this part of England show. A team, established under the auspices of the British Ministry of the Interior, assigned to evaluate community cohesion researched the towns of Oldham, Burnley, Southall, Birmingham, and Leicester, where riots had erupted in the spring of 2001. The results of their study, made public on December 11, 2001, are alarming.[6] They describe whole communities turned in on themselves, deeply frustrated by their poverty and the inequality of their social and economic opportunities vis-à-vis the rest of the country. "You will be the only white person I will meet today," said one man of Pakistani origin from the town of Bradford, when interviewed by the team. Whether in the areas of housing, employment, schooling, or social services, the report describes an England segregated according to the twin categories of race and religion.

A frightened isolationism, as well as the sometimes reactionary use of Islam, is the frequent response to anti-Muslim racism. The absence of communication between ethnic groups and the local political community, particularly on delicate questions of culture, race, and religion, serves only to exacerbate the situation. For many Muslims, the proper response to such ghettoization is to form their own associations based on an ethnic identity linked to Islam. The imagined community and ethno-familial culture that has crystallized around Islam is thus a response to the way in which religion has taken on a racial dimension. The concentration of populations in urban areas, and the constant—real or imaginary—contact with the culture of the country of origin, support the separatist use of Islam. Thus, in many cases, the imposed ghettoization is accepted and even desired. M. Krishnan quotes Wasim Ahmad of Bradford: "'We want to keep our religious beliefs, not becoming Muslims just in the way many Christians treat their faith.' For Ahmad, the only way to do this is to isolate himself from the outside environment. Wasim, and thousands of others like him, do not want to be treated any differently than anyone else. 'I am aware of myself as a Muslim, not hostile to anyone but just wanting to give myself self-respect,' he adds. That sentiment is true. All they want is to be in their city and want to help it by working peacefully there."[7]

Paris, Berlin, and Amsterdam are admittedly different from New York and Bradford; nonetheless, the perception of social difference in terms of ethnicity is just as prevalent in the urban space of continental Europe. In the large metropolises of the developed world, such as London and New York, the labor market is increasingly divided according to the criteria of ethnicity, religion, and gender. Whereas the industrial town tended to dissolve ethnic and cultural groups in favor of more universal aggregates (working class vs. owner class, private employees vs. civil servants), the global city tends to foster and preserve ethnic differences. The importance of ethnicity also increases as the various forms of self-employment in the service sector provide economic opportunities to the masses of newcomers at the heart of large cities. As a result of these new urban contexts, the forms of socioeconomic integration can no longer be accurately described solely by categories of economic class. Instead, they increasingly relate to categories of ethnicity. Any reflection on social interaction in the contemporary urban environment cannot but take into account the ethnic aspect of social groups, whether these groups are made up of immigrants or not. In the current context, the persistent connection between ethnicity, religion, and poverty exacerbates the victimization of the Other, even as it encourages the self-isolation of minorities according to ethno-religious categories.

Self-identification as a Muslim is, in many cases, a consequence of the ethnic solidarity maintained or preserved by the socioeconomic conditions of segregation. Avoiding the stigma attached to segregation requires dissociating from the dominant culture as far as possible, reclaiming the stigmatized identity and inverting it into a positive attribute. Marginalized ethnic or religious groups takes both the isolation imposed upon them by the dominant culture, and the binary and essentialist categories with which the dominant culture characterizes them, and turns these disadvantages into positive elements of identity. In such conditions—and contra the theory of Portes and Zhou of "segmented assimilation"—the maintaining of ethnic ties does not make for a smooth transition into the dominant culture.[8]

The Nation of Islam and the Separatist Impulse

In the case of American Black Islam, Islam also serves as a reinforcement of the racial barrier. In spite of considerable social and economic progress in the last 30 years, the economic and social situation of black Muslims continues to be one of social and urban segregation. This group is still beset by poverty, drug use, and delinquency. Note also that blacks make up a third of those living under the poverty line in America, and represent more than half of all arrests for robbery and murder.[9] In such circumstances, conversion to Islam seems like a viable way to transform racial stigma from a liability into an asset. In the ghettos and prisons of the United States, Islam is gaining rapid converts. According to Wendy Murray Zoba's figures, nearly 80 percent of conversions to Islam in America take place among the black community. This statistic means that nearly one African American in fifteen describes him- or herself as Muslim.[10]

This attraction is not new. Since the nineteenth century, many American blacks have been drawn to the message of Islam—first in the cotton fields of the South, today in the ghettos of the North. The descendants of slaves are still very much in search of a place within American society, and being black in America still carries the stigma of discrimination. Islam initially satisfied the desire for a distinct identity within American society. More than just a spiritual movement, Islam allowed African Americans, in the years following emancipation, to address the question of their roots by creating a myth of black superiority and the black race's original devotion to Islam.

These facts also serve to explain the success of the Nation of Islam, whose history begins in the 1930s.[11] The Nation of Islam preaches a separatist millenarianism, according to which, at the end of time, the superiority of the black race and of the Islamic faith will be recognized and the white race, product of the devil, will disappear from the face of the Earth. In 1934, the Nation of Islam already claimed more than 8,000 followers. This same year,

Elijah Muhammed, chief minister and second-in-command of the movement
took over leadership from Wallace D. Fard. Elijah Muhammed's reforms gave
the movement its distinctive features.[12] His insistence on discipline and elit-
ism provided the most disenfranchised members of the black community
with a positive means of identification. Through the prohibition of alcohol,
drugs, tobacco, and gambling, together with the valorization of family life
and conjugal fidelity, he fought against social and moral degradation. Thus
the success of the Nation of Islam is due less to its religious aspects than to
its ethnic ones: the Nation of Islam's message fosters the communal cohesion
of a group that has been and remains both socially marginal and excluded
from American economic prosperity.[13]

After Elijah Muhammad's death in 1975, his son, Wallace Deen, took
over as head of the movement. In a dramatic move, he abandoned the elitist,
separatist, and racist lessons of his father, and directed the movement toward
an orthodox Sunni pietism; he renamed the organization and changed his
own name to Warith Deen Mohammed.[14] Louis Farrakhan, broke with
Warith Deen Mohammed in 1977 and rebuilt the Nation of Islam under his
leadership. Despite the Nation's notoriety, only 20,000 black Muslims—out
of nearly 2 million self-identified Muslims—were members of the Nation of
Islam at this time. More than 20 years after Farrakhan's restructuring of the
organization, this proportion remains nearly the same. Out of nearly 3 million self-identifying black Muslims, only 1-3 percent are members of
Farrakhan's movement. The current majority of black Muslims follow the
teachings of Sunni Islam, through organizations developed by Warith D.
Mohammed and others.[15] For the most part, they no longer call themselves
"Black Muslims," but simply Muslims.[16]

Thus Warith Deen Mohammed's role, though less visible in the media,
has without a doubt been the more decisive one for the black community
itself. The bulk of Mohammed's efforts were aimed at the reinstatement of
African American Muslims in the *Ummah*, or world Islamic community.
This goal resulted in a shift toward the doctrines of orthodox Sunni Islam.
Temples were renamed mosques; ministers became imams. The practice of
fasting during the month of Ramadan was revived according to the lunar calendar,[17] as was the tradition of praying five times a day. To prevent racist ideologies from overwhelming the Nation of Islam, Warith Deen Mohammed
opened every mosque of the organization to all Muslims, regardless of skin
color. He also changed his attitude toward the United States, arguing for
African Americans' integration into the national community rather than the
founding of a separate nation. This new stance was reflected in the successive
name changes of the movement: the 1976 *World Community of Al-Islam in*

the West became the *American Muslim Mission* in 1981, and the *Muslim American Community* in 1990. Today, Mohammed's movement is extremely decentralized; each mosque affiliated with the organization enjoys a great deal of autonomy. In 2002, the name of the organization was changed once again to become the American Society of Muslims. In September, 2003, Warith Deen Mohammed stepped down as head of the movement; since then, the movement has been without centralized leadership.[18] Mohammed's decision came as little surprise from a leader who has always advocated for local communities to take charge of the movement's direction.[19]

Yet despite their membership in a universal community of believers acting in submission to God and to the Prophet Mohammed, African Americans' devotion to Islam remains a means of reinforcing their separation from white and dominant America. Islam thus continues to act as a religion of resistance in opposition to the dominant white, Christian culture. The foundational myth of the Nation of Islam perfectly illustrates the inversion of racial stigma. Blackness is a positive attribute, the symbol of progress and superiority: in opposition to whiteness, which is associated with regression and the Devil. "So the religion we have, the religion of Islam, the religion that makes us Muslims, the religion that the Honorable Elijah Mohammed is teaching us here in America today, is designed to undo in our minds what the white man has done to us. The Black man was on Earth before the White man. The lost tribe of Shabbaz."[20] "I always knew that the whites were the devil," one member of the Nation of Islam, whose father's house was repeatedly demolished in racist attacks, affirmed.[21] Once again, Islam is a way to elaborate upon an externally imposed racial boundary and to create, in every aspect of society, a separate black nation within the nation.

The question that follows is whether the adoption of Sunni Islam can be a way to overcome the temptation to separatism. Robert Dannin has posed the question: is there an Islamic pedagogy that would benefit the black population?[22] Since the advent of the Nation of Islam, conversion to Islam has acted as a form of rehabilitation for a community afflicted by drug addiction, alcoholism, delinquency, and the dissolution of the family unit. The Islamization of the African American community has allowed it, in a way, to rediscover its moral center; ironically, Islam has also facilitated its adjustment to the core values of American society, such as the value of work, professional success, and family stability. By the same token, however, the continuing strength of the racial divide means that this correlation exists on separatist terms; in other words, African American cultural change has remained within the black community, without any real communication between it and other segments of American society.

In December of 1999, we interviewed Ayesha, the president of the Women's Association of Islam in Harlem. She is around 40 years old and became a Muslim in 1971. Born into a Methodist family from Alabama, she arrived in New York at the height of Malcolm X's preaching career. As she recounts:

> I was raised in Alabama and when I finished school I came to New York to pursue some goals. And it was at the time when Malcolm X was just starting. And that was all just the story in my subconscious: I wasn't consciously interested in doing anything religiously in terms of the Nation. But the political education that I was getting was absolutely awesome. The social education was very important. . . . The world has changed. But it was wonderful, you know. So, there was this climate, with Malcolm during this social critique of American society. . . . And it was after he was assassinated, much after, that I became Muslim. I never consider becoming Muslim when he was with the Nation. It never crossed my mind. But I was absolutely committed to the talks and lessons that he was giving about injustice in American society and in the world. It was years later that I embraced Islam. One day I just went to the Islamic center and I went into this room and there was a custom that we had . . . I just [went and took *Shahada*[23] for the] first time . . . I was married; my husband and I both we became Muslim together. It was lovely. So, after that we had this habit of going to the mosque every Sunday for classes at 72nd Street and Riverside Drive. We would sit around this room And we [would ask], oh, why did you come to Islam? It was a common practice, and when I was asked why I came to Islam by one woman that I knew, it just came out of my mouth: I am just following Malcolm. Right this was after he came for Hajj and all that stuff. I don't know why I said that. It just came out. So, then she said . . . there was this lady sitting next to her she said, well, meet Malcolm's wife.[24]

We should also note the appeal of the Nation of Islam outside the United States, in particular in the United Kingdom, where the twin message of social and economic and issues has resonated within many of the black communities of London for over a decade.[25]

As a rule, Islam tends to attract communities in the West that are vulnerable on both a material and a symbolic level. It is interesting to note, for example, the increasing attraction of Islam for Latino immigrants, beginning in the early 1980s. Allianza is a Puerto Rican Islamic association active in East Harlem since the late 1970s. The *sermons (khotbas)* at Allianza are conducted in Spanish. The imam, Omar Abdurahim Ocasio, was born in the Bronx. He was forty-five years old when we met him in April, 1999, and a college graduate, working for a New York railroad company. His principal function as imam at Allianza is teaching Islam to new converts. This is how he describes the sentiment of these new Muslims:

> But we know they don't think of us as Americans, I mean, . . . I remember my wife's grandfather came up to me and says, remember this . . . he said that in Spanish. He said remember this always. They [white, non-Latino Americans] will never look upon you as an equal. You will always be a second-class citizen. Those are the kind of things that my grandparents or our elders would pass onto us. That we remember they will never look upon as an equal. But basically that's how the average Puerto Rican sees it. When they become Muslim, that's another thing because now, they are [one] minority within [another] one.[26]

Ocasio's testimony demonstrates his perception of Islam as a way to resolve the thorny question of nonassimilation with mainstream American culture; it also shows how in the process, Islam can become a way to bind a community together in the midst of an unwelcoming society.

The Resurgence of Xenophobic and Racist Nationalism

In the past two decades, the debate on issues of race has reemerged in every European country that is home to Muslim populations. As in the previous century, this debate is used to justify the opposition between Europeans and non-Europeans. This time, however, the non-European is not Jewish, but Muslim. We should note here that anti-Semitism has not disappeared. It is sometimes disguised as a critique of Israeli policy regarding the Israeli–Palestinian conflict, or else it takes the form of doubts regarding the reality of the Holocaust.[27] Nevertheless, it is Islam that is henceforth the anathema religion in European societies. Once again, the conflation of race, religion, and ethnicity is a standard part of discourse. The reemergence of the issue of race in national discourse first materialized in the 1980s with the return of Far-Right political parties. This return coincided with the influx of Muslim immigrants into Europe. Most of these political parties had already been present as fringe elements in the political arenas of the various European countries, but their popularity grew once they linked the issues of the need to defend national identity and the recent increase in Muslim immigration. One of the oldest and most established parties of the European Far Right is France's National Front, which has played a prominent role in the political and electoral life of the country since 1984. Toward the end of the 1990s, the National Front's visibility and influence seemed to be waning, largely due to the departure of Bruno Mégret, the party's second-in-line, in order to establish another organization, the National Movement for the Republic. However, the fact that, in the April 21, 2002 presidential run-off elections, National Front candidate Jean-Marie Le Pen came in second only to incumbent president Jacques Chirac (16.89 percent of all votes cast) demonstrated, if proof was needed that the party continues to have a strong political influence on the French electorate. However, the regional elections of March 28, 2004, in which the National Front won only 5.7% of all votes—as well as the European elections, in which the party carried 9.81% of the vote—seems to indicate a decline, due in part to internal conflicts within the party's leadership.[28]

The German National Democratic Party (NPD: Nationaldemokratische Partei Deutschlands), currently 4,000-members strong, has been in existence since 1964 and is Germany's oldest Far-Right party. In October 1995, its leader, Günter Deckert, had to resign as head of the party following accusations of financial corruption, not to mention accusations of historical revisionism (apropos of the Nazi Holocaust) and incitement to racial hatred. In 1997, the NPD reelected Udo Voigt as party president. The NPD has been especially influential at the local level, where it coordinates various demonstrations of a militant Far-Right nature, and consistently tops opinion polls in issues against both mosques and the drug trade.[29] The other Far-Right party in Germany, the Republikander Party, made a comeback in the 1992 elections in the state of Baden-Württemberg, where it won more than 12 percent of the vote. The Austrian Freedom Party (Freiheitliche Partei Osterriechs, FPO) also rebounded in the mid-1980s under the leadership of Jorg Haider, who won 22.6 percent of the vote in Vienna in 1991. He entered into coalition with the People's Party after his own party carried 27 percent of the vote in 1999. This entry of an overtly racist and anti-Semitic party into the Austrian government led European authorities to cut off all contact with Austria until the Party could prove its political "normality."[30] Haider has remained active in the government despite the fact that his party lost votes in the 2002 elections.

The Vlaams Blok in Flanders also enjoyed an increase in popularity, winning 6.6 percent of the popular vote during the 1991 parliamentary elections. Since then, its influence has grown, especially at the local level: in Antwerp, where the party has a loyal constituency, Vlaams Blok votes rose from 18 percent to 30 percent between the local elections of 1988 and 2000. (Approximately one-third of the party's members are Antwerp natives.) In the June 2004 European elections, the party won more than 14% of the vote, a five-point increase over the European elections of 1999[31]. The Danish

People's Party, an outgrowth of the former Progress Party, which dissolved in 1999, has also gained in popularity as a direct consequence of its adoption of an anti-immigration platform. In a report published in 2000, the European Commission for the Fight Against Racism noted that there was cause for alarm, especially given the recent rise in anti-immigrant and anti-Muslim discrimination in Denmark. In Italy, too, the arrival of immigrants has prompted the return of Far-Right parties and political stances. The Far-Right Lega Nord party received 9 percent of the vote in 1992. Its true electoral victory, though, came in the June 1993 Milan local elections, where it received more than 40 percent of the vote. Lega Nord's strategic alliance with Silvio Berlusconi further helped it to obtain 8.4 percent of the vote in the 1994 national elections.

Even the Netherlands, long viewed as tolerant toward its Muslim immigrants, now claims a party on the Far Right. On March 6, 2002, the Leefbaar Rotterdam Viable party obtained 36 percent of the vote during the first round of municipal elections. The party's leader, Pim Fortuyn, a sociology professor and open homosexual, was the first in the history of Dutch politics to have publicly expressed anti-Islamic sentiments. His remarks warning of the presence of Muslims as a danger to Dutch society[32] resulted in his exclusion from the national party, Leefbaar Nederland, shortly before the 2002 elections. But the author of *Against the Islamization of our Culture* remained as candidate for the party at the local level and eventually founded his own party, Lijst Fortuyn, in order to compete in the municipal elections. On May 6, 2002, Fortuyn was murdered under mysterious circumstances. Despite his death, his party came in second place in the May 15, 2002 parliamentary elections, just behind the Christian Democrats, with 26 seats (out of 150) in the Chamber of Deputies. In the January 2003 elections, however, Fortuyn's party only won eight seats, or 6 percent of the vote.

In spite of these electoral ups and downs, the parties of the Extreme Right seem to have gained a firm foothold in European political life. Several factors combine to explain this resurgence of the Far Right in Europe. The most important is the ability of these movements to present Islam as an unyielding force, incapable of being assimilated into the national culture, by emphasizing both the fragility and the importance of European cultural values. This is how, as of 1985, 47 percent of the (native) Danish population believed that Muslims were too culturally different.[33] Polls in Germany consistently show a fear of foreigners, and the general approval of statements such as, "we must preserve the purity of the German people and stop populations from mixing."[34] In 1991, 10 percent of people polled in Germany were recorded as being in complete agreement with this statement, and 14 percent were in partial agreement.[35] An opinion poll taken in the Netherlands shortly before the March 2002 municipal elections indicated a similar attitude. According to the poll, which was published in February 2002, nearly 46 percent of those aged 18–30 were in favor of a zero immigration policy.

The rhetoric of absolute incompatibility between different cultures is the common denominator of all European parties on the Far Right. "What we have is over-foreignerization," said Mr. Haider in March 2001. (The German term is *Uberfremdung*: a word dear to anti-immigrant parties.) "Perhaps a 12% foreign presence is enriching, but 33% is a burden. When you have 200 Muslims in the park cooking lamb, we do not understand it. And when we eat pork, they say it stinks."[36]

However, Far-Right parties hardly have a monopoly on the language of conflict between civilizations. Such language is common to whole swathes of the European political arena, including those unconnected with right-wing groups. It is so widespread, in fact, that Europe could be considered the Chosen Land for the Clash of Civilizations argument—even more than the United States, Samuel Huntington notwithstanding. The American perception of Islam, in contrast, is largely based on a form of externalization tied to foreign policy and the troubles in the Middle East. A racialized perception of Islam is not as common in the United States as it is in Europe, and hostility in the United States is less the result of competing national identities and more something that stems from the constant redefinition of and shifting balance between ethnic groups. Following the attacks of September 11, 2001, however, the traditional place accorded to religion in American society has undergone a significant shift. The gap between American and European experiences in matters of Islam, it would seem, is shrinking.

The correlation between race and nation has been a recurring motif in the rhetoric of post–Cold War European politics, even in those countries that have traditionally shied away from emphasizing ethnicity and ethnic differences. "The Indian and the Asian do not become English by being born in England," declared Enoch Powell in 1968. In 2000, a report known as the Parekh Report (after its author, Bikhu Parekh), commissioned by the Runnymede Trust (an independent research organization), created a violent controversy by denouncing of the "insidious" racism of British society, and by recommending that, as much as possible, English or British identity should be dissociated from the notion of whiteness. In the October 18, 2000 issue of the *Daily Telegraph*, Bikhu Parekh noted that since Great Britain was for centuries, an essentially white nation, British identity so-called retains an implicit assumption of race. At the same time, controversy was brewing in Germany over the definition of German culture. Friedrich Merz, the Christian Democrat President of the CDU-CSU (Christian Democrat Union/Christian Social Union) coalition, stated in October 2000 in the *Rheinischen Post* that a precise definition of

German culture was necessary, so that immigrants could know what it was they were supposed to integrate into. In November 2000, the CDU adopted Merz's proposal and included it as a fundamental point in its platform on integration and immigration.[37] These statements caused an uproar in the media, as well as among prominent Muslim organizations, representatives of the Jewish community, and workers' associations. Merz's statement effectively recalled Germany's Nazi past and the Nazi ideology of one people (*Volk*) based on an ethnic conception of nationhood. CDU's new approach to immigration further referred to "Western values," characterized by Christianity, the tradition of Roman law, and the Enlightenment: an association between Christian culture and the German nation that had previously been a cornerstone of the language of the Far Right.

Similar defenses of national and European identity, based on an essentialist idea of culture, are found throughout Europe. Barrera, a key figure of Catalan political life and an early recruit to the cause of nationalist militancy, declared in March 2001 that the collective Catalan identity was being threatened by the influx of illegal immigrants, and that Jorg Haider was right to maintain that too many immigrants constituted a threat to traditional Austrian society.[38] Enrique Fernandez-Miranda, Spain's minister of immigration issues (Delegado del Gobierno para la Extranjería), stated that conversion to Catholicism was a key element in successful integration of immigrants.[39] In Italy, the ruling Forza Italia party and the Catholic Church have increased the number of associations seeking to defend national identity and the dominant religion. In September 2000, in language recalling the Crusades (i.e., speaking of Christendom versus Islam), Cardinal Biffi called for limits to be placed on Muslim immigration in order to defend Christian Europe:

It is obvious that Muslims must be treated as a separate case. We must have faith that those who are responsible for the public goodwill not fear to confront it with eyes open and without illusions. In the vast majority of cases, and with only a few exceptions, Muslims come here with the resolve to remain strangers to our brand of individual or social "humanity" in everything that is most essential, most precious: strangers to what it is most impossible for us to give up as "secularists." More or less openly, they come here with their minds made up to remain fundamentally "different," waiting to make us all become fundamentally like them . . . . I believe that Europe must either become Christian again, or else it will become Muslim. The "culture of nothing," of freedom without limits and without meaning, of skepticism praised as intellectual conquest, seems to me to have no possible future. This culture seems to be the dominant attitude of the European peoples, all rich in material goods, but poor in the truth.[40]

Similarly, during his September 26, 2001 visit to Berlin, Italian Prime Minister Silvio Berlusconi described Western civilization as superior to Islamic civilization and recommended that the entire world be Westernized.[41] In the same vein, Italian and Polish dignitaries were responsible in May 2004 for a letter—signed by more than ten members of the European Union and addressed to the president of the European Commission—demanding the inclusion of an explicit reference to Christianity in the preamble to the future European Constitution. This letter however produced no results.[42]

Well before the National Front's success in the first round of French presidential elections in April 2002, the spread of Far-Right ideas in French political and cultural thought was denounced in the late 1990s as "ideological lepenization" (after the leader of the National Front, Jean-Marie Le Pen). This phrase, from senator and former, miniser of justice, Robert Badinter, is a criticism of the complacency of a political environment that favored the National Front in matters of electoral strategy and allowed for a particular set of political themes (immigration and security) to take on a disproportionate emphasis. But such "ideological lepenization," is also a result of a society fixated on issues of race and racial difference. In Far-Right discourse, the foreigner is no longer guilty merely of his/her "foreignness"; he or she is also guilty of a cultural heritage supposedly incompatible with "French cultural tradition." The foreigner cannot even be relieved of this incompatibility by becoming a citizen—in fact, quite the contrary. This rhetoric is where the integration of immigrants from North Africa into the Republic reaches a limit: people are perceived as simply different depending on their respective place of origin. And this position is not exclusive to the National Front, even if the National Front is capable of exploiting it to its advantage.

The Vichy regime of World War II and the end of the French colonial empire in the 1960s shattered France's belief in a "universal" French culture and its corresponding symbols, the direct result of the defeat and shame associated with these inglorious periods of history. Since then, the continued demand that the formerly "dominated" be "naturalized" has damaged the effectiveness of the Republic's role as melting pot. For more than 20 years, the debate on immigration in France has emphasized this inability to make a space for the "Other" within the context of "equality and fraternity." The widespread use of the term "second-generation" to refer to people who—according to French laws on nationality—should simply be considered French citizens, is a case in point. It is worth remembering that at no point in the (significant) history of immigration to France have the children of Polish, Italian, or Portuguese immigrants been so habitually described as "second-generation." Similarly, it is difficult to understand the frequent distinction made between French citizens of foreign origin and "true French citizens." According to the logic of democracy, such a distinction should simply not exist. Why, indeed, should ethnic criteria be a key factor in the social administration of the low-income suburbs? As terminology gets confused and meanings slip into one another, the equation Poor = Suburbs = Immigration = Arabs comes into being. This equation then subtends even the most ostensibly liberal political discourse, and leads to dangerous uses of the term "integration," which has become reserved exclusively for people of immigrant origin. It is nonetheless the identification with Islam, not ethnicity or the fact of being foreign-born, that has become the mark of impossible difference (see chapter 3).

The persistent rhetoric on the cultural (and even racial) incompatibility of Muslims and Europeans is part of an essentializing meta-narrative sweeping through the most varied segments of European societies, from the intellectual, political, and journalistic spheres down to ordinary citizens. Such rhetoric is a definite obstacle to understanding, and prevents a true appreciation of the mechanisms of Islamic integration in European culture, particularly with respect to multiculturalism and secularization.

Europe's "Bin Laden Effect"

This rhetoric reaches its height in the international conception of Islam as The Enemy. This rhetoric was more or less implicit throughout the 1980s—particularly in France, in terms of the rise of Islamicism in Algeria—and became explicit, even hostile, after the attacks of September 11 and the claiming of responsibility by Osama bin Laden and Al Qaeda. What has been termed the "Bin Laden Effect" consists mainly of casting all Muslims within the United States and Europe in the role of The Enemy, transforming them into scapegoats for the entire society. After September 11, 2001, hundreds of verbal and physical assaults against Muslims were reported in the United States. Several people with only physical resemblances to Arabs or Muslims (such as Sikhs) were also murdered. In Europe, fewer physical assaults were less common, but verbal insults and attacks were reported in almost all European countries, especially Great Britain, Germany, and the Netherlands. According to FBI statistics, attacks against Muslims increased to 16 times their previous frequency between 2000 and 2001. Instances of discrimination against Muslims in public spaces, including public transportation, have also increased.

Despite these statistics, it seems as if the attitude of both the citizenry and the governments of various countries has actually become more, not less, ambivalent in regard to Muslims. Repression and discrimination have led to a desire for understanding and dialogue, even in the United States. Most public opinion polls in Europe indicate that there was *not* a reversal of opinion concerning Muslims after the events of September 11. People's image of Islam was already negative, in Europe and in the United States, and it remained so after September 11. In France, for example, the non-Muslim population has associated Islam with fanaticism more or less consistently since 1994. Similarly, in the United States, recent surveys show an association between Islam and fanaticism in popular opinion.[43]

Nevertheless, the "Bin Laden Effect" may also prove beneficial in certain respects, namely, in regard to the increased interest in Islamic culture and civilization. This fact is reflected in the exponential rise in Islam-related book sales,[44] as well as in public discussion and media. Even after September 11, Islam continues to attract converts in the United States.[45] On the other hand, suspicion toward Muslims increased in countries like Germany, the Netherlands, Portugal, and Sweden, as well as in the United States. Muslims themselves were suddenly under a permanent obligation to prove their disapproval of terrorism. Media attitudes also helped to reinforce hurtful stereotypes about Islam, particularly in the Netherlands, Greece, Ireland, and Italy.[46]

Governments, for their part, were mostly able to distinguish between international events—specifically, events in the Middle East—and the condition of Islam within their own countries. Initiatives to create spaces of rapprochement and dialogue between Muslims and other religious groups have been launched in Denmark, Germany, Italy, and the Netherlands. In countries such as France, the United Kingdom, or Belgium, where dialogue already existed, efforts were made to reinforce lines of communication. In the United States, on the other hand, the events of September 11 has resulted in a shutting-down of dialogue and has strained communication between Muslims and government authorities.

At the same time, however, it is clear that the September 11 terrorist attacks have made discussion on immigration (in Austria, Denmark, Germany, Greece, Italy, and Portugal) and security more difficult. The USA Patriot Act, passed on October 26, 2001, extended the powers of the government to monitor U.S. residents—including and especially resident aliens and their families. This bill was followed by similar initiatives in Europe. In Great Britain, a law on terrorism, crime, and security was passed on December 14, 2001. The law sparked widespread debate on the restriction of public freedom, due to the increased power it gave to the police force regarding information gathering and the monitoring of citizens. In Germany, two security-related laws were passed: the first on December 8, 2001, and the second on December 20. These laws not only increased funding for security forces, they also provided for greater police freedom in conducting investigations, allowed armed security agents on German planes, and instituted revisions into the process of incorporation for certain religious organizations and the privileges that entailed. In France, the debate over national security has been dominated by the events of September 11 and the consequent awareness of the need for antiterrorism measures. While the law proposed in France on November 15, 2001 was initially intended to address issues of everyday security, a whole series of antiterrorism regulations had been introduced by the time it reached debate in the National Assembly. Issues of national security, terrorism, and ordinary delinquency suddenly find themselves conflated, a cultural confusion that has only added to the ostracism of young people in the suburbs. Two provisions of this law in particular—one concerning noise in the common areas of apartment buildings, the other stipulating a maximum penalty of six months prison time to "serial" subway turnstile-jumpers—seem to have no relation to terrorism at all, nor will they have an impact on high-level delinquency, much less terrorist practices.

Still, in France, as in many other parts of Europe, an ambivalence reigns in the perception of Muslims and of Islam. The debate in France may certainly seem weak on issues of civil liberties, particularly compared to those in the United States and Great Britain. With the exception of dissent from a few intellectual figures, the increased police surveillance in day-to-day security issues failed to generate much public discussion in France.[47] And yet in terms of a vision of Islam as a viable religion within French civil society, signs of reconciliation are indeed appearing, signs that even the events of September 11 have not been able to weaken. Could it be that a new, more tolerant attitude toward Islam is emerging in France, precisely out of these traumatic events?

. . . and the Hardening of American Opinion

This kind of paradox is also visible in the United States, where studies have found that, while Americans may have a negative image of Islam in general, they often have good image, on the other hand, of American Muslims.[48] In any case, one definite consequence of September 11 in the United States has been the appearance and sudden centrality of the American Muslim minority in public discourse.

It is also in the United States, however, in which the events September 11 have had the harshest consequences for Muslims. Racial crimes toward Muslims unquestionably increased after September 11: the Council on American-Islamic Relations (CAIR) cites more than 1,717 acts of discrimination against Muslims in the year after the attacks, particularly in the workplace and at airports.[49] Another CAIR report of May 2004 testified to an unprecedented increase in crimes and acts of violence toward Muslims, which more than doubled between 2002 and 2003.[50]

But it is the "War on Terror" that has been the greatest source of Muslim stigmatization. Antiterrorist measures in America have included the increased surveillance of immigrants and visitors coming from Muslim countries, racial profiling, and Department of Justice interviews, and investigations of Muslims already present in the country. These practices are just a few of the many elements contributing to anti-Muslim discrimination in the United States.[51] Two years after the World Trade Center attacks, protest continues against governmental attacks on civil liberties, the victims of which are primarily immigrant Muslims or people of immigrant Muslim origin. Nearly 1,200 resident aliens of Muslim origin were arrested in America after September 11, 2001 largely due to their ethnicity or country of origin. Even if these discriminatory practices have since tapered off, they continue to spark intense debate on the tension between the necessity to respect human rights and the concern for national security.[52]

Since September 11, the Bureau of Immigration and Nationalization Services (INS) has exercised its power to hold and/or deport any resident alien or visitor who overstays his or her visa with increasing diligence, in particular for citizens of Muslim countries. Immigration control procedures have been significantly tightened by requiring immigrants to register at immigration offices and making them notify the government of any change of residence during their stay within ten days of moving. In December 2002, more than two hundred Iranians were held for several days in California before being turned over to the INS for registration. Under the terms of the Patriot Act, the government can hold people in detention on unspecified charges for indeterminate lengths of time, and has the power to conduct investigations in ways that threaten to endanger Fourth Amendment protections against illegal search and seizure.[53] The Patriot Act also gives the FBI the power to question anyone, including any citizen who works in highly sensitive professions such as aviation or government administration. In November 2001, General Attorney John Ashcroft announced that the government would conduct investigations of nearly 5,000 foreign Muslims living on American soil. By the end of 2002, more than 3,000 additional investigations had been announced. According to official sources, only around twenty people from the first group were arrested and accused, and those for reasons other than terrorist activities.

Many Muslim charitable organizations have also been the target of police investigations. On December 4, 2001, the government designated The Holy Foundation for Relief and Development (HLF) as a terrorist organization and froze its assets, alleging that the foundation had ties to Hamas, listed as a "terrorist" organization under U.S. diplomatic regulations. The Global Relief Foundation (GRF) and the Benevolence International Foundation (BIF) were also penalized financially. More than 50,000 people were affected by the shutting-down of these three organizations. Indeed, it has become increasingly difficult to practice *zakat*—the Islamic duty of charitable giving—without being subject to scrutiny, even to the point of an FBI investigation. On March 20, 2002, FBI agents searched several Muslim offices and houses in Virginia and Georgia, looking for evidence of terrorist support. Even academic institutions like the International Institute of Islamic Thought (IIIT) and the University of Islamic and Social Sciences were among the targets. These investigations were part of the Green Task Initiative, whose objective is to dismantle the financial resources of terrorist groups. During the first four months of Green Task Initiative's operation, more than 10.3 million dollars in assets were seized.

As it happens, the implementation of these security measures frequently involves discriminatory practices. A particular example is the case of airport security. The practice of forcing Muslim women to remove their veils or headscarves no longer registers as discriminatory abuse, and there have been numerous instances in which people have been forced to leave an airplane because members of the crew regarded them as "suspicious." The highly publicized story of one of President Bush's own secret agents—expelled from an American Airlines plane on December 25, 2001—is only the most extreme example of such prejudicial treatment.

Immigration policy in the United States has also become more restrictive. On November 2001, the government instituted a 20-day waiting period for all men between the ages of 18 and 45 coming from Muslim countries. The upgrading of procedures for welcoming foreigners into the country, announced on June 5, 2002, consists of the following steps: taking the visitor's photograph and digital fingerprints at passport control, regular surveillance of any foreigner in the country for less than 30 days, and increased power on the part of the INS to deport foreigners whose visa has expired. These measures apply to visitors from all Muslim countries, and have been the object of intense criticism, particularly when they are wrongly applied to American citizens.

The Rise in Reactive Identity-Formation Among Western Muslims

The increase in the number of arrests and detentions of Muslims has been accompanied by public debate on the importance of protecting fundamental civil liberties, particularly in local media and on the Internet. This debate has been at the heart of the ACLU's massive campaign against Attorney General John Ashcroft's Homeland Security Act. In December of 2001, the ACLU, along with 18 other human rights organizations and Muslim lobbying groups, filed a civil action suit against the federal government. On January 27, 2004, it filed a complaint with the UN against the U.S. government's arbitrary detention policies. Similarly, the In Defense of Freedom Coalition, a massive coalition of more than 150 human rights organizations (including the ACLU) and 300 lawyers, was created on September 20, 2001, to fight against the erosion of fundamental civil liberties due to the War on Terror.

The current anti-Muslim rhetoric among American public figures is much more pronounced than it was before September 11. Attacks on Islam by prominent fundamentalist and evangelical Christians—who have gone as far as calling Islam the Antichrist—have been both increasingly visible and increasingly virulent since September 11. According to a 2003 survey, 77 percent of all evangelist Christian leaders have a negative image of Islam and perceive it as inherently characterized by violence. At the same time, however, these same people are ready to accept Muslims into the American community, and 79 percent of them consider it very important to protect the rights of Muslims.[54] This apparent contradiction nonetheless conforms to the national pattern, in which a general poor opinion of Islam is juxtaposed with an acceptance of individual Muslims. The contradiction is tied to the fact that anti-Islamic rhetoric concerns itself mainly with religious principles and values: essentially, the realm of philosophy or theology. But it rarely touches on those questions of racial and ethnic prejudice that affect the daily lives of Muslims. In other words, though the current popular discourse may be extremely hostile towards Islam, those who believe in this discourse do not necessarily also approve of discrimination toward Arabs, Asians, or Blacks. This is explained in part by the fact that the standard perception of Muslims is highly ethnically determined. Muslims are by and large perceived as members of an ethnic minority (Arab, Asian, Latino, etc.) and not as the messengers of a world religion. Of course, it is important not to overestimate this "tolerance" toward Muslims. Surveys such as those described above also reflect the widespread American attitude of "political correctness," which entails the somewhat automatic denunciation of any form of racial or ethnic discrimination (even if one's actual opinions are more or less to the contrary).

The anti-Islamic discourse of evangelist and fundamentalist Christians has been particularly visible and virulent, and has served to crystallize certain aspects of American public opinion. American Islamophobia tends to focus more on the religious aspects of Islam, in contrast to European Islamophobia before September 11, which was largely focused on cultural issues.

The American emphasis on religion is exemplified by the proliferation of literature, including several works by Muslim converts to Christianity, all insisting on the following two points. These works make the claim that: (1) Islam is an essentially violent religion; and (2) the God of Islam is fundamentally different from the Christian or Jewish God. One of the most popular of these books, *Unveiling Islam* (2002) which sold more than 100,000 copies, insisted on the utter lack of congruency between the God of Mohammed and the God of Christians,[55] and asserted that Mohammed thought of Christians as the children of Satan. Islamophobia reaches all the way up to the highest levels of government. U.S. Attorney General John Ashcroft was said to have stated, "Islam is a religion in which God requires you to send your son to die for him. Christianity is a faith in which God sends his son to die for you." This statement was repeated by a radio journalist in November of 2001, who insisted that he heard the words from Ashcroft himself. The journalist's allegations sparked a massive protest campaign, led primarily by Muslim organizations, including, among others, the Arab American Institue (AAI). On February 8, 2002, the AAI sent an open letter to President Bush, demanding either an official apology from the attorney general or his resignation. On February 13, 2002, Ashcroft issued a weak denial of the allegations, stating that the reported remarks "do not accurately reflect what I believe I said."[56] U.S. Army General William Boykin, deputy undersecretary of Defense and a professed evangelical Christian, similarly stated in October 2003 that the current political situation is a religious war: the Christian world against an idolatrous Islam.[57] A Department of Defense report, released on August 19, 2004, says that speeches made by the top general claiming that Muslims worship an "idol" violate Pentagon rules and warrant "corrective action."[58] Boykin has since also come under fire in regard to the mistreatment and torture of Iraqi prisoners by U.S. Army soldiers.[59]

Such an extreme climate of suspicion poses a new challenge for Muslim immigrants or Muslims of immigrant origin, who have, without question, felt more vulnerable since September 11, 2001. Some have spoken out against their ghettoization, comparing their situation—in the words of the Muslim Public Affairs Council (MPAC) President Salam Al Marayati—to confinement in a "virtual camp."[60] The once common view—particularly within the immigrants of middle- and upper-class origin—of America as an environment relatively favorable to Islam, is gone. Not only do Muslims now feel vulnerable in the United States, they also experience a feeling of being watched and the constant threat of arrest. Hussein, a tradesman of Indian origin who now lives in Brooklyn, has been a victim of panic attacks ever since FBI agents entered his place at six in the morning on June 26, 2002, looking for a suspect who was not, apparently, him: "I constantly live with fear, as soon as I hear a noise, my heartbeat accelerates. I have the feeling that I can be accused of anything and that I do not have true means to defend myself."[61]

In the well-known process of reactive identity-formation (already observed in the case of French Muslims after the Paris Métro attacks of 1995), such hostility toward Islam results in an intensification of one's personal attachment to Islam as the reference point of one's identity. This attachment is all the stronger when the individual has been personally a victim of discrimination, since s/he is not acting against merely an abstract hostility of government policy and media discourse.[62] Adherence to Islam is not always accompanied, however, by the strengthening of religious practice and belief. Instead, it is essentially a way to establish personal identity in relation to the outside environment and the discrimination it presents.

A consequence of this reactive identity-formation is that the "American Muslim" identity comes to take precedence over all other ethnic ties. Several organizations with the aim of introducing a Muslim voice into American political discourse, such as "Muslims Against Terrorism," have been created since September 11. Asma Khan, a 31-year-old lawyer and the founder of this association, devotes the majority of her time to issues concerning Islam and American Muslims. As she has said, "I am part of this generation that does not hesitate in asserting its American identity, and I am not afraid to be a Muslim and an American citizen."[63]

The crucial question here, however, is whether this recombination of identities will prove lasting and lead to the formation of a stable American Muslim identity—following the social model of Jewish American identity, which has come, with the passage of time, to supercede other ethnic and cultural differences. In the case of American Muslims, it is still too early to tell. Before September 11, such a development was far from inevitable. Muslim social organization up to this point has more resembled that of American Catholics, who preserve ethnic differences within the context of a common religious affiliation. Moreover, the split between black Muslims and Muslims from foreign nations presents an obstacle to the development of a pan-Islamic identity.

CHAPTER 3

The Secularization of Individual Islamic Practice

Another factor to be considered in the transformation of Islamic identity and practice is the influence exerted on Islam by the secular character of European and American societies. The legitimacy of Islam's establishment in Europe and America—often described as spaces devoid of God—continues to raise questions and doubts. In many respects, Islam is considered to be the diametrical opposite of the principle of secularism, viewed as an inherent attribute of the Western world. It is, certainly, true that it was in Europe that the principle of religious freedom developed, through blood and tears, from the sixteenth century on. This struggle for religious freedom led to that gradual separation of the political and religious spheres, which is now a fundamental aspect of democracy from Europe to the United States, Canada, and Australia. This separation includes both religious organizations' independence from most forms of political authority and the protection of religious freedom, guaranteed by that same power. This process of separating Church and State, otherwise known as secularization, is based on the philosophical principles of tolerance and respect for religious beliefs. It should be noted that the European history of this separation is rather more complex and contentious than the corresponding American history, as the social systems of Europe were long characterized by the congruence between State's roles and those of a dominant Church. In contrast religious pluralism in the United States is one of the basic elements of the national ethos.

Secularization, however, represents more than the separation of the religious and the political spheres. It also, and more importantly, stands for the diminished social influence of religion and its institutions in public life. In Europe in particular, the term secularization has an ideological function and manifests itself as an element of European identity in a variety of political and cultural narratives, including the sociology of religion. Consequently, the establishment of Islam is perceived as a potential threat to this cultural norm. Most of the justifications offered in support of this fear invoke *ad nauseam* the idea that "for Islam, there is no separation between politics and religion."

Certainly, Islamic thought is far from having achieved the same degree of skepticism that marks the course of Christian thought. The development of the concept of a religion independent of the State, and the primacy of a politics based on individual rights (as opposed to a politics focused on the common good), mark the triumph of a liberal Protestant vision of the self (the Kantian moral agent) situated within a secularized public arena.[1] No similar evolution has taken place in the Muslim world. It is tempting, perhaps, to consider the absence of this evolution as evidence that the Islamic mind is resistant to secularization *in toto*. Our approach makes no claims for the *a priori* ability or inability of Muslims to adapt to their new context, and additionally takes care to distinguish between Islam as it exists in Muslim States and Islam as a minority religion within non-Muslim countries. The politicizing of religious thought is often considered to be a characteristic inherent to Islam; in fact, however, this politicization has only emerged in the last quarter of the twentieth century as a deliberate policy of the post-colonial nations.[2]

There is no nation within the Muslim world that does not claim Islam as a foundational element of national unity. In every country of the Muslim world, Islam is either a State religion or under State control, even in ostensibly secular nations such as Turkey and Iraq under the former administration of Saddam Hussain. In light of this fact, the State is almost always the primary agent responsible for the authoritative interpretation of tradition. As a consequence, Islamic thought loses a certain vitality, not only in questions of government, but also in topics of a cultural or social nature. Thus it is not that "the Muslim mind" is naturally resistant to critical thinking, but rather that analysis and judgment have too often been the exclusive privilege of political authority. A further factor to consider is the prevailing view of international relations, which depicts Islam and the West as opposing forces, creating a "siege mentality" among Muslims and turning Islam into a tool of political resistance. Religious discourse becomes a key element in wartime rhetoric, a fact amply illustrated by the otherwise explicitly secular Saddam Hussein during the 1990 Gulf War.

Muslim emigration to Europe and the United States provides release from the "iron grip" of Muslim States on Islamic tradition. This "liberation" can take a variety of forms. Rather than attempt the pointless enumeration of Islam's failings *vis-à-vis* modernity, then, the more constructive method is to analyze the cultural and political principles that shape religious life in Western culture, and the ways in which these principles have influenced Muslims in their adaptation to the secular nations of the West. From such an analysis, two surprising facts emerge. The first is the increasing secularization of individual Islamic practice. More and more, religious practice tends to become a private matter, freed from the social conventions and standards of Islam as practiced in officially Muslim countries. The second fact has to do with the handling of *shari'a* in European and American court systems.

The Individualization of Religious Choice

To be Muslim in Europe or the United States means to lose one's relationship to Islam as a cultural and social *fait accompli*, and instead to open it up to questioning and individual choice. This is not to say that such individualism is a characteristic solely of Western Islam: in the Muslim world, too, people make individual choices and question their relationship to tradition. Nevertheless, the context of such individualism is quite different in the West. In secular democracies, the multiplicity of possible—and sometimes contradictory—choices is not only more noticeable, but also more accepted. While first-generation immigrants lived in a state of relative harmony between religious, social, and national identity, their children face a divergence, if not an outright contradiction, between the layers of individual, collective, and national identity. In a society at best indifferent, at worst hostile, to be Muslim no longer seems a given.

The individualization of religious choice thus leads to a range of possible Muslim identities. Danièle Hervieu-Leger[3] has described four types of Islamic practice: communal Islam, ethical Islam, cultural Islam, and emotional Islam. Communal identification with Islam emphasizes orthodoxy and the performance of ritual, in which observance of the five pillars, circumcision, food prohibitions, and rules regarding dress are the crucial elements of religious praxis. Ethical Islam, on the other hand, emphasizes communal and personal values that may have little or nothing to do with ritual and religious prohibitions. Cultural Islam refers to identification with all those elements that make up a culture: language, heritage, and the various modes of behavior within a group or society. In emotional Islam, identification is based on the reaction, sometimes spontaneous or short-lived, to particular events. One illustration of this form of Islam is an identification with political causes in which Muslims face oppression, from Palestine and Bosnia to Kosovo and Iraq. The minority status of Muslims in the West, and the continual reflection on what it means to be Muslim that this status entails, often triggers these kind of emotional attachments. These attachments, in turn, come to prevail over other forms of identification, especially when Muslims or Islam are victims of prejudice.

In the postmodern West, it is the more personal forms of Islam— emotional, cultural, and ethical—that dominate. Indeed, for the often silent majority of Muslims in Europe and America, identification with Islam and Islamic tradition does not necessarily entail a corresponding religious observance. This tendency certainly also exists in the Muslim world, but due to Islam's official status (with the possible exception of Turkey), never reaches the level of a general cultural trend. In the West, however, this tendency is both visible and explicit. In the same way as Catholicism and Protestantism developed personalized and secularized versions of themselves,[4] we are now witnessing the emergence of an individualized and secular Islam.[5] Within this trend, Muslims can be divided into three types: those who practice a private version of their faith, nonpracticing Muslims who nonetheless identify on an ethical or emotional basis, and fundamentalists who embrace a totalizing version of communal Islam.

Private Faith: "I Wear the Veil on the Inside"

Many Muslims who have been educated in Europe or the United States make distinctions between Islamic customs based on the customs' social visibility, adapting their observance to the boundaries between public and private of the country in which they live. It is common to meet young people of both sexes who perform "*Shahada*":[6] they follow dietary prohibitions, pray occasionally, and fast during the month of Ramadan, but refuse to be singled out as Muslims in social relations. This type of practice usually requires a certain knowledge of the Islamic tradition, so that the believer understands exactly what practices and customs exist to choose from. Although this trend is found in Muslims of all social backgrounds, it is most pronounced among people with a higher level of education.

D.,[7] 30 years old, has dual French and Moroccan nationality, and came to France five years ago to get her doctorate in Social Psychology.[8] After receiving her Ph.D., she was hired as a professor of gymnastics at an elementary school. She is not married, does not drink alcohol, does not eat pork, and fasts for Ramadan, but does not do the five daily prayers. To her, wearing the headscarf seems inappropriate in France, though she is sympathetic to the practice. S., 33, also binational, arrived from Morocco when he was three. He tries to pray five times a day—even though he may not always manage—but refuses to wear a beard or to dress "Muslim style."[9]

Two of the most visible signs of the division between private practice and religious fundamentalism are dress codes and the relationship between the sexes. Thus it is that, there are many young women who observe the five pillars of Islam but do not cover their head. "I wear the veil on the inside," says one.

Asma was born to a Pakistani family in New Jersey. She is a masters student in Economics at New York University. Her roommate is also Muslim, of Iranian origin. Asma eats *halal*, prays every day, and refuses sex before marriage, but wears jeans and does not cover her head. "I can be Muslim and still take part in every aspect of social, cultural and political life," she says. "For many girls my age, to wear the *hijab* is to give up taking part in things or to see themselves as limited in their capacity for action. Even if we want to participate, people judge us; our individuality disappears under the veil."[10]

Assia is 34 years old. A divorced mother of four, she lives in Manhattan, where she works for an organization for the prevention of domestic violence. She is a naturalized American citizen, having arrived in the United States from Palestine more than 27 years previous. She fasts during the month of Ramadan and observes the main holidays, mostly to set an example for her four children. Her children, however, attend the Islamic Noor school, in which a strict Wahhabi Islam is practiced and taught.[11]

The choice of education for children is also a decisive factor in differentiating between different types of Islamic practice. Families usually choose public schools or, if the option exists, an Islamic school. For Islamic schools, especially in America, there is then the choice between those influenced by the very conservative Salafi movements, inspired by Saudi doctrine,[12] and those, still very much in the minority, that are more receptive to American society and culture.

Ethical and Cultural Islam

A second type of Islamic practice consists in combining maximum individual autonomy with belief in a higher power. These Muslims live a life more or less secular, but observe the major Islamic rites of passage: circumcision, marriage, and burial. They define themselves as "nonpracticing believers," neither rejecting nor truly keeping to the ethnically-based Islam passed on to them by their parents, but tied nonetheless to Islam through the observance of holidays and traditions.

This type is further subdivided into those who can be classified as "nonpracticing orthodox," and those who move toward a departure from Islam entirely. Those in the first group, more numerous, treat their religious tradition as a cultural norm, but feel either that they are somehow unworthy of this tradition, or that the environment and the society in which they live prevent them from properly keeping the faith. This group is largely composed of working-class immigrants, who have little knowledge of Islamic tradition and ritual practice. Most have not received any teaching in the Qu'ran, either from within the family or outside of it (*madrasas*, religious organizations etc.).

The ethical approach is defined by an adherence to the moral and humanistic values that underlie religious practice—without, however, adhering to this practice itself. Many of the interviews presented in this book can be summed up by the following statement: "I am Muslim, I believe in Allah and his Prophet, but I do not practice." The more educated the person, the more this statement is explicit and asserted without a sense of guilt. Maryam is Ismaeli and a student of Anthropology at Rice University in Texas. She is active in her community and her mosque (Jama'at Khana), but does not fast for Ramadan. She subscribes wholeheartedly to the moral values of Islam—particularly to the concept of voluntarism, a central feature of Ismaeli practice. For Maryam and others, voluntarism consists in devoting a part of her spare time to the religious, educational, or social activities of the community.[13]

Adherence to Islam also involves the recognition of cultural heritage. Nadir was born in India but is Pakistani by nationality. He arrived in the United States in the 1970s for a postdoctoral program in Medicine. He is married and the father of a nine-year-old child. He first found work in a California hospital; at present, he is the director of a film company that makes videos about Islam. He describes the founding of his company:

In 1985, we started the Islamic information service. The idea was to inform the greatest society here about issues related to Islam and Muslims. And also not only to inform the non-Muslims, but also to increase the awareness and knowledge of Muslims themselves on contemporary issues, and how it would fit within the values system [of Islam]. So, we started a television program called "Islam in English Language," which showed locally for quite sometime: it was broadcast every week for half an hour. The money for the program was raised by Muslims themselves, because here everything is privatized and to buy air time. . . I mean, you have to purchase air time and you have to pay the production costs and all that. And then we also thought that if we can acquire our own technology cell—meaning, our own production facility—we could get into more content development in the English language. Because if you look at anything in the medium of television or video on Islam in English, there is very little.

Since 1985, we have produced more than seven hundred, eight hundred programs and documentaries. We invested our own money to acquire this studio. . . . So we became operational, and since then, we have broadcast every week. Not only that: for the last four or five years, we expanded the broadcast to one hour to five hours. And we are now in at least two hundred cities; we have a web site on which people ask us questions and comment on the program or the issues that we have presented. We have also encouraged interfaith dialogues with visits by university students and church groups to discuss issues we have in common, and how each community looks at a given set of issues. Those have been very successful programs. Next month there are two or three groups coming in. We tape those programs and show them without commentary. We let the discussion stand where it is. The program is basically values-based, dwelling more on the common ground that we share than on the differences. But that does not mean that we water down the differences.[14]

Leila is Arab, though she refused to say from which country.[15] An anthropologist working in a university, she also hosts a radio program for an independent New York radio station. She defines herself as both a non-believer and nonpracticing. For some years, however, she has hosted a special program for the month of Ramadan: "I subscribe to a lot of, let us call them, Muslim-oriented magazines," she says.

There are a lot out there. And I identify people: you know, I bring them on my program as experts on an issue. Or I publicize their work. Or when Ramadan comes . . . now, most people at the station know that it is Ramadan, which is a big thing. They are not fasting, but they see us fasting and have a few programs about it. We have a few other Muslims in here doing programs during Ramadan. And people are just . . . [there is only] a little bit of awareness. So, I feel that a lot of my work is just general education. It is not easy. Someone gives you four hours during Ramadan and says, do something for us. It's public radio station, and most of the listeners are not Muslim. How are you going to creatively educate people?

So, I have tried to get sometimes . . . we will read stories of Muslim history, the life of the Prophet or . . . I do fair amount of Sufi [material], because it is more creative, you know, more sensuous. There is a lot of good stuff in terms of the Sufi music. I combine Sufi music with readings from Rumi and other kinds of Sufi readings. Whenever I go to the Middle East I get Sufi music of various kinds. We also have one poet, a white convert. His name is Abdul Al-Hai Noor. He wrote a book called

Ramadan Sonnets, one poem for every day during Ramadan. And that's what I did for Ramadan. Every day of the month, I did a four-minute piece. And that worked very well. Another time we'll have Muslim children on the program. There are no many children who are religious, plus radio is not a children's medium in general. But I found that when children are singing Ramadan songs and talking about fasting, just for half a minute, two minutes, three minutes, not much more, that is also very nice. But once we had a program on women in Islam, and . . . you know, it's a big thing, very sexy: "Women in Islam." So I won't do that any more. I mean, I don't care if somebody is male or female. But we had this special on women in Islam. It was not a particularly good program. The women who came were very defensive. They said I am not . . . and you people do not understand . . . they were very defensive, because they were reacting to this thing out there. I won't do that. I am very, very careful, as an anthropologist I think, to not be reactive in that way.

The way Muslims relate to Islam can also result in a certain militancy. Salam Al-Marayati was born in Iraq but raised in Arizona. He majored in Biochemistry at the University of Los Angeles, but has since devoted his entire career to defending the public image of Islam[16]. His public activism is entirely in the service of Islam. In 1989, Al-Marayati founded the MPAC: "The Muslim Public Affairs Council was founded, out of the need of Muslims to relate to the media and to public officials, to get involved in design-making and opinion-shaping," Al-Marayati states. "In America, public opinion is the central element of how designs are made. And Muslims do not have a voice in that public opinion apparatus. The Mosques cannot do it on their own, because they're so burdened with religious services and social services for its membership. So I decided to form the Council as a vehicle to disseminate accurate information about Islam and Muslims to the public, and to begin the process of creating an effective American Muslim constituency in U.S. politics."

This kind of activism in the name of Islam has no true equivalent in Europe. In the United States, on the other hand, emphasis is placed on public and active expressions of religious membership, an emphasis that encourages public engagement in the name of religion even if this engagement is not always accompanied by religious practice.

The Hybridization of Islam

The trend of individualism can also be seen in the emergence and development of certain syncretic practices, most notably Sufi or mystical orders.

In the West, the search for a transcendental union with God may not necessarily take the form of group membership via the transmission of specific knowledge or practices. Although Sufi sects obviously have a group and sometimes also a method, an individual can join or leave the group at will, sometimes without even the requirement to be Muslim. Particularly in American society, syncretic Sufism attracts a considerable number of middle-class and educated individuals from cities like New York, Los Angeles, and Boston. From a psychological perspective of religion, joining a Sufi group follows a pattern of the search for self-transformation and rehabilitation. Whatever form the practice takes, they all share the idea that humans need to find a way to live in harmony with a higher power that provides meaning and direction in life.[17]

Marcia Hermansen has used the term "Perennial Movements," to describe groups, such as the Sufi Order of Pir Vilayat Khan, for whom being Muslim is not a requirement of membership. Vilayat Khan was born in Europe to an Indian father (The father, Hazrat Inayat Khan, arrived in the United States in 1910) and an American mother. He died in the town of Suresnes on June 17, 2004. According to his sect, the divine revelation transcends that of the Prophet Muhammad and includes other traditions such as Hinduism, Zoroastrianism, and Christian esoteric traditions, especially as described in the writings of Henry Corbin. Marcia Hermansen uses the term "hybrid movement," in contrast to "perennial movement," to describe groups that respect orthodox procedures of conversion to Islam and a strict Islamic ritual practice, usually based on the *dhikr*.[18] Sufism also takes exigencies of the non-Muslim world into account in its idea of the initiate's gradual progression in the faith.

One example of the "hybrid" tendency is the Naqshabendi movement, founded by Cyprus-born Shaykh Nazim Al Kibrisi. Since the 1970s, the movement has found more and more disciples within Europe and in United States. Since 1991, the American branch of the movement has been run by founder Hisham Kabbani's son-in-law. This latter made a name through his lobbying efforts on behalf of Islam, in contrast to both Saudi and more conservative movements. Another example of a hybrid movement is the Bawa Muhaiyadden Fellowship, founded by Guru Bawa Muhaiyaddeen. He left Sri Lanka to settle in Philadelphia in 1971, gathering around him a group of mostly American disciples. He was organizing *dhikr* sessions by 1976, and by 1981 had also established the practice of five-times-daily prayer.

The entrance of a non-Muslim into a Sufi brotherhood is almost always the result of a search for a syncretic or hybrid spirituality, and is not necessarily accompanied by orthodox religious practice. Instead, it has more to do with the adoption of a certain philosophy, lifestyle, or way to better know oneself. Followers emphasize the idea of inner change and virtues such as self-control, courage, and wisdom as the means of reaching divine knowledge.

Hoda converted to Islam and entered the Nakshabendi brotherhood as a result of her intellectual and artitistic attraction to Islam. She explains her transformation: "I met Sheikh Nazim al-Haqqani in Damascus, Syria in 1978, at which point Islamic Sufism ceased to be a spectator sport. I began to eat the food instead of the menu. For me, commitment to inner change is the heart of submission to God's will, the very heart of life here and hereafter. What it means in my daily life boils down to some very simple goals mainly just to be, to be sincerely in my right spot, to be this little sand grain in harmony with the great wheeling pattern whose light I barely register."[19]

Bagha was born into a Muslim family. A charismatic sheikh's teachings attracted her to Sufism: "His first objective was to unfold the reality of Islam for us," she explains. "His students were mainly western-oriented new-age people in search of truth. Being an architect-engineer, the sheikh was trying to relate esoteric Islam and jurisprudence to science and modern belief systems, in order to better relate to the new-age group. On the esoteric side, he confined himself to the remembrance of God (*dhikr*), which he said is the most powerful tactic for emergency conditions like the ones we faced. He told us to do our spiritual practice of remembrance of God twice a day, twenty minutes in the morning and at night as beginners."[20]

Sheikh Bentounes, the current head of the Alawiya brotherhood and a member of the CFCM (Conseil Français du Culte Musulman), describes Islamic identity in the following terms:

> More than a religion, Islam is a state of consciousness. It creates a consciousness of being. It's not some catalogue of rules like the Highway Code, even if some would prefer it to be. Islam is above all an act of faith, an inner conviction, a living spirituality. Islam exists so that man can reach more and more developed degrees of consciousness to pacify his ego, to quiet his ego in order to live according to the Divine Will, by making man His Lieutenant, the lieutenant of God on earth: the caliph of God. To attain this concept of *khalifat*, man must transcend all things. The question was posed to the Prophet: "O Prophet of God, tell us what is to be Muslim." His answer was: "A Muslim is one of whom one fears neither the hand nor the tongue." He does not define the Muslim by fasting or prayer. Those are precious tools that are offered to us so that we may work on ourselves to arrive at an inner awakening of consciousness. Such spiritual exercises make change possible. But they are not obligations. Most Muslims experience them as obligations. Because their Islam

is an Islam based on tradition and not an Islam based on experience. It is not an Islam we have found ourselves, but an Islam we inherited from our parents. This kind of Islam is lived as a monolith of habits and traditions, whether they are African, Turkish, or South Asian. But they have nothing to do with the spirit of the religion."[21]

Orthodoxy and the Totalized Religious Life

Secularization, so-called, can also consist in choosing an integralist approach to tradition. Integralism here means following all religious regulations and living one's religion as a way of life, a style, in all senses of the term. Codes of dress and a refusal to mix the sexes in social relations are the two primary elements of the espousal of a totalizing message of Islam, in contrast to more private versions.

Once again, there are degrees to this integralist identification. The observance of Islamic customs and practices does not necessarily imply the refusal of the world. Thus the choice to cover one's head or to refuse the mixing of men and women in public areas does not always mean a corresponding refusal to work or be socially engaged. Sara studies Law at Harvard University. Her father is a Pakistani immigrant and her mother is American, converted to Islam. Sara is married and the mother of a two-year-old little boy. Depending on the season, she covers her hair with pretty scarves or hats, and usually wears pants. Her husband is an Iraqi Shiite. "We are both American, educated here. Because we are also Muslim, I get the best of both worlds."[22] She is an active member of Karama, the association of Muslim women lawyers, and is proud to claim that she once sat in the California State Supreme Court with her head covered.

This kind of orthodoxy, adapted to the requirements of a pluralist society, is a particularity of American Islam. The orthodox elite in the United States is more numerous than its European counterpart, and tends to combine a self-examining and introspective approach to Islamic tradition with an active participation in society. One might describe it as "modern orthodoxy." "It *is* more difficult to respect all the traditions and at the same time be part of the society around us," Sara emphasizes. "It is important for me to show that one can be a modern woman and at the same time cover her head, because it contradicts the idea of the woman oppressed under the law of *hijab.*"

This kind of fundamentalist and yet open-minded lifestyle is mostly found among the university-educated elite in America, and applies to quite a number of Muslim students, particularly those who wear the *hijab*. Leila came to Missouri at the age of seven. Her father is a doctor of Bangledeshi origin, and she attends the University of Chicago as a Religious Studies major. Leila covers her head and wears long tunics in the Pakistani style, but does not shy away from active involvement in the social life of her campus. She remembers how other students stared at her the first time she wore *hijab* on campus. Some asked her why she had decided to wear "that thing": "I told them that it was part of my religion, that it was a way to be a bit more sincere, and so that from now on, people would pay attention to who I am, instead of what I look like."

In most cases, however, the choice of a totalized Islamic practice is accompanied by a rejection of the non-Muslim world. Paradoxically, fundamentalism can be said to have a postmodern quality, in that it often proceeds from the deliberate rejection of worldliness and its excesses. In other words, fundamentalism is, more often than not, a freely chosen identity, not something imposed by the community, tradition, or the family. A puritan and separatist version of Islam is appealing to many young people, and in certain cases can even be a response to cultural and social ghettoization.

If the prevailing western meta-narrative bases itself on the opposition between Islam and the West, Muslims, for their part, have their own binary, in which the West is associated with impurity, depravity, and the arrogance of rule by the strongest. This opposition—in which Islam is positive and the West is negative—is accompanied, in sectarian interpretations, by a totalization of religious life. Many marginalized youth, both men and women, are beginning to create communal ties between peers specifically chosen for their intransigence in the face of an impure environment. This sort of sectarian relation to the outside world is part of the Salafi and Wahhabi systems of belief, for example. Today, the ideologies of Salafi, Barelvi, and Tabligh Islam attract many Western-acculturated youth: or, rather, *de*culturated, insofar as such groups give a concreteness and a legitimacy to the rejection of the world by sealing themselves off from all products of culture. Their stated goal is to recreate the idealized community of the Prophet, independent of all historical context. In these sects there is an obsession with wholeness and purity, neither of which can be achieved without the meticulous observance of Islamic regulations, in every aspect of life. Above all else, relations between the sexes catalyze this obsession with purity. Dress codes, as well as a retreat from the outside environment in all matters of life—work, leisure activities, lifestyle—are tailored to reflect this binary vision.

The sectarian worldview is based on a hierarchy of world religions that places Muslims at the top and tends to evaluate all areas of social and political life according to their religious character, or lack thereof. All relations with the outside world are conducted exclusively from the standpoint of religion. In other words, every aspect of behavior, be it in the family or in society, is judged according to its degree of conformity with the laws of Islam. The world is divided into "believers" and "infidels," the latter term referring not just to non-Muslims but also to Muslims who do not sufficiently observe the Law.

Nonetheless, in secular societies, the choice of a fundamentalist approach is a reversible one, as the case of Nada demonstrates. Nada is a masters student at the University of California, Berkeley. She was born in Jordan, but grew up in Detroit. Her father, a software engineer, is remarried to a non-Muslim who recently converted to Islam. Nada explains that she had always been very conservative in her religious choices:

> I always observed the five pillars, wore the headscarf. My father never forced me, but he was proud when I made the decision to wear it. In the summer of 2000, I went to a camp for young Muslims, and I discovered that all my Indo-Pakistani friends knew more about religion than I did. I was embarrassed, because for some stupid reason I had thought that as an Arab I would know more than them, which was wrong. Then I wanted to learn more. I started to read everything that fell into my hands, most of which were Wahhabi or Salafi publications. I started going to extremes: I didn't wear bright colors any more, my scarf covered not only my hair but also my chest (which was already covered by a long tunic), I didn't listen to music any more, I no longer watched TV. I isolated myself in a bubble along with my college roommate. My father was very critical of my choice: whenever I saw him he tried to get me to wear less unappealing clothing, to be more reasonable. I refused to listen to him because I thought he didn't understand anything about Islam and I understood everything. I was also encouraged by the imam at my mosque, who congratulated me on my choice and held me up as an example for other girls.
>
> I wanted to take a trip to Cairo in the summer of 2001 to really study Islam at Al-Azhar University, and I had the good luck to be invited to live in the house of X, a famous female forensics expert. I asked the imam at the mosque and he told me not to go, because it was *haram* for a woman to travel alone. I talked to my father about it, who encouraged me to go and wanted to have a talk with the imam. So there I am in Cairo. I was studying at Al-Azhar under a very religious woman, and I was staying at the house of a widow who was also an expert in *fiqh* (Islamic jurisprudence), but with more liberal views. So every day I was getting two completely different interpretations of the same questions, from makeup to clothing or whatever. . . . I remember asking my imam once if a woman was allowed to show her feet. . . . His response was, "no, no matter what the school of

jurisprudence says." But in Cairo I discovered that for Hanafis, a woman is allowed to wear sandals. I felt betrayed by this person I had looked up to so much. I had expected him to teach me everything about the Law and the different interpretations that existed, not just to give me the strictest interpretation as if it were the only one. That summer in Cairo was the turning point. I realized that there was not just one, but many possible interpretations of the Law. When I got back to Dearborn, I wore colors and pants again, and I saw that my imam was disappointed by my change. I left my bubble and went back to a more balanced view of things, even if it's not always easy and I'm always worried about making a mistake. I'm still conservative, but now I live in the world.[23]

The Secularization of Shari'a

The individualization of Islam can also be seen in the practice of *Shari'a*, whose application and administration in the tribunals of Europe and America is dramatically different from that in the courts of the Muslim world. It is an unprecedented, but underappreciated, fact that Islamic legal norms are being reconstructed in the West as a function of the principles of dominant European law. Up to now, separatist claims—that is, demands for Islamic law to be applied in a way that departs from the legal framework of host societies—have been rare. One example of this occurred in Britain in the 1970s and 1980s, when the Union of Muslim Organizations requested that special statutes be applied to Muslim individuals; or, more recently, in 1991, when the Muslim Society of Canada requested certain rules governing personal status to be included in Canadian law. In June of 2004, the province of Ontario agreed to consider allowing an Islamic association (The Islamic Institute for Civil Justice) to represent Muslim families on issues of civil law.[24] But in general, such extremely marginal demands have come from radical, highly politicized groups, whose objective is to establish an Islamic State—thus making any effort to reflect upon *Shari'a* in a non-Muslim context irrelevant. This is the case, for example, of the Hizb AP Tahrir group of Great Britain, which explicitly calls for the creation of an Islamic State, and anticipates that this process will be accelerated by the imminent conversion of Prince Charles. The Universal Declaration of Islamic Rights[25] also takes a similar position to these groups; but this document, it should be said, still has little influence in the daily lives of Muslims. In general, the marginality of such claims attests to the fact that divine rights do not yet take precedence over human rights in mainstream society.

For the majority of Muslims who accept the legal and institutional framework of the country where they live, on the other hand, the adaptation of

Islam to national laws is indeed in progress. Surprisingly, this adaptation has been, in most cases, a passive one. That is, it does not come from Islamic legal experts or Muslim theologians, but from European and American judges.[26] The consequence is the slow and "invisible" construction of a new form of Islam, an Islam that has been translated according to Western laws. The contours of this evolution can be more or less clear, depending on the country and the Islamic group concerned. Pearl and Menski call the hybrid legal system now coming into being in England *"Angrezi Shari'a"*[27]: "While English Law is clearly the official law, Muslim Law in Britain today has become part of the sphere of unofficial law. This analytical paradigm indicates that Muslims continue to feel bound by the framework of the *Shari'a* and value it more than Western concepts. . . . Thus, rather than adjusting to English law by abandoning certain facets of their *Shari'a*, South Asian Muslims in Britain appear to have built the requirements of English Law into their own traditional legal structures."[28] This emergent hybrid product is stamped with the seal of Western individualist culture: in other words, it is marked as compatible with the principle of individual freedom. The recognition (even implicitly) of such a principle, is currently redefining Islamic regulations with regard to the status of the individual and the family, the two main areas in which discord arises between Western legal norms on the rights of individuals and the legal norms of Muslim countries.

Marriage, Polygamy, and Divorce
Islamic precepts regarding the family and the individual have been profoundly altered by life in the West. In matters of family law, most Muslim countries privilege a system that authorizes polygamy, that gives priority to the husband in divorce proceedings, and that does not recognize civil or interreligious marriages. Conflicts usually arise regarding international laws on the rights of individuals when the legal prescriptions of certain Muslim countries are in open contradiction with those of the European or American legal system. When such disputes arise, two scenarios are possible: either a ruling or legal precedent from the country of origin is recognized, or else the law of host country is applied. Thus it can happen that such customs as polygamy or wife repudiation can be accepted in Western democracies in the cases of immigrants who arrive in the host country having already practiced the customs in their country of origin. However, there are still restrictions to this recognition of foreign laws: if officials or government employees consider the foreign rulings to be excessively discriminatory, particularly in matters of gender equality, they may refuse to recognize them. Thus the degree of tolerance for polygamy may vary from country to country and

situation to situation. The refusal to recognize polygamy is most categorical in England, where no polygamous marriage whatsoever may enter the country. Surprisingly, it is French judges who have tended to show the greatest leniency, particularly during the 1980s. Interestingly, between 1983 (arret Rohbi, Cass. Ire civ, 3Nov 3, 1983) and 1994, the trend was toward an acknowledgment of *talaqs* (repudiation) pronounced overseas. However, since 1994 (Cass. Ire civ, June 1, 1994), the trend has been reversed. Today, the increasing hostility of the judge to recognize the effects of a repudiation carried out in a foreign country is quite patent in France. The shift is partially caused by the adjustment to the principles of the European Convention of Human Rights: equality of the partners (art 14) and the right of the woman to a due divorce procedures (Art. 6).[29]

As a general rule, the refusal to offer legal recognition of certain phenomena (polygamy, repudiation, etc.) is justified by the argument that they constitute a threat to public order. It is also interesting to note that in certain countries, such as in Belgium, repudiation is legally recognized if it has been mutually consented to.[30]

But what happens when new Muslims of European or American origin have to adapt Islamic law to their own western legal systems? In no Western country does Islamic law apply in matters of marriage, divorce, inheritance, and so on. Attempts to reconcile the legal norms of the host country with those inherited from Islamic tradition continue to grow in number, and attest to the pragmatic outlook of most Muslims. In most cases, the law of the country is formally followed; meanwhile, an informal respect is paid to Islamic law, from marriage contracts and divorce to the custody of children.

Although there are various schools of Muslim law, the principles of Islamic marriage are everywhere the same. Marriage is seen as a contract based on mutual consent. Individuals who are to be married communicate their wishes through *wali* (proxies), whose role are generally determined according to levels of male kinship on the bride and groom's side. According to existing civil laws, forced marriages are forbidden in the Muslim world, though coercion by a guardian can often be an efficient way to restrict freedom in matters of marriage. And it is indeed true that the family (the mother in particular) wields significant influence over the choice of the child's spouse. It is the mother, for example, who brokers transactions and organizes meetings. In Europe and the United States, Islamic marriages increasingly follow the logic of individualism, marking a break with the dominant practice in Islamic countries. The influence of the family is thus on the wane, and marriage is increasingly a matter for the individual and his/her own feelings—more or less similar to the situation for non-Muslim young people of the same generation.

The conflicts that emerge around the issue of marriage thus tend to be more cultural, and less directly related to Islamic law. Theologian Zaki Badawi[31] gives the example of a young Pakistani woman in England who refused to marry her cousin. The young man immigrated to England on the basis of a civil marriage. The woman's father married her, in a religious ceremony, against her will. She decided to run away, so as to escape before the marriage could be consummated. Her father died and her brothers put pressure on her in a variety of ways (including death threats) to make her respect her father's wishes. The husband returned to Pakistan, where he married another young woman, but the first woman was never allowed to have another religious marriage ceremony since her husband continued to refuse to grant her a divorce.[32]

The Islamic marriage ceremony consists in reading the *Fatiha*, the first *sûrah* of the Qu'ran; this consecrates the marriage. The ceremony generally takes place at the bride's parents' home, with only a few guests in attendance. In countries where Islam is a State religion, a religious authority (i.e., with official status) performs the reading. The same is not true for Europe or the United States, where any acknowledged believer can read the *Fatiha* and thus make the marriage official. In cases where religious marriage has the same status as civil union (as in Spain or Italy), marriage based on Islamic code is legally binding. In Spain, the recording of the marriage in the civil registry, a requirement for Jewish and Protestant minorities, is not mandatory in the case of Islam. Consequently, polygamy can be given a kind of hidden approval. Any marriage that occurs after the recording of a first marriage in the civil register will obviously have no legal status, but since marriages do not actually have to be registered, contracting more than one cannot be considered illegal.[33]

In the cases of Belgium, the Netherlands, France, Holland, and Germany, religious authorities may not proceed with a religious marriage until a civil marriage ceremony has first been carried out by a government official. It is often the case that this order (civil marriage *then* religious marriage) is not respected by the couple, though such divergent practices remain officially illegal. A judge will sometimes even recognize an existing Islamic marriage on the grounds that official acknowledgment was being sought.[34] Our own research shows that many young people are exchanging religious vows, then allowing a certain amount of time to pass before taking their official vows before mayor or public official. These young couples are not yet married in the eyes of the law, but they can live together as a married couple and take time to get to know each other, as if they were simply cohabiting. Thus if they do decide to split up, there are no legal proceedings to be undertaken.

In France, the reading of the *Fatiha* may also precede the civil marriage ceremony, in contravention of the law—but since imams have no official status in France as of yet, this practice cannot actually be regulated.

In Great Britain, purely religious marriages have no legitimacy under the law. Marriage must take place in a legally recognized location,[35] and must be recorded in the marriage registry, although the person officiating at the religious ceremony may also fill out the documents for civil marriage. In the United States, too, the person officiating at a religious ceremony has legal authority to preside over the corresponding civil wedding. The law makes no conditions about the person officiating; the choice is considered an internal issue for the community. Any Islamic ceremony led by a civilian is thus perfectly acceptable in the eyes of civil law, so long as the person has registered beforehand with the municipal authorities. In this respect, the American procedure is more flexible than that of European countries. Some States in America even go so far as to recognize Islamic marriages without requiring any prior civil registration. This is made possible by the principle of common-law marriage, which states that a husband and wife who recognize themselves as such and have lived together for a certain length of time constitute a married couple. In the case of Ohio vs. Helps, for example, a wife was not allowed to testify against her husband even though they were not married under civil law. Since there was proof that they lived together and that they were married under Islamic law the court declared their marriage to be valid.[36]

It is within the domain of repudiation (i.e., divorce) that arbitration or attempts at reconciliation between religious law and civil judgments most often become necessary.[37] Repudiation is prohibited by law in all Western nations. In well-organized minority groups, however, a judge may take into account the recommendations of certain religious decision-makers. In England, a body for reconciliation, the Shariah Council,[38] was established in 1982 in order to settle disputes between forms of religious and civil marriage. If a husband refuses to consent to his wife's demand for a divorce, the wife can take her plea to the Shariah Council, which then summons the two parties and tries to offer a form of arbitration. A system of arbitration also exists in the United States, where the Fiqh Council of North America[39] has sought solutions to cases of conflict between Islamic regulations and prevailing American norms since 1995. American courts are also expanding their mediation efforts by calling upon social workers, religious authorities, and Muslim lawyers. It does seem that legal conflicts around polygamy will continue to go down in number, however, as the practice is followed less and less often by Muslims integrated into Western society.

More surprising are the current arguments being presented by female legal experts that the Qu'ranic laws on marriage actually favor monogamy. Azizah al-Hibri refers to legal experts of the classical period, who considered that a second marriage was not recommended if it was prejudicial to the first wife. Similarly, Amina Wadud, in her exegesis of the Qu'ran, proposes an interpretation according to which polygamy is justified only in very limited cases, such as the just treatment of orphans.[40] Still others, such as the members of the Muslim League of Women, assert that since the second wife is not legally recognized under civil law, she cannot be afforded equal status: which means the situation does not conform with Islamic law *a priori*, given that polygamy is only considered legitimate if all wives receive strictly equal treatment.

Other sources of potential conflict regarding Islamic family life concern the religious education of children and child custody regulations, particularly in cases of interfaith marriage. In Islam, it is the father who passes on his name and his religion to his children. He is thus legally entitled to custody of the children in the event of divorce from a non-Muslim woman. In general, however, Western courts do not recognize such a principle, unless it happens to be in the best interests of the child.

A new set of Islamic norms is thus being forged in European and American courts of justice. In most cases having to do with family life, negotiation is still the strategy of choice. The recognition of individual freedoms and the consideration of each party's best interests lead to compromises that change not only the letter but also the spirit of the Islamic laws, stripping them of the meanings they have in Islamic societies. One example of this transformation, in which Islamic regulations are "acclimatized" to Western legal norms, concerns the acceptable period of time one's widowhood should last. Traditional Islamic law specifying the amount of time that must elapse before one is allowed to remarry cannot be strictly enforced in European societies.[41] Laws governing inheritance offer another example of the flexibil-.ity involved in translating old practices into new contexts. Once again, the Islamic precepts (which specify that for every part of an heritance given to a daughter, two parts must be given to each son) cannot always be strictly adhered to, especially in legal systems influenced by Roman law (Roman law ensures that each descendant be provided for equally).[42]

It is in matters of divorce that changes in Islamic law have been the most significant, but also the most difficult to identify. Even though a divorce can still be officially carried out within religious law, unofficially, it may have been already initiated by the wife herself in the civil court system. In addition, divorce is increasingly a topic of discussion for both members of the married couple. The fact that husband and wife both abide by traditional Islamic law does not necessarily determine the degree of oppression or inequality within a marriage.

The status of polygamous marriages and negotiation in divorce proceedings are the two main categories in which Islamic laws find themselves transformed within the context of Western democratic societies. Even more important, the connections between religion, morality, and religious law are becoming more and more relaxed, hinting at a secularization of Islamic norms. The codes of behavior traditionally associated with Islamic observance can no longer be a requirement, once the Law of the Prophet has been adjusted to fit a secular code of national laws. In most Western societies, in fact, Islamic tradition is transformed into a collection of legal rules having mainly to do with the observance of ritual; consequently, it loses its sacred character. The question then becomes: which rules are not in open contravention of the host country's legal statutes? And, by extension: which rules do not contradict the dominant secular culture?

Circumcision and ritual slaughter are two prescriptions within Islamic tradition that frequently come into conflict with the legal system of certain countries. Although no democratic nation explicitly outlaws circumcision, the topic is still often a subject for debate.[43] Indeed, in 1992 a bill was proposed in Belgium that sought to classify circumcision as a form of sexual mutilation punishable by law. Unlike male circumcision, female circumcision is illegal everywhere, on the basis of respect for individual physical integrity.[44]

Laws regarding the ritual killing of animals are also usually recognized under host country law, with the exceptions of Switzerland, Norway, and Sweden. In most cases, existing legislation on *Kashrut* (Jewish dietary law) has been broadened to include references to *Halal* meat; in some countries, such as Belgium and the Netherlands, special legislation has been created for Islam. Resistance to the ritual slaughter of animals (in countries such as Germany, Austria, and Belgium) is generally not born of legal constraints; more frequently, it is the product of opposition from the civilian population (e.g., animal rights movements). In certain cases, this criticism gathers such power that the right to the ritual slaughter of animals is called into question entirely. In 1995, Hamburg's administrative court ruled that ritual slaughter was not part of Islamic law. The defendants, from a company run by practicing Muslims, appealed the decision. They took their case to the Federal Administrative Court, which rejected the appeal, stating that the principle of religious freedom had not been violated.[45]

Most Islamic laws, however, enjoy legal protection in Europe and in the United States. This is shown, for example, in the supplying of *halal* food to schools, prisons, and the army.[46] In the same vein is the acknowledgment of key festivals such as *Eid al Fitr* that marks the end of the month of Ramadan. Furthermore, in clashes over the issue of daily prayers and the workday, most court cases have decided in Muslims' favor. More serious conflicts tend to arise when there is a tension between the public nature of certain prescriptions and the secular character of the host country's dominant culture. One example of this situation is the wearing of the Islamic veil, which has been a recurring problem within French society, as well as in other European countries (see chapter 4).

The paradox, however, is that in officially multicultural countries, legal recognition for Islamic cultural practices is often easier to obtain than an acknowledgment of Islamic law. In Bakhitiari v. The Zoological Society of London, for example, a young Iranian woman lost three fingers after being bitten by a monkey. In a 1991 decision, the court took into account the fact that in Iranian society, the woman's marriage prospects were now much slimmer as a consequence of her handicap. The plaintiff thus received a significant sum in damages. In Seemi v. Seemi (1990) a Muslim woman received £20,000 in damages in a case against her husband, who had falsely accused her of not being a virgin at the time of their wedding.[47]

This overview of Muslims in secular societies again raises the question: How can Islam and Muslims be integrated into Western culture while still maintaining the latter's principles of equality and individual freedom? Paradoxical though it may be, the secularization of Islamic *institutions* seems less problematic. The secularization of Islam also means its official establishment in European society. An unprecedented situation is thus beginning to emerge: the cooperation between Muslims and the secular Western state. In the United States, this cooperation is further manifested in Islam's inclusion in civil religion, as well as by a growing number of Islamic lobby groups.

CHAPTER 4

The Secularization of Islamic Institutions in Europe and the United States: Two Approaches

European Islam and the Church Model

It is a significant fact that throughout Europe, the arrival of Islam has reopened the file—up to now considered "case closed"—on the relationship between Church and State. The great diversity of Euro-Islamic scenarios, however, reflects the cultural and political specificity of each country more than it sheds any light on the so-called special nature of Islam. The relationship of the government to religion in Europe tends to pattern itself on one of three principal types: the cooperation between Church and State, the existence of a State-sponsored religion, or the total separation of religion and politics. No matter what the type of relationship, however, the European question of Islam's institutionalization has no real equivalent in American culture. European secularism does not consist merely in the protection of religious freedoms and the political independence of religious organizations, as it does in the United States. It is also, if paradoxically, accompanied by a collaboration between Church and State. The secularization of Islam, therefore, is seen particularly in the emergence of Muslim Organizations adapted to preexisting structures of Church–State relations within the host country.

State Recognition of Religion: Austria, Belgium, Italy, Spain, and Germany

The development of Islamic institutions is facilitated in countries such as Belgium, Italy,[1] Spain, and Austria, where all religions are already legally recognized.

Islam was officially recognized in Austria in 1979. The Islamic Law of 1912[2] provided the basis for this recognition, and Muslim Social Services (Moslemische Sozial Dienst) was, with the help of several other religious and political associations, influential in pushing this recognition through. After Catholicism and Protestantism, Islam is now the third largest religion in the country. There is an Islamic Consistory (religious governing body), and since 1983, courses in Islam have been taught in the schools by more than 230 state-appointed teachers.

The Belgian government recognized Islam as a religion in 1974. This recognition was, however, merely in principle, since the religion had no official means of representation within the government. The Islamic Center of Brussels, a branch of the World Islamic League and financed by Saudi Arabia, has played the de facto role of spokesperson for Islamic affairs, though it never received any official acknowledgment. The main practical consequence of the recognition of Islam has been the hiring of teachers of Islam for public schools. But in the absence of a real representative body for Islam, these teachers, approximately 800 in number, enjoy no official status. They were hired and financed by local Belgian officials after passing an examination in either French or Flemish language, pedagogy, and theology, and appointed by the Director of the Islamic Center of Brussels.

The assassination, in February 1989 of the imam-director under mysterious circumstances exposed the shortcomings of the current situation. Drawing inspiration from the initiatives of the French Minister of the Interior, Pierre Joxe, who had recently created the Council for Reflection on Islam in France (Conseil de Réflexion sur L'Islam en France, CORIF), the Belgian Council of Ministers established on March 30, 1990 a provisional advisory committee. This committee would be made up of 17 members, chosen by the Minister of Justice to reflect all of the different linguistic and political divisions within Belgian society, as well as the different sensibilities of Islam.

Despite these measures, the process of institutionalization has been long and difficult. The December 13, 1998 elections for the Belgian General Islamic Assembly were held in 105 mosques, chosen at random, as well as 15 selected public spaces. Voter participation came to 64 per cent (45,000 voters)[3]. In turn, the Assembly elected an internal executive council (l' Exécutif des Musulmans de Belgique) composed of seventeen members: seven Moroccans, four Turks, three Belgians, and three members chosen from other nationalities. In order to be eligible for the executive council, approval from the Ministry of Justice was required. It was this stage most of all that placed the council's autonomy and legitimacy in doubt, as the Belgian government rejected in advance the candidacy of almost half of all the members of the Assembly, due to their "fundamentalist" leanings. This situation led to tensions between the partially appointed executive council and the elected General Assembly. The crisis came to a head in 2002, effectively preventing the Council from functioning and bringing the Assembly's activity to a standstill. The Ministry of Justice intervened as go-between, and in 2003 created an interim Council to fulfill the previous Council's functions until new elections could be held before the end of 2004. On June 25, 2004, the Belgian Council of Ministers approved a royal decree creating a commission that would be responsible for organizing the re-election of a representative body for Islam[4].

In contrast, the process of Islam's institutionalization in Spain has been surprisingly trouble-free. Two conditions must be fulfilled for an agreement to be reached between the Spanish government and any organized religion: the religious organization must be registered as such, and it must be able to claim a certain number of members who can prove their residence in Spain. The Spanish Federation of Evangelical Associations and the Federation of Israelite Communities already benefit from such agreements. On January 26, 1992 Islam was granted official recognition via the Islamic Commission of Spain (CIE), an umbrella group comprising the majority of Muslim federations and associations in the country.

Official recognition in Spain offers financial as well as legal advantages (such as the inviolability of religious spaces). It also gives religious marriages the same legal status as civil marriages and provides for the introduction of religious education in public schools, though as of 2004, this last measure has not yet been put into practice.[5]

The rapidity of Islam's institutionalization in Spain is even more remarkable given that Spain has only been a destination for Muslim immigrants since the 1980s. The special nature of the relationship between Spain and Islam partially explains the rapid official recognition of the religion. Spain's long history with Islam (Spain was entirely under Muslim control from the eighth to the twelfth centuries, and the Arab kingdom of Grenada fell as late as 1492) makes the religion something not entirely foreign, not to mention the existence of Ceuta and Mellila, the two Spanish cities on Moroccan territory. The fact that the first Islamic organizations in Spain were created either by converts or naturalized citizens was an additional factor in the easy acquisition of State cooperation. The Islamic Commission that signed the 1992 accord was formed by the merger of FEERI (Spanish Federation of Islamic Religious Organizations), established in 1989, and the UCIE (Spanish Islamic Community Union), which came into being in 1990. These two groups came out of the very first Spanish Muslim organizations, made up of converts or Spanish Muslims from Ceuta and Melilla, as well as middle-class immigrants from the Middle East, who make up a large section of both professional and diplomatic cadres. In spite of this, the 1992 accord has not been respected by the government of Spain; moreover, the disputes between Muslim immigrants and converts to Islam have done little to facilitate its enactment.

In cases where religion is officially recognized by the State, it appears that resistance to the official recognition of Islam is tied more to current attitudes and the degree of acceptance Islam enjoys in general, rather than to any actual legal or institutional obstacles. The non recognition of Islam in Germany is a classic case.[6] No Islamic association in Germany has managed to achieve the status of public organization, despite the goodwill efforts of groups such as the Central Islamic Council (*Zentralrat*), who in 2002 drew up a charter declaring Islam's compatibility with the constitutional principles of Germany.

Islam's struggle for institutionalization in Germany has largely been fought over the issue of religious education in public schools. According to German law, all religions are entitled to courses in the public school system, under state administration.[7] In Bavaria, North Rhine-Westphalia, Hesse, and Rhineland-Palatinate, Islamic education is provided as part of a Turkish-language educational program for children of immigrants, organized in cooperation between the German States (*Länder*) and the government of Turkey, or other countries with nationals residing in Germany. The Turkish government, or the government of the country in question, provides the course content; the German States provide logistical support and occasionally contribute funds. Negotiation for the programs was carried out with representatives of the Turkish government, under the rubric of treaties with the home countries of *Gästarbeiter* (immigrant workers), and with the initial purpose of facilitating the acculturation of *Gästarbeiter* children upon their return to the country of origin. (Other German states, such as Sarrland or Bade-Würtemburg, follow a different method, in which the Turkish government provides both personnel and logistical support through the Turkish consulate.)

These programs, however, have not proven entirely satisfactory, due largely to the fact that textbooks and curricula for the programs were imported directly from Turkey. For this reason, the German States have begun to seek alternative solutions. In 2000, North Rhine-Westphalia made the decision to transform its Turkish-language program into a course on Islam conducted in German. During the same period, Hamburg launched a program of religious instruction for everyone: that is, a course on all religions, aimed at promoting interfaith dialogue. The state of Brandenburg similarly established a course on religion ethics.[8]

Since the 1990s, the strongest critics of these programs have been the main Islamic organizations in Germany, who had expected to be asked by the government to create the educational programs for the public school system. The most active of these organizations has been the Islamic Federation of Berlin, which has campaigned since the 1980s to obtain community status, in order to be able to provide a program of education in Berlin's public schools. Created in 1980, the Federation is made up of between 25 and 30 member organizations. Although close to the Islamic movement Milli Görüs,[9] it is careful to keep such alliances at a distance, in light of the "crackdown on fundamentalism" atmosphere in Germany after the attacks of September 11, 2001. The Federation was initially refused religious community status due to a lack of teachers and textbooks, until a February 24, 2000 Federal Court decision recognized the organization's right to provide religious education in Berlin's public schools. This recognition was granted despite an appeal by the municipality of Berlin, who asked the Court to rethink its decision, on the grounds that the Islamic Federation was suspected of being an extremist organization and had been under surveillance by German Secret Service well before September 11.[10] The school administrative authority in Berlin was already engaged in a fight against the Federation, and continued to try to discredit it as an organization more political than religious in nature. Doubts about the Federation even arose in Turkey. As soon as the Court's decision was made public, Turkish journalists launched a campaign of protest, asking readers to keep their children away from the Federation's "clutches." The Association of Turkish Parents similarly declared that it could not accept the Federation's educational program because of its political agenda. The Federation, for its part, made the announcement that its classes were open to everyone. Once its status as a religious community was official, the Federation designated several pilot sites in the Kreutzberg district of Berlin, declaring its intention to provide around forty new teachers to selected schools. Two elementary schools received Islamic courses provided by the Federation as early as the 2001–2002 school year.[11] Since this date, the Federation has expanded its programs to 28 schools throughout Berlin.[12] The program remains controversial, however, and relations between the Federation and the Berlin Ministry of Education have once again become tense, after it was discovered that in 2003 the Federation had distributed a form, taken from the Internet, to Muslim families to request that their daughters be exempt from co-ed classrooms.[13] Nonetheless, this model (cooperation between the Ministry of Education and Islamic associations to create programs of religious education in the German language) continues to be used with increasing frequency. In Lower Saxony, at the beginning of the 2003 school year, the Ministry of Education announced the introduction of German-language Islamic classes in eight elementary schools, under the direction of the main local Islamic organizations. Similarly, in Bavaria, the government is in the process of transferring authority to local Islamic associations and away from the Turkish government for the teaching of Islam in public schools.[14]

In cases of strict separation between Church and State, the institutionalization of Islam can be considered something outside the political sphere, and primarily dependent on initiatives led by Muslims themselves. In these countries, the government gives no support of any kind to religious institutions, offering itself solely as the guarantor of religious freedom and equal treatment for all religions. This is the case in the United States, where the question of Islam's governance and official legitimacy is not an issue. The federated nature of the United States precludes the need for a centralized Islamic body under the control of a "Grand Mufti". Furthermore, religious affairs are considered an aspect of civil society. It would thus be inappropriate, even improper, for the State to involve itself in the administration of a religious institution.

The Special Case of France

This is not the case, however, in that other country with a strict separation between church and State—that is, France. France's long colonial history still exerts a strong influence on the French administration of Islam,[15] which has always been treated as a "special case." One must also take into account the prevailing idea of religion as a menace to public order—in contrast to the United States, where religion is seen as a unifying force. The administration of Islam has been the State's responsibility since 1989, when several Ministers of the Interior began an initiative to stimulate dialogue and rapprochement between leading branches and associations of Islam in France. But after the attempts of the CORIF, other initiatives have had little success. Since the failure of CORIF, subsequent efforts have waffled between the choice of a general dialogue among all the currents of French Islam, and priority given to the Great Mosque of Paris, (closely tied to the Algerian government), even though the latter option has received a fairly cold reception among most French Muslims. The 1995 Charter of the Muslim Religion, proposed by the then Minister of the Interior, Charles Pasqua, had the potential to become an important symbolic document, particularly through its declaration that it was possible to be at once a Muslim and a good French citizen. But despite its meticulous description of a potential representative body, this document did little to advance the cause of Islamic administration in France, in part because it was the product solely of the Mosque of Paris and not the result of a collective effort.

If the Mosque of Paris could no longer be considered the primary agent of French Islam, however, the question of a suitable representative body remained unanswered. In October 1999, Jean-Pierre Chevènement reinitiated dialogue with Islamic leadership. These talks led to the signing of a document, on January 28, 2000, once again affirming the compatibility of Islam and the French Republic. The May 2002 presidential elections marked by the victory of Jaques Chirac and the Right, delayed the process yet again for several months. On the 19 and the 20 of December 2002, however, the new Minister of the Interior, Nicolas Sarkozy, called together the main institutions of French Islam to create the French Council on Islam (CFCM, le Conseil Français du Culte Musulman). This so-called historic agreement consisted in getting those Islamic associations involved in the previous delegation to give their consent to the document already approved by the Minister of the Interior and the three main Islamic organizations. This fact serves to explain why the board of directors of what was to become the French Council on Islam was not elected: the presidency went to Dalil Boubakeur, Rector of the Great Mosque of Paris; the two vice presidents were Fouad Aloui, from the Union of Islamic Organizations in France (UOIF), and Mohmed Bechari, of the National Federation of French Muslims (FNMF).

In any event, the agreement confirmed the principle of vote by mosque for all future elections of the Council, which have since included elections for its representative assembly, its administrative council, and its second board of directors (though some of the board will still be appointed). On April 6 and 13, 4,000 electors, representing more than 900 houses of worship, elected the CFCM's General Assembly. Each mosque chose a certain number of delegates according to its size: less than 100 m² of floor space, one delegate; 100–200 m², two delegates; and so on up to large mosques whose range reaches over 800 m², entitled to 15 delegates; and lastly the Mosque of Paris, with 18 delegates. Nine hundred and ninety-five mosques chose 4,032 delegates to make up the regional electoral assembly. In the elections, the Mosque of Paris came out behind the FNMF (with links to Morocco), and the UOIF, which follows the ideology of the Muslim Brothers. However, on May 4, 2003, the General Assembly of the CFCM confirmed the choice of the French state in reelecting Dalil Boubakeur, rector of the Mosque of Paris, as president of the new Council.

In the mind of the French authorities, the CFCM should allow for dialogue between all the different camps of Islam, following the model of the Catholic, Protestant, and Jewish faiths, who have similar representative bodies. In an interview for the French daily *Libération* (February 21, 2003),

Nicolas Sarkozy described the CFCM's role as one of giving Islam "a public face, which will lead to integration and, from there, a form of normalization." He emphasized the necessity of "understanding the place Islam occupies in French society." The creation of the CFCM responds to the desire to remove Islam's stigma as an "underground" religion. Sarkozy affirmed his "rejection of the current conditions that force Islam to develop out of cellars and garages," adding that "we should all fear a secrecy [which] leads to radicalization." The June 15, 2003 elections for regional council presidents confirmed the dominance of the UOIF, which, along with its allies, captured the presidency in 11 out of 25 regions, including the two most important: Île de France and Provence-Alpes-Côte d'Azur. This success demonstrates the lack of support and trust that the Mosque of Paris (seen as too much a tool of the Algerian government) has among the Muslim population in France. The discrepancy between the results of the popular vote and the favorites of the French government led to the first crisis within the new Council. The day after the elections, Dalil Boubakeur threatened to resign, only keeping his post due to pressure from the Ministry of the Interior.

The second serious crisis faced by the new Council regards the headscarf debate of and the proposed ban on all visible signs of religion in the public schools. Dalil Boubakeur initially expressed CFCM's disagreement with this bill, upon the release, by the Stasi Commision, of a study recommending the bill's approval. However, after President Jacques Chirac's speech on December 17, 2003, supporting the Stasi Commission's position, Boubakeur changed his position and made an announcement asking Muslims to respect the law if it passed, and urging them not to protest. Other members of the CFCM, on the other hand, such as vice-president Fouad Alaoui, expressed their disagreement with the proposed law (as representatives of the UOIF). They have lent their support to the demonstration held on January 17, 2004, as well as to other forms of protest against the proposed law, which was eventually adopted by Parliament on March 15, 2004.[16]

Countries with a State Religion: Great Britain, Denmark,[17] Greece[18]

The third model for the relationship between religious institutions and the State in Europe involves the existence of an official State religion, as is the case in England, Denmark, and Greece. But, just as in Spain or Italy—where the Catholic religion has dominated for a variety of cultural and historical reasons—other religions are not therefore deprived of their rights by any means. In all areas of government in which the dominant religion is a factor, the minority religion is accorded all the same rights—albeit with a "delay effect" of greater or lesser length, and more or less overt forms of resistance. As the State religion, the Church of England enjoys a number of privileges: 2 archbishops and 24 bishops are members of the House of Lords; the Anglican Church is the only one to preside over all ceremonies of the Royal Family, and the reigning king lays claim to the title of "defender of the faith"—even if Prince Charles has repeatedly stated that he considers himself the "defender of all faiths."

The debate over Islamic schools demonstrates how the extension of religious education laws to the Muslim minority can generate resistance before finally being accepted. Under British law, any religious organization or school of thought has the right to create private schools. Accordingly, there are 110 Islamic schools in England at present, enrolling approximately 10,000 Muslim students.[19] To be accorded the status of "Voluntary-Aided School," however, is a different matter. To receive the State funding that voluntary-aided school status confers, the school must both conform to a state-issued curriculum and be open to all students. Yusuf Islam, a.k.a. folk singer Cat Stevens, was one of the first to get involved in the Muslim fight for State authorization. The government several times refused funding to the schools he founded, on the basis of arguments that had never been applied in other minority cases.[20] On January 30, 1998, however, Al-Furqan Primary School in Birmingham and Islamia Primary School in the Brent district of London were finally given official status. On May 10, 2000, Prince Charles officially inaugurated the Islamia Primary School, in the presence of Yusuf Islam. Since then, the state has authorized two additional schools: Feversham Girl in Bradford and Al Hijrah in Birmingham.[21] According to the most recent 2004 statistics, only four Islamic schools received authorization,[22] an indication that despite official recognition, resistance to Islamic schools has not died out. The authorization of Al Hijrah was far from unanimous. One of the dissenting members of the municipal council, Tory James Hutchings, stated that such an institution would only serve to reinforce the social and cultural segregation of Muslims.[23] In May of 2004, an Islamic high school in Oxford was similarly refused State assistance, once again due to the fear of encouraging separatism between different cultures and religions.[24] The attacks of September 11, as well as the rioting in the cities of Northern England in the spring of that same year, only strengthened this resistance, and Islamic education was often described as a potential means of promoting Islamic extremism, and even unrest, among Muslim youth.[25]

The question of equal status between the State religion and a minority religion can also arise in unexpected places—for example, in the "Rushdie

Affair," in which certain representatives of the Muslim community demanded that the law against sacrilege, until that point associated exclusively with the Anglican church, be applied. What is perhaps most surprising is that, by and large, Muslims, along with other minority religions, do not want Anglican Church privilege abolished, but on the contrary extended. In 1996, the Policy Studies Institute of London organized a debate on "Church, State, and Religious Minorities." Most of the participants, and particularly the Muslims, criticized the project as an attempt on the part of political liberals to eliminate the State's role in religious matters. They argued against the idea that religious equality required the absolute separation of government and religion. They cited examples to the contrary from English history, and demanded instead of separation, a pluralization of government involvement in religion: in other words, State intervention and protection not merely for Anglicanism but also for all other religious represented in the United Kingdom.[26]

It is also worth noting the "hybrid" case of the Netherlands, where the principle of secularization has been a part of the Constitution for two centuries, but where the cooperation between the State and the churches is equally well established due to a long history of pillarization.[27] This tradition of cooperation is expressed in several different ways. Religious schools, for example, have received State funding since 1917 under the constitutional principle of religious equality. Such a practice, however, is hardly unanimously popular, and the endless debates on financial ties between religious organizations and the State led, in 1983, to a revision of the Dutch Constitution instituting seperation of the State and religious institutions. Ironically, this provision forced the government into negotiations with several religious organizations, who required State assistance as a direct result of the cutting of financial ties between the government and the churches. Among other decisions, the money previously designated for religious leaders was replaced by a comprehensive allowance. The participation of Muslim organizations in these negotiations was an important watershed in the institutionalization of Islam, even if no permanent agreement was reached. In light of this failure, the government set up an advisory committee in 1988. Among the recommendations made by the committee was the need to provide financial assistance for the building of mosques, in order to rectify the inequality between the Muslim minority and Christian denominations. These recommendations, however, have not been followed upon by action.

In contrast to funding for mosques, the funding of activities dealing with general spiritual guidance, such as Islamic schools and Islamic information broadcasts on public television, has been retained. In 1998, the State provided funding for two imams to work as chaplains in the army, and two others in the prisons. Since then, however, the status of imams has remained controversial, particularly with regard to the compatibility of their teachings with the core values of Dutch society. In May of 2001, a Moroccan imam declared on television that homosexuality was a disease and a danger for Dutch society. These statements caused a public uproar, and a massive debate on freedom of religious expression and the necessity for imams to respect the values of Dutch society. This controversy, which was only heightened by the September 11 attacks, led to the adoption in January 2002 of a law requiring training in Dutch language and culture for all foreign-born imams entering the territory. (It is optional for those already living in the Netherlands.) The first class, consisting of around thirty imams from Morocco and Turkey, graduated in January 2003.[28]

Finally, let us note that Islam can also gain official status through other means, such as laws protecting ethnic minorities. Noteworthy among these is the law granting time off in businesses for the observance of Muslim holidays.[29]

Islam and Secular Ideology

To fully comprehend the role of religion in Europe and the United States, we must look to more than the institutional arrangements described above. Beyond the official separation of Church and State and the principle of religious neutrality, the *ideology* of secularism, part of the legacy of the Enlightenment, rules in the West. The vision set out by Auguste Comte in his book, *The Religion of Humanity* (1851), typifies the belief in the power of secular humanism, a doctrine that confirms the triumph of the rational human being over the forces of religion and functions as a sort of counter-model for religious faith. Comte even writes of "Priests of Humanity," men who would be responsible for spreading the gospel of progress and ensuring sociocracy's victory over theocracy.

The age of Positivism may be long gone, and the battles with the churches finished, but the continued influence of this past on current perceptions of religion should not be underestimated. A common denominator of Western European societies is the tendency to discount or ignore matters of religion in social interaction between citizens. One characteristic of the secularist mindset is the idea that religion has no share in the common good of societies. This attitude is practically unanimous in Western Europe, no matter what the relationship between the State and organized religion.

One consequence of this view is to make problematic, or even unacceptable, the various manifestations of Islam in Europe. Muslim demands are automatically perceived as suspect, or sometimes even retrograde, and can provoke highly emotional reactions from the public. The headscarf is interpreted as a symbol of the rejection of progress and women's emancipation. It thus draws the *ire* of those groups most explicitly concerned with defending secular ideology: teachers, intellectuals, feminists, public servants. Islam's entry into European society rekindles the fight against all religions: a fact shown, for example, in a petition submitted in 2002 by a Norwegian atheist organization to the municipality of Oslo to be permitted to proclaim for a few minutes each day that God does not exist, specifically in order to compete with the muezzin of Oslo.[30]

France's Headscarf Controversy

Secularist ideology reaches a fever pitch in France, where—as the escalation of the headscarf affair demonstrates since the 1980s—it has even become part of official policy. Positivism's influence on the architects of French secularism revealed to them, in effect, a new entity: the collective social being. This discovery allowed them to establish voluntary submission to the principles of positivist science and human progress as the basis of all democratic activity. They thus effected a complete reversal in epistemological thinking, the corollary of which was the rejection of all transcendental philosophies. This change implies even more than the principles of individual liberty, social equality, and religious neutrality; it also means the "will to place man as the source and the center of all necessity."

For reasons particular to France's historical situation, most notably the resistance of the Catholic church to the law of separation, this rejection of religion eventually took on a radical character. The conception of secularism in France[31] is thus an extremely rigid one, in which any and all signs of religion must be eradicated from public space. Not only are classes on religion banned in the public schools—making France an anomaly among democratic nations—but even the wearing of religious symbols has become a subject of controversy. The appearance of Islamic headscarves in French schools has provoked an impassioned argument about secularism of a kind not seen since the separation of Church and State. More important, perhaps, is that the headscarf controversy has brought to light the glaring disparity between the dominant sociocultural conception of secularism and its legal expression. In other words, the way in which most French citizens understand secularism is not at all the same as the law itself. The law merely provides for the separation of Church and State—and therefore, religious neutrality in public institutions—and for the legal protection of all religious expressions.

In keeping with its long tradition as the guardians of the law, the Conseil d'État[32] has regularly drawn attention to this gap between public perception and legal statute. In a November 27, 1989 ruling, it reminded the government that it is only public servants, not the consumers of public services, from whom the principle of secularism obliges religious neutrality. Thus the infamous headscarf, as a symbol of religious faith, does not in any way violate this obligation. In a ruling with wider implications than the headscarf case *stricto sensu*, the Conseil d'État stressed that "the wearing of religious symbols is not incompatible with the law of secularism," the only limitation to this being in cases in which the symbol becomes a threat to public order.[33] Additionally—and this is the crux of the matter—the court essentially contradicted the sociologically dominant conception of religion's role in society. In fact, the principle of secularism provides a legal basis for the free public expression of all religions, and forbids the State from interfering in this process. The expectations of the general public, however, diverge significantly from this ruling. For the majority, secularism means the illegitimacy of all public protestations of religion generally, and the religion of the Other in specific. The proof is that the Conseil d'État has regularly been called upon to review decisions of the administration that potentially violate the principle of secularism. On November 2, 1991, for example, the Conseil overturned a ruling by the Administrative Court of Paris that upheld a regulation of the school at Montfermeil stipulating that any student wearing a headscarf would be expelled. The Conseil's overturning of the decision was on the grounds that any such absolute prohibition, including prohibitions against religious symbols (because it was only the headscarf that was in question) violated the principles of secularism. The war in the schools intensified after the Minister of Education, François Bayrou, issued a memorandum to school administrators on September 20, 1994 stating that "the ostentatious display of any symbol of religious, political, or philosophical belief is forbidden in places of public education." What, then, constituted an "ostentatious" symbol? Wasn't any symbol ostentatious by definition? Was it only the Islamic headscarf at issue?

In 2003, the debate went to the next level with the introduction of a bill to ban ostentatious religious symbols in the public schools, eventually passed in March 2004. The Stasi Commision, a delegation of scholars and experts created in July 2003 at the initiative of the French presidency, came out in favor of the law. In a televised speech on December 17, 2003 President Chirac himself endorsed the Commission's decision. Such a law seems to hope to bridge, by legislative means, of the gap between the law and public perception. It reveals an authoritarian conception of the law, henceforth charged with the protection of individual freedom—including the protection of individual freedom against the individual's will—and above all with imposing a definition of freedom of conscience based on an idealized and homogenous vision of society. In other words, to be a modern citizen means to reject all public sign of religion. The headscarf law seeks to "liberate" young Muslim women from the oppression of religious symbols.

France's intransigence on the headscarf is a crystallization of already-existing crises regarding the meaning of the Republic and the function of democratic institutions. Public schooling in France was to be not merely an institution for the transmission of knowledge; it was also intended to be a vehicle for the propagation of a universal, science-based morality, which stands in opposition to religious teaching. The idea was to create a program of total transformation of citizens through State education: a program that, religiously neutral though it is, will nonetheless completely transform both the individual and civil society. It thus functions as a kind of anti-Church with ambitions to monopoly, the creed of science serving for dogma.

As the utopian structures of modernity begin to crumble, however, this vision of the State is no longer possible. Thus the question arises: what now constitutes social cohesion? In an atomized society, where ideas of accomplishment, of self-realization, of progress are deeply in doubt, on what basis can individuals come together to think about their common destiny—and, by the same token, their collective memory? The public schools are no longer able to provide definitive or unanimous answers to these questions. Muslim opposition to the French headscarf law have been strong, both in Europe and the Muslim world, and heralds the worldwide emergence of popular opinion on this issue.

France's inflexibility on this issue has also served to bring Islam's more radical tendencies into the public sphere, as shown by the demonstration organized for January 17, 2004 by Mohamed Latrèche's French Muslim Party. This party, created in 1997 by the Syrian-born resident of Strasbourg, had until recently never succeeded in finding a voice within the Muslim community. Now, however, it is becoming a player in the French political scene both through its opposition to the law, and through its support of the two Aubervilliers high school students, Alma and Lilla, whose expulsions in the fall of 2003 reactivated the headscarf debate.

The Question of Freedom of Conscience

Similar debates are occurring all over Europe. This is largely due to the fact that for many, Islam has come to symbolize all the possible evils associated with the social conditions of women. The status of women in Islam appears, in effect, as the opposite pole of the principle of non-discrimination (including discrimination on the basis of gender) which regulates all interpersonal relations in French society. This negative image can be carried to such an extent that the headscarf appears on the same level as symbols such as the swastika. In a 1992 ruling, a member of the Conseil d'État wrote that the scarf expresses nothing in itself. It therefore cannot be equated with symbols such as the *swastika*, which are direct incitements to hate. The headscarf is only experienced as an assault on women's dignity within the *reconstruction* of everything one knows—or thinks one knows—about Islamic religion and society. But in fact, this interpretation of religious symbols without any consideration of those who actually wear it is *in itself* a violation of the principle of freedom of conscience. The negative image of the headscarf, perceived as an attack on the values of equality and universality, is common throughout Europe. In July 1998, the minister-president of Baden-Württemburg upheld the decision of a Stuttgart school not to hire a Muslim woman as a teacher, because she wore a headscarf. The minister declared that the headscarf was more a political symbol of women's subjugation than a religious prescription.[34] On July 4, 2002, the Federal Administrative Court ruled against the wearing of veils by public school teachers. But in a surprising September 2003 decision, the Federal Constitutional Court refused to uphold the principle of barring women teachers who wore the headscarf from the schools, and delegated the decision to the States on a case by case basis.[35] Since then, Baden-Württemberg has banned headscarves for teachers in a law of April 1, 2004. Other States, such as Bavaria, Berlin and Lower Saxony are also in the process of forbidding teachers to wear the headscarf. At any rate, these decisions do not affect students who wear the headscarf, and cannot really be compared with the French position, as Chancellor Gerhard Schroeder has himself pointed out.

The real difference of opinion on this issue, however, is between Europe and the United States. Freedom of conscience certainly also comes under attack in the United States, where controversies over the wearing of headscarves often also arise in places other than the public schools, particularly in the business world. Instead, the difference is in the strong judicial tradition of the United States in defending religious freedom. When, for example, in March 2004, a Muskogee, Oklahoma 6th-grader was temporarily expelled for having continued to wear *hijab* despite a rule prohibiting all headcoverings, the Justice Department supported the complaint filed against the school district by the girl's parents, which invoked the 14th Amendment (Equal Protection) and the need to defend constitutional freedoms. The American judiciary can thus rule on cases of religious discrimination without it creating a nationwide debate. The public role of religion nevertheless continues to be a contentious issue, pitting those who, in the name of the separation of Church and State, want religious references eradicated from public space, against those who believe that this option does not reflect America's political and cultural history. This perpetual controversy was recently illustrated by the public outcry following a June 26, 2002 decision by a San Francisco federal appeals court, declaring unconstitutional the phrase, "One Nation under God," included in the Pledge of Allegiance since 1954.

The discrimination that American Muslims have faced since September 11, 2001 must also be factored into the changes in the status of religion in public life. For perhaps the first time in the United States, an entire religion is not only subjected to widespread public suspicion, but also to governmental surveillance of its activities and associations. The actions carried out in the name of the War on Terror include police searches of organizations' offices and arrests of people accused of belonging to militant Islamist organizations, and have been denounced by Muslim leaders and others as just so many attacks on civil liberties. This public scrutiny of a religion is unusual for the United States, and brings together for the first time the American and European experience in their treatment of religion in general and Islam in particular.

"Professional Muslims" and American Civil Religion

In the United States, the strict separation between Church and State means that Islam's struggle for legitimacy is not a question of establishment in official institutions. The religious diversity of the Founding Fathers[36] precluded the establishment of a national church. Religious pluralism has characterized American society since its beginnings, in contrast to the traditional religious homogeneity of most European societies. Even among the first Protestant settlers on the American continent[37] there were numerous religious differences, whereas European societies are marked by the historical predominance of one religion, or occasionally dual religions, as is the case in Belgium and Holland. David Martin classifies nations either as Catholic societies, which are based on religious monopoly, or as Protestant societies, which are most often duopolies based on the concept of pluralism.[38] Despite the pluralism of American religious life, however, the question of Islam has nonetheless been divisive, particularly and very obviously after September 11.

The Emerging Public Face of American Islam

The emergence of a Muslim minority within American society is fairly new. One reason for this is that, despite the considerable number of African American converts to Islam, African Americans are more commonly seem as being defined by their skin color or ethnicity rather than their religious practice and beliefs. This perception is partially explained by the fact that the Nation of Islam, as well as other, more short-lived organizations such as the

Islamic Party, has always advocated for segregation and the rejection of civil religion. The founder of the Nation of Islam, Elijah Mohammed, was imprisoned during World War II for having exhorted the black population not to vote or serve in the military. African-American acceptance of American society and its underlying political principles is a relatively recent phenomenon. Among those black leaders who have been influential in this shift is Warith Deen Muhammad, the former head of the Muslim American Society[39]. The second reason for the relatively recent emergence of the American Muslim minority is that Arab or other Muslims who immigrated to America from the 1920s through the 1950s were for the most part progressively assimilated into American culture.

It was only after 1967 that Islam became a central element of collective identity in the United States. For immigrants who entered the country after 1965, Islam was the primary means of cultural and political identification—in contrast to their predecessors, who had built their identity more on the basis of Arab nationalism. Thus Arab activists, formerly concerned with issues related to the Middle East, and Palestine in particular, have begun instead to form Islamic associations. The Federation of Islamic Associations (FIA), founded in 1953, played a pioneering role in this area, but never quite succeeded in overcoming the tensions between first- and second-generation immigrants.

The 1963 creation of the Muslim Student Association (MSA) by students from throughout the Muslim world—inspired by Islamic revivalist movements such as the Muslim Brothers—was the true birth of Islam's public face, and many Islamic associations have since developed out of the MSA.

The Islamic Society of North America (ISNA) was created in 1982 as a result of diversification and specialization within the MSA. It is a coalition of different types of local organizations, including Islamic centers and professional associations (such as lawyers' or doctors' groups). The third reason for Islam's sudden visibility has been the influx of Muslims from the Asian Subcontinent—Indians, Pakistanis, and Bangladeshis—less familiar with pro-Arab lobbies. Today, these three ethnic groups (Indian/Pakistani/Bangladeshi) represent more than 24 percent of Muslims in the United States, and over 12 percent of all immigrants.

Since the 1970s, Muslims have taken one of two paths to inclusion in American civil religious society: Islamic organizing in various coalitions and associations, and political lobbying. One must distinguish between those groups with a professed religious character—which generally bring different associations together under one heading on the basis of categories such as profession/area of expertise or geographic region—and those that specifically define themselves as lobby groups. Of the former, the two most important are the ISNA and the Islamic Council of North America (ICNA).

In 2000, we interviewed Muzammil H. Siddiqi, president of the ISNA from 1996 to 2000, at the offices of the Islamic center he runs in California. Born in India, he has lived in the United States for the past 30 years. He studied Medicine and Islamic Studies in India, and Social Sciences through the American university system, receiving his Ph.D. from Harvard University in 1976. His doctoral thesis dealt with the Muslim perception and interpretation of Christianity. He currently teaches Islamic and Religious Studies at the University of California, Fullerton. He explains:

> ISNA is the oldest and the largest federation of Islamic organizations in the United States and Canada. It started with the MSA, around 1962 or '63. Then the MSA evolved: many students became residents here; they immigrated, raised families. So, after twenty years, in 1983, the MSA developed into the ISNA. The MSA remained, as a wing of a major organization, a bigger organization. Now we have the ISNA as an umbrella group, and under it are various constituent organizations: the MSA, the Muslim Student Association; the IMA, Islamic Medical Association; the AMSS, Association of Muslim Social Sciences; the AMSE, Association of Muslim Scientists and Engineers; MAYA, Muslim Arab Youth Association; and MYNA, Muslim Youth of North America. These are the various constituent organizations. This is how the ISNA has grown, by involving many people. There are many other organizations in this country, such as the Islamic Circle of North America and the Nation of Islam. When the Nation of Islam came under Imam Warith Deen Muhammad leadership, they became mainstream Muslims, and changed their name to American Muslim Mission. We are very happy because last year, Imam Warith Deen Muhammad [from the American Muslim Society] also joined the ISNA. So, he is now also in our *Shura*, our constituent assembly. He is one of the members.[40]

One of the ISNA's most important activities is its Annual Conference, usually held at the end of August, which brings together thousands of people who come to participate in a wide variety of workshops and discussions. It is also a vast marketplace for Islamic goods, with booths selling books, cassette tapes, clothing, and other related items.

The ICNA, on the other hand, was inspired by the Islamic party Jamaat-Pakistani Islamiyya,[41] and emerged on the American religious scene in 1971. In 2000, we met with the secretary general of the organization,

Zaher Uddeen, in Queens, New York: "We have about 65 to 70 chapters in different cities all over the U.S. and Canada," he states. "The basic objective of our work is to take the message of Islam to the rest of humanity. We want to share our heritage. We would like to share our Islamic beliefs and teachings with the rest of the population in the U.S and Canada. Our main objective is towards humanity, therefore we organize our different programs and activities to reach out to the maximum number of communities."

Uddeen describes the difference between ISNA and ICNA as follows: "ISNA is basically a federation of different professional organizations. They have the Islamic Medical Association, the Social Scientists Association, the Muslim Engineers Association. So, they are basically a kind of federation. And they have two major activities: one is their monthly magazine, Islamic Horizon, and the other is their annual convention. But we have a more grass-roots approach. We have our own chapters under one *Ameer*, which what we call the leader, the president. We have our own consultant body, or Shura, we call it, Majlis Al-Shura, where we make policies and decisions for the future. Then we have the Executive Council, which implements those decisions on a day-to-day basis. Our organization is basically open to any Muslim, although to be elected to office, you have to first be a member of the General Assembly. Members have to fulfill some basic requirements in terms their studies and how good they are in their day-to-day duties as a Muslim."[42]

Since the 1980s, there have been a growing number of Islamic organizations active in U.S. political life. Liberty of conscience and freedom of expression are the cornerstones of American civil society, and are represented by specific legal provisions that have been acquired over time. Thanks to these provisions Muslims in America may express themselves with a freedom unknown to European Muslims, not to mention, those living in the Muslim world.

One consequence of this has been the considerable number of organiza-tions, journals, and institutes created in the past 15 years to counteract the prevailing demonization of Islam in American culture. The efforts of CAIR have been particularly representative, in this respect, of the emerging Muslim voice. The Council was created in 1994, in order to document instances of bias against Muslims and Islam and to confront anti-Muslim prejudice. Their lobbying efforts have consisted in using existing public laws to defend the rights of Islam, including the right to practice Islam in the name of reli-gious freedom. CAIR has brought numerous lawsuits before the courts in defense of Muslims—against the government, businesses, and the media— on First Amendment grounds, as well as those of the Civil Freedom Legislation Act of 1964, and Equal Opportunity laws. The organization has won countless victories in high-profile lawsuits against corporations such as

Nike and Budweiser, convicted of having used Islamic images to attack the beliefs of Muslims or of treating Muslim employees in a discriminatory fashion. After September 11, the group's primary focus has been the struggle against anti-Muslim discrimination in the name of "War on Terror."

European Muslims have not been nearly so successful in making their voice heard through political and legal advocacy—to the point where CAIR had to intervene in 2000 in the case of a young French Muslim woman who faced discrimination in regard to her headscarf at the French consulate in Chicago. Thanks to CAIR's intervention, the young woman was able to have her passport photograph taken with her headscarf on. The irony here is that French Muslims have never succeeded in getting this kind of dispensation in France itself.[43] To understand such a discrepancy, we need to look at the differences between the two countries in terms of their attitude toward civil law. Without question, it is easier for a victim of religious discrimination to obtain compensation in America. The role of the American judiciary in religious matters is crucial in this regard. The protection of religious minorities in America is guaranteed by adjustments to existing legislation, and based on a philosophy that considers freedom of religious belief as the cornerstone of individual dignity. Such a situation works in Muslims' favor; they are able to use America's long history of judgments supporting the free expression of religion to their advantage, even when Islamic beliefs themselves are ridiculed or disparaged.

The establishment of an active Muslim lobby has also been one of the priorities of the American Muslim population. In less than a decade, lobbying groups such as the AMA (American Muslim Alliance, formed in 1989), the AMC (American Muslim Council, 1990), and MPAC (Muslim Public Affairs Council, 1998) have multiplied. The AMC was founded by a network of intellectuals and militant Muslims from a variety of backgrounds, convinced of the need for political mobilization to end discrimination and hostility towards Islam. They made a name for themselves after lobbying in the White House and Congress to include the preservation of identity and the rights of the Muslim community within the terms of American pluralism. Their goal has been to set themselves up as an intermediary between the Muslim community and institutions of power. One of their primary demands has been for the political acknowledgment of equal status between Muslims and other religious communities, as well as to transform the well-known description of society, "Judeo-Christian," into "Judeo-Christian-Islamic"—in the understanding that the Muslim tradition holds dear the same values as do Judaism and Christianity, whose contributions to the cultural and social fabric of America are incidentally not in doubt.

The goal of these lobby groups has been to defend the interests of Muslim populations in the halls of government, as well as to protest U.S. policy in the Middle East. They have also worked to mobilize the Muslim community through regular voter-awareness campaigns. For the 2000 presidential elections the various Muslim lobbies banded together in coalition under the name AMPCC (American Muslim Politics Council Coordination) in support of the Republican candidate George W. Bush.[44]

Disillusioned by the Bush Administration's politics after September 11, 2001, no Muslim organization to date has officially endorsed a candidate for the 2004 presidential elections. Nonetheless, AMPCC continues to be politically active. In an open letter to the Muslim community during the 2003 ISNA convention in Chicago, the organization announced its intention to raise the issue of the deterioration of fundamental civil liberties as a result of the War of Terror. Since then, it has worked to encourage Muslim Americans to become active in the presidential campaign. According to a June 29, 2004 CAIR survey, the majority of Muslims surveyed expressed a preference for Democratic candidate John Kerry (54%), followed by Ralph Nader (24%). A July 15, 2004 survey conducted by the Zogby Institute from a cross-section of the Arab-American population confirmed this preference for Kerry (51%)[45].

These Muslim political and religious associations are not representative, however, of all the currents of American Islam. Despite the ecumenical claims of its president, the ISNA has never been able to reunite the American Muslim community. One continuing division in American Islam is between African American Muslims and immigrant Muslims, a fact marked by the two separate congresses held on the same day by the MAS (mostly representing the former) and the ISNA (one of the main groups organizing Muslims with an immigrant background) in Chicago, on September 4, 2003. The ISNA has also been criticized for leaning too much to the right in terms of global Islam. The majority of books and tapes sold at the ISNA's Annual Convention are indeed strongly biased toward the Salafi movement, and leave little space for more liberal or progressive options. This criticism is also a reflection of the absence of representation within the ISNA of minority movements, such as Shiite or Sufi Islam, and sectarian groups such as Ahmadiyya.[46] In other words, the ISNA is the image of the Muslim immigrant elite: conservative, Sunni, and responsive to the messages of Saudi/Wahabi Islam or of the Muslim Brothers.

New Challenges for Islam After September 11
Before September 11, the number of associations promoting the entrance of Islam into American civil religion was on the rise even before September 11.

In the past two decades, these groups have made significant changes to their strategy and the content of their message. Throughout the 1970s and before the First Gulf War, there was an internal conflict—not always visible to the outside observer—between the Society of the Muslim Brothers and the Wahabi movement, a conflict that reflected certain tensions in the Muslim world. For Wahabi, the internal structure of the Muslim community should take precedence over any kind of inclusion or participation in American society; those associated with the ideology of the Muslim Brothers, on the other hand, felt that communication with the non-Muslim community was essential. After the first Gulf War, however, domestic issues and the image of American Islam as a minority religion became most important. From that moment on, the debate has been defined as a conflict between liberals/progressives and conservatives/fundamentalists. This opposition refers not only to these camps' interpretations of religious tradition, discussed in greater details in parts II and III, but also to their acceptance or rejection of American political life.

The fight to define the legitimate Muslim community—regardless of whether this definition is based on ethnic, linguistic, or religious considerations—has at times been intense. The case of Sheik Hisham Kabbani is a perfect illustration of these internal conflicts and their political consequences. In the late 1990s, Kabbani, of the Nakshabendi brotherhood,[47] had achieved a certain visibility in some political circles as well as the White House. In a meeting with State Department representatives during Clinton's second term of office in January 1999, the Sheik categorized the majority of Islamic leaders in America as "fundamentalists." These words were widely reported in the media; the Sheik subsequently faced violent opposition and censorship from the American Islamic elite, self-appointed guardians of the orthodox definition of the Muslim community.

Muslim strategy in the American public sphere has generally taken one of two principal routes: lobbying, and moral persuasion. Moral persuasion takes the form of discourses justifying Islam's place in American culture through an appeal to the shared values of monotheistic religions. In other words, Muslims want to show that they, too, subscribe to the fundamental values of American society: "Internally, the U.S. is the most Islamic State that has been operational in the last 300 years. Internally, it is generally seeking to aspire to its ideals, and the growing cultural religious material health of American Muslims is the best testimony to my claim."[48]

Muslims also continue to exert political pressure in international issues, particularly in the case of Palestine. Muslim lobbyists experienced a moment of symbolic victory in 1999 when they temporarily blocked the opening of a Burger King in the Occupied Territories by threatening a boycott. But Islam's entry into politics comes at the price of tensions and conflict with Pro-Israeli and Jewish organizations. Daniel Pipes—essayist and public intellectual involved in several think-tanks, as well as a self-declared enemy of what he calls "militant Islam"—is outspoken in opposing President Bush's repeated statement that Islam is a religion of peace[49]. On November 29, 2001, he made the claim that 10 to 15% of all Muslims sympathize with the "militant Muslim agenda"[50]. Through his internet site, Campus Watch, he reports on universities and intellectuals who are too sympathetic, in his opinion, to Islam or the Palestinian cause. On April 1, 2003, his nomination by President Bush to the board of the United States Institute for Peace (USIP) raised strong opposition among Muslim organizations, who launched a campaign to block his appointment.

The case of Salam Al-Marayati, president of MPAC, further demonstrates how the conflict between Muslims and Pro-Israeli organizations can reach all the way to the highest levels of government. In 1999, Al-Marayati was nominated to the National Commission on Counterterrorism. After several Pro-Israeli organizations launched a virulent campaign against his appointment, he was quickly removed from his post.

The period after September 11 has been a crucial one for the public status of American Islam. Since then, the number of Muslims involved in political life has steadily declined. In the 2000 elections, 152 people of Arab or Muslim origin were elected to various offices. In 2002, the number fell to 10 people (out of 70 candidates). In 2004, there are only 15 candidates for political office of Muslim or Arab descent. Furthermore, and despite their vigorous public denunciation of the attacks, Muslim leaders came under fire for their inability to take a position on Islam other than a defensive or apologist one. Since the terrorist attacks, both official and popular interest has increasingly focused on religious or intellectual figures who "read" Islam from a legal or theological standpoint. Hamza Yusuf is one of those who owe their rise in the media and in political circles to their status as religious leader. Born in Washington State, raised in California, converted to Islam at the age of 17, he did his training in Islam in Algeria, Morocco, and Mauritania, and now runs the "Zaytuna Institute" in the San Francisco Bay Area. His charismatic religious authority attracts crowds of young Muslims to each of his lectures. Since September 11, he has been a frequent guest at the White House. One of his most striking arguments, post–September 11, has been the critique of the monopoly on discourse held by doctors, engineers, and other "men of science" who know little or nothing about either religion or Islam. He has repeatedly stated that Islam has, for the most part, been interpreted by inexperienced and ill-informed individuals, and sees the terrorists who executed the attacks of September 11 as enemies of Islam.[51]

One of the greatest challenges after September 11 is the building of consensus and the sharing of resources within the Muslim community, in order that racial and religious disagreements—particularly those between blacks and immigrants—may be overcome.

PART 2

The Imagined Community

CHAPTER 5

The Absolutized Community

Cultural globalization means the development of deterritorialized cultures and communities based on categories of race, gender, religion, and even lifestyle. This phenomenon is in continuous tension with the opposing trend, just as powerful and even more visible, of widespread Westernization, epitomized by the standardization of consumer culture and by the way of life often termed "McDonaldization."

Cultural globalization is thus "the intensification of worldwide social relations which link distant localities in such a way that local happenings are shaped by events occurring many miles away and vice versa."[1] The consequence is that the usual correlation between spatial and social distance has been destroyed. To live "globally" means to live in a world where social proximity is constructed over and in spite of geographic distance, and where geographic proximity no longer leads *a priori* to social ties.[2] In this context, Islam acts as a powerful element of identification, one that creates ties of solidarity among gender, age, or class groups, who may nonetheless be separated by vast differences in nationality, country, or culture.

The point here is not that Islam has become a world religion. In fact, Islam was a global religion from the very beginning, as seen in the concept of the *Ummah*, the community of believers that brings together not only all Muslims currently living on Earth, but also all past and future generations. Even the creation, at the beginning of the postcolonial period, of new nation-States could not completely break the power of the *Ummah*. Today, ease of communication and travel—not to mention the decline of nationalism, which had taken precedence over Islam as an ideology of the Muslim world throughout the last quarter of the twentieth century—has made the

Ummah an even more effective unifying force. The power of the *Ummah* remains strong despite the continued fragmentation and pluralization of interpretations of the Islamic message. Unlike Protestantism—where schisms in theological interpretation led to the creation of distinct communities and the proliferation of sects—the unity of the *Ummah* as an imagined community with a common and constantly renewed destiny remains intact.[3] It is thus a paradoxical time for Islam. On the one hand, Islam is more exposed than ever before to Western influence; on the other, it enjoys better conditions than ever for the transnational diffusion of its message. The first result of this transformation—seen, for one, in the recent proliferation of Islam-themed websites—has been the increased importance of spirituality in Islam and the practice of Islam as a matter of personal faith. In particular, Western influence on Islam leads to an increased visibility and expression of subjectivity as it relates to Islamic belief. Of course, all Muslims have a personal and subjective experience of Islam, but this fact is more often than not obscured by Islam's role as a communal, cultural, social, and political force in Muslim countries. But in certain circumstances self-examination in terms of religious faith can come to take precedence over one's own cultural heritage. This kind of renegotiation—between the personal and the collective approach to religious practice—is a central element of Western Islamic identity.

This renegotiation, however, may not always be concretely transformed into the individualization of religious practice or innovations in theological thought. Indeed, Europe and the United States have favored ground for certain puritanical and fundamentalist movements of Islam. As Arjun Appadurai notes, the globalization of culture means that more options are open to the imagination, and one's vision of possible lives expands correspondingly.[4] In an "information society"—hyperreal, driven by computer and Internet technology, and in which social interactions are often simulated or mediated—people feel the risk of losing their sense of identity and idea of what they know. The feeling of moral relativity becomes acute.[5] One possible reaction to the bewildering range of available moral choices is a certain rigidity of thought and the total rejection of cultural pluralism. Faced with this dilemma, many Western Muslims develop an attraction to conservative or reactionary interpretations of Islam, and even to "theologies of hate" as propagated by movements like Al Qaeda.

The Theology of Intolerance

The paradox of Islam in Europe and the United States is that these countries have proven to be fertile ground for the growth of puritanical and intolerant interpretations of Islam. This is only an apparent contradiction, however, as the globalization of culture tends to promote fundamentalism or puritanism in almost all religions, not just Islam.[6] The different strains of Islamic fundamentalism can be distinguished from one another according to whether they rely on the achievements of the Islamic legal tradition, or whether they reject them in favor of a direct relation with the Qu'ran and the Sunna. The former includes movements as diverse as the Deobandi, the Barelvi, and Jamaat Al-Tabligh. In the latter category are the Wahabi and Salafi movements.[7] This division is as much cultural as theological. Movements coming out of the Indian subcontinent, for example, often incorporate mystical elements into their ideology, whereas movements from the Middle East, such as Wahabism, tend to reject all suggestions of mysticism.

Deobandis, Barelvis and Jamaat-at-Tabligh

For groups that follow Islam through its legal precedents, the Islamic experience—in the West as elsewhere—is mediated through a deep knowledge of the life and the actions of the Prophet, as transmitted by a chain of recognized and approved interpreters respective to the particular school. The Deobandis, one example of this trend, are named after the city of Deoband, in India, where founder Haji Mohammad Abid established his *Darul Al Ouloum* (Knowledge Center) in 1866. To this day, the center still serves as an active place for the teaching of Islamic tradition. Since the center's creation, more than 65,000 Muslims have come to study there, and it is estimated that there are an additional 5,000 or more Deobandi schools scattered throughout the Indian subcontinent. While they insist upon an extensive knowledge of Hadith, Deobandis also believe that the souls of the Prophet and the saints are immortal, and that they act as mediators between believers and God. But the Deobandi movement is primarily concerned with the teaching and transmission of Islam through the creation of its Qu'ranic schools. The Taliban in Afghanistan took the Deobandi as their inspiration. The Barelvis, founded in India by Ahmed Raza (1856–1921) also emphasize the figure of the Prophet and the saints as mediators.

Another group that takes a traditionalist and legalistic approach to Islam is the Tabligh, sometimes referred to as the "Jehovah's Witnesses of Islam." The Tabligh is usually described as a pietist and apolitical movement whose primary aim is to strengthen Muslim orthodoxy.[8] A subsect within the larger Deobandi movement, the Tabligh movement was founded in 1927 by Maulana Muhammad Ilyas, a devout Muslim scholar who lived in

New Delhi and died in 1944. The essential principle of Tabligh is that every Muslim can be a vehicle for the values and practices of Islam.[9] The most important aspect of its practice is the mission, which consists in the missionary devoting one hour of his day, one day out of the week, one week each month, or one month out of the year to go and spread the world of Islam. The mission can take place in the city of the missionary, in his country, or in more distant destinations as far as India and Pakistan. The annual gathering of Tabligh in Lahore brings together the largest amount of Muslims at any one time, second only to the pilgrimage to Mecca.

Today, the West is the center of Tabligh proselytizing. The success of Tabligh is particularly noticeable among acculturated Muslims or Muslims in search of Islam. For these people, the Tabligh method proves effective for learning the basics of the Islamic faith, due to its centralized structure and its emphasis on secrecy. In fact, the pyramid structure of Tabligh provides an alternative to the absence of religious institutions that characterizes diasporic Islam. For many Muslims of the diaspora—looking for a way to practice Islam, but unable to access the universities and centers of learning of the Muslim world and not yet having created comparable institutions in Europe or the United States, Tabligh comes to fill a particular void.

Secrecy is an important element of Tabligh religious teaching in an environment that is perceived as at best indifferent, at worst hostile. The idea of practicing one's faith in an inhospitable environment, a remnant of Tabligh's origins as a minority religion in India, happens to be perfectly suited to the minority condition in the West. The common denominators of most adherents of Tabligh are: their marginal social and cultural status, and their lack of prior knowledge about Islam. The effectiveness of Tabligh essentially stems from its ability to provide an intensive religious training for individuals who have never attended a madrasa or read the Qu'ran. It should hardly be surprising, therefore, that an increasing number of conversions in both Europe and the United States (including both converts from other religious traditions and from those who were born Muslim) are due to the proselytizing activity of Tabligh. In this context "marginal status" does not refer to the poor or the outcast; instead, it refers to those people, even people from the educated classes, who have not been able to find their symbolic place in society. In Zygmunt Bauman's metaphor,[10] they are vagabonds, illicit travelers—or, more precisely, those without even the right to go anywhere, in contrast to tourists, who can travel in all legitimacy and with all the necessary resources.

All of these fundamentalist movements place a great deal of emphasis on proper ritual practice and conformity to strict Islamic dress code (for women, head-covering and loose garments revealing only the face; for men, long tunic, head-covering (*kuf*) and beard). The movements differ in their degree of receptivity to aspects of Islam such as Sufi teachings or the role of divine mediators between human beings and God. Barelvi doctrine, for example, accepts the existence of *pirs*, or Muslim saints, whereas Deobandi doctrine rejects it. Because of this disagreement, the former consider the latter to be aligned with the Wahhabis.

Wahabis and Salafis

In contrast to the traditionalist branches of Islam, Wahabis and Salafis reject the importance of juridical schools, instead advocating a direct relation to the revealed Text. In their literalist interpretation of Islam, nothing must come between a believer and the Text. Customs, culture, Sufism, and so on: everything must be gotten rid of Wahabism emerged in the eighteenth century in the Arabian peninsula with the teachings of Abdel Wahab, which acquired a political dimension from to Wahab's alliance with the Saudi monarchy. Wahhabism is characterized by an extreme hostility to any kind of intellectualized criticism of tradition. Mystical approaches and historical interpretations alike are held in contempt. Orthodox practice boils down to the literal interpretation of the revealed Text, with no recourse to the historical contributions of the various juridical schools (*madhab*).

The modern heirs of this rigorist and puritanical line of thought in the Arabian peninsula (as well as in Syria, Jordan, and Egypt) are known as Salafi. The only real difference between modern Salafi Islam and the original Wahhabi period, therefore, is a difference in audience: what this means, however, is that Salafi decisions and interpretations are no longer limited to the Saudi kingdom, but are now followed by Muslims allover the world. *Salaf* refers to the devout elders who served as companions to the Prophet Mohammed. The irony, however, is that *salafiyya* was initially a reformist movement created in the nineteenth century. Though the early Salafi leaders, including Mohammed Abduh, Al-Afghani, and Rashid Rida, promoted a return to the revealed Text and the *Hadiths*, (the words and deeds of the Prophet Mohammed), they were not by any means antiintellectuals, and were in their time even considered progressive. Nonetheless, by the end of the 1970s, the Saudi government had succeeded in transforming *salafiyya* into a conservative theology. The fatwas of Sheikh Abdul Aziz Ibn Baaz, Grand Mufti of the Saudi Kingdom, who died in 1999, and of Sheikh Al-Albani are the shared points of reference for their disciples in Europe and the United States.[11] (In contemporary Salafism, the *salaf* are the first three generations of Muslims, comprising the companions of the Prophet (*Sahabah*), their immediate successors (*Tabiun*), and the generation after these. The term "*Salaf*" is also used to refer to those sages who guarded the spirit and the letter of this original Islam: including, among others, the founders of the four juridical schools, as well as Ibn Taymiyya).[12] The movement has succeeded in imposing their beliefs not as one interpretation among many, but as the orthodox doctrine of Sunni Islam. The considerable financial resources of the Saudi government have certainly also helped in creating this situation of religious monopoly.

In the past two decades, the rivalry between Saudi Arabia, India, Pakistan, and Iran over control of the Muslim world has rapidly intensified. Within this atmosphere of competition, Europe and the United States have become crucial battlegrounds, as evidenced by the massive rise in the sum of petrodollars distributed in this part of the world. The proliferation of brochures, free Qu'rans, and new Islamic centers in Malaga, Madrid, Milan, Mantes-la-Jolie, Edinburgh, Brussels, Lisbon, Zagreb, Washington, Chicago, and Toronto; the financing of Islamic Studies chairs in American universities; the increase in the number of Internet sites: all these elements serve to facilitate access to Wahabi teachings and to promote Wahabism as the sole legitimate guardian of Islamic thought.[13]

One must not, however, overestimate the influence of these movements. According to experts quoted in the *New York Times*, less than 25 percent of all Muslims in America who attend mosque follow Wahabi doctrine.[14] However, in this case, influence may not be merely a matter of numbers. In a minority culture—lacking both institutions for religious education and the means by which to produce new forms of knowledge—the easy access to theology that Salafism presents is one of the primary reasons for its great success. The widespread diffusion of Salafi teachings results in a situation in which even non-Salafi Muslims evaluate their Islamic practice by Wahabite standards. In other words, even if most Muslims do not follow Wahabite dress codes—white tunic, headcovering, beard for men, *hijab* and *nikab*[15] for women—orthodox Salafi practice-nonetheless often becomes the golden standard for what a good Muslim should be.

Today, competition rages in the West between Tablighis and Salafis, and anathemas rain down on both sides. One fatwa from Sheikh Ibn Baaz,[16] in particular (issued in 1997), named the Tabligh, as well as the Muslim Brotherhood, as one of the 72 heretical sects of Islam.[17]

This "theology of intolerance" is defined, above all, by an exclusive and hierarchical vision of the world, as well as by a taxonomy of religions that places Islam at the top. For example the expanded use of the term "*kafir*" (infidel, heretic) is very common among salafis (more than tablighis). This term was initially used only for polytheists, not for members of competing monotheistic faiths. But Salafism now extends the term to Jews, Christians, and sometimes even nonpracticing Muslims.

A typical example of this way of thinking is the following fatwa ruling on whether Jews and Christians can be considered infidels, published on the Belgian website Assabyle.com. After making reference to several applicable *sura* (chapters of the Qu'ran), the Sheikh concludes, "Jews and Christians who do not believe in Mohammed and deny his Prophesy are infidels." But the argument goes even further, eventually coming to the conclusion that "He who does not consider to be a infidel one who follows a religion other than Islam, such as the Christians, or who doubts their vileness or approves of their ways, he himself is a infidel."[18]

The world is thus divided into Muslims and infidels, and the West, seen as the breeding ground for moral depravity, is always placed in a negative light. Such logic also informs an essay entitled "The Choice Between the Burka and the Bikini," by Abid Ullah Jan,[19] in which the author contrasts women's status in Islam as figures of respect to their status in the West, bound to the dictates of fashion and made the constant objects of western sexual depravity.

According to Sheikh Abdur Raman Abdum Khaliq, in a text translated from Arabic on Assabyle.com, the role of every good Muslim is to declare that Muslims are members of the greatest nation that humanity has ever known, and to proclaim the superiority of Islam throughout the world: "It suffices to note that the call to unify the religions, the effort to bring the various religions together, and their presentation as a homogenous and unified vision is a ploy on the part of the infidels that seeks to confuse truth and lies, and to eradicate Islam by torpedoing its foundations and leading Muslims into wholesale apostasy."[20]

Another characteristic common to these movements is a way of thinking that partitions off the different aspects of life—family, work, leisure—and sorts everything according to the opposition between *haram* (forbidden) and *halal* (permitted). Everything that did not already exist or happen during the time of the Prophet is an innovation, and thus haram. Khaled Abou El Fadl has called this "The Culture of *Mamnu*' ('It is forbidden')."[21] Islam as it existed during the time of the Prophet, especially during the residency in Medina, is idealized and essentialized, functioning as an "epic past"[22] and gold standard for life in the present. Every aspect of this era must serve as the foundation for the present day: "In this era, everything is good, and all the good things have already come to pass."[23] Celebrating one's birthday, for example, is considered *bida*' (an innovation) by the Salafis, and is thus forbidden: "Celebrating Birthdays has no source whatsoever in the pure Shari'ah. In fact it is an innovation, since the Messenger of Allah (sal-Allaahu 'alayhe wa salaam) said: 'Whoever introduces anything into this matter of ours that does not belong to it shall have that action rejected.' This was recorded by both al-Bukhaaree and Muslim."[24]

Reactionary Views of Women's Status

Another characteristic common to both Tablighis and Salafis is their extreme inflexibility regarding the status of women. The rules determining proper dress for women are presented as absolute and may never be questioned. Salafis take the dress code further than the Tablighis; for the former, a woman must cover not only her hair but her face and hands as well. The *nikab*, gloves, and long tunic fashionable in Saudi Arabia distinguishes the Salafi Muslim woman from the Tablighi Muslim woman. The latter also wears a long tunic, but in a neutral color (not necessarily black), and covers her hair with the *hijab*. Tablighi men, for their part, wear tunics that go down to their ankles, while Salafi tunics come just below the knees.

The puritanical interpretation of women's behavior regulates not only dress, but also women's roles as a wife, as a mother and daughter, and as a participant (or nonparticipant) in the community. Mixed-gender interaction is forbidden in both public spaces and schools, and male superiority is constantly reaffirmed, along with the Qu'ranic legitimacy of corporal punishment for women.[25]

Answering a question on the propriety of mixed-sex education in the university, the Salafi site Islam Q&A responds that attending coed institutions is forbidden for the Muslim: "Studying in mixed schools, institutes and universities is not permitted. The evils that exist in these institutions because of that mixing are no secret, let alone the fact that people do learn much, if anything, in these institutions. Wise people even in *kaafir* countries have called for segregation between the sexes in educational institutions because of the moral damage they have noticed and the weakening of educational standards. Trustworthy scholars have issued fatwas stating that this kind of education is not permissible."[26]

Even more than political issues, it is this question of women's status within both the family and society that allows the various interpretations of Islam to be placed on a spectrum, from the most reactionary to the most liberal. Women can, it should be said, enjoy a certain emancipation within Islam, notably in the Tabligh movement. In Tabligh, a woman may leave her house to go on a mission, so long as she travels with a group of women and is chaperoned by a male relative. These excursions are the occasion for intense study. In other words, if the Tablighi ideal of woman is that of wife and mother, the actual life of women within the movement can often come to contradict these principles.[27]

An additional criterion is the respective opinions of the various movements on political participation and citizenship in Western societies. Salafi doctrine, at least in the West, espouses isolation and separatism, in contrast to more open-minded movements such as the Muslim Brotherhood. This separatist attitude is explicit in groups such as the Qur'an and Sunnah Society, the Al Hijrah Society, and in the United States, the Society for Adherence to the Sunna (SAS). As an example of this separatist tendency, Khaled Abou El Fadl cites the fatwa issued in 1996 by the SAS approving the actions of Abdul Rauf, a black Muslim basketball player who refused to rise for the singing of the national anthem.[28] However, one can also find sectarian Muslim groups or individuals who are engaged in civic activity, again notably within Tabligh. A follower of Tabligh, for example, sits on the French Islamic Council, the representative body for Islam in France. By the same token, in the course of our research we have encountered many Salafis, men and women, who are active in interfaith or anti-racist groups.

Global Orthodoxy

Since September 11, the apolitical nature of these fundamentalist groups has been increasingly questioned. The reason for this questioning is not, however, the oft-cited argument that the several Europeans and Americans who joined the Taliban's ranks first went through a training in Tabligh Islam.[29] The crucial issue is the fact that these movements profess a theology of intolerance, which can easily become, in turn, a theology of hate. The fundamental question is whether these versions of Islam based on the anachronistic and ahistorical reading of scripture, have a necessary correlation with the unleashing of intolerance in general. Both Tablighi and Wahhabi Islam are anchored in a defensive and reactionary attitude toward a modernity automatically associated with the West and its depravities. This defensive attitude is translated into an apologist advocacy of tradition and Islamic history.

Among these apologist arguments, the most widespread is that the institutions of modernity were themselves first created by Muslims. According to this argument, it is Islam that liberated women, invented democracy, acknowledged pluralism, protected human rights, and guaranteed people's safety—well before such things were even conceivable in the West. During the latter half of the twentieth century, when colonized Arab peoples were fighting for their independence and Arab nation-states were first emerging, this argument was a powerful way to resist Western hegemony and claim an authentic and autonomous Muslim identity. The primary aim was to strengthen Islam in its fight against its Western enemy. The consequence is that the idea of public good is used to justify any distortion to religious tradition. As Khaled Abou El Fadl has stressed, the consequence is that Islamic tradition has degenerated into a self-satisfied and morally arrogant theology, and Islam itself is detached from its historical, national, and political contexts and turned into a kind of universal and absolute orthodoxy.[30] Post-1970 doctrines of Salafism have greatly contributed to the strength of this attitude. In essence, Salafism responded to the feeling of defeat and powerlessness that has plagued the Muslim world since 1967 (in other words, since the defeat of Arab nations in their war against Israel) by radicalizing their rhetoric on non-Muslims and on women. The self-assurance of Salafism is grounded in a binary and ahistorical reading of scripture. The result is an overriding puritanism that overcompensates for humiliation with a self-righteous arrogance, and in which good Muslims are constantly contrasted with the western, democratic, secular, depraved and immoral Other. When this arrogance is combined with the call for war against the Infidels, the conditions for both radicalism and a warlike attitude come together as one.

The Appeal of the Theology of Hate

One of the biggest surprises of the September 11 attacks was the revelation of the role played by European—and, more rarely, American—Muslims in the support for Al Qaeda. Who in the West was not shocked when they saw the gaunt face, the staring eyes, and the rigid jaw of John Walker Lindh, captured in November 2001 by the American army near Mazar-al-Sharif from within the Taliban's ranks? Several Europeans—including seven French and a number of British citizens—are among the Talibani prisoners held at the U.S. Army Prison in Guantanamo. Up to several hundred European-born or—educated young men appear to have joined the Taliban army in Afghanistan at some point. Among these, for example, is 27-year-old Jerôme Courtailler of Savoy, found guilty in absentia on June 21, 2004 by the Hague Court of Appeals (after having been acquitted by a Rotterdam court in December 2002). He is charged primarily with having participated in Al Qaeda activities and having helped to plan terrorist attacks against the American embassy in Paris.

Jihadis of the West

The appeal of jihadist movements for young European Muslims did not begin with Al Qaeda, however. Mujahedin resistance to the Soviet occupation in

Afghanistan attracted Muslim youth from all over the world starting in the1980s. Redouane Hammadi and Stephane Ait Iddir, French citizens sentenced to death in Morocco for killing two tourists in an attack on a Marrakech hotel in 1994, received their training in Afghanistan. In 1992, Joseph Jaime and David Vallat, both converts to Islam, met in a camp in Afghanistan.[31] At their 1998 trial in Chasse-sur-Rhône, they both received prison sentences for having given logistical support to the Algerian Islamicist networks responsible for the 1995 Paris subway bombings. Khaled Kelkal, a French-Algerian born in a suburb of Lyon, rediscovered Islam in prison, subsequently becoming involved in the GIA, the group responsible for the Paris bombings. Kelkal remains the prototype for this generation of disaffected European-Muslim youth who, unable or unwilling to integrate themselves in Western society, hope to find some sort of answer in the movements of jihad.

Taking up arms for a transnational political cause is, of course, nothing new. These men are, in many ways, reminiscent of the young people who came from all over Europe to participate in the Spanish Civil War, as well as those who fought for the anticolonialism movements in the Third World after World War II. But what is more surprising in the case of Islam is that many of its demagogues and ideologues live, not in the Muslim world, but in countries of the industrialized West.[32] The most vocal and virulent proponents of jihad against the West, in fact, live—in the West. We must, therefore, make a distinction between the ideologues of *jihad* and its foot soldiers. The foot soldiers are those who go take up arms in Afghanistan or Bosnia, who plant bombs, and so on. The ideologues deliver *fatwas* and preach inflammatory rhetoric against the West.

Some of the soldiers who take up arms in the name of *jihad* are the sons of Arab or South/Central Asian immigrants; others are recent converts to Islam. It is tempting to attribute the attraction to movements like Al Qaeda and the violent rejection of the West to social and economic frustration, a pattern which would mirror those that exist in the Muslim world. The fact is, however, that many Western Talibanis are neither marginals nor delinquents. John Walker Lindh, for example, is the only son of a well-off family in California. He was raised in a liberal environment—both in terms of his religious education and his schooling—in Mill Valley, a town north of San Francisco known as a refuge for former hippies who have "arrived." After he refused to attend Catholic school, his parents placed him in an alternative school that provided him with a great deal of educational freedom. At the age of 12, he saw Spike Lee's film *Malcolm X*, which led to his developing an interest in Islam. At the age of 16, he converted to Islam and began to attend the mosque in Mill Valley. He adopted the name Suleyman al Lindh, in

Afghanistan later taking on the *nom de guerre* Abdul Hamid. His coreligionists in Mill Valley describe him as being extremely determined in his desire
to educate himself about Islam. He went to Yemen to learn Arabic, and from
Yemen, to a *madrasa* in the north of Pakistan. His teacher at the *madrasa*
describes him as a student completely devoted to Islam. In May of 2001, he
left for Afghanistan. He had already been recruited by Al Qaeda to train in
one of the centers of instruction directed by Osama bin Laden. According to
his own statements on CNN, he fought with the Pakistanis in Kashmir in
the summer of 2001. During the war, he was sent to Kunduz to fight the
Northern Alliance.[33]

Zaccarias Moussaoui, the alleged "twentieth hijacker" of the September 11
attacks, had already been arrested in the United States on August 16, 2001.
Born in 1968 at Saint Jean de Luz, the French-Moroccan Moussaoui was
raised by his mother, who divorced his father when he was very young. He
went to England to complete his university training and learn English,
receiving his degree in international business from the South University in
London in 1995. It was during this time that he became an Islamic militant.
Like Richard Reid, the so-called shoe bomber who boarded a flight from
Paris to Miami with explosive devices in his shoes, he frequented the Brixton
mosque. The mosque eventually expelled Moussaoui for his extremist positions, as did the Muhajiroun-run mosque of Finsbury Park. Between 1997
and 2000 he made frequent trips to Pakistan and Afghanistan and cut off
relations with his mother.

Richard Reid, born to an English mother and a Jamaican father in a poor
suburb to the south of London, fits somewhat better the profile of the social
and economic outsider. His father was in jail for the greater part of his childhood, and he himself spent time in prison for a variety of petty crimes. It was
in prison that he converted to Islam, taking the name Abdel Rahim. He, too,
attended the Brixton mosque—known for being home to many converts—
and eventually came into contact with members of the jihadist movement.
In 1998, he left for Pakistan.

Nomads of the Global City
One of the common denominators of these young people attracted to
jihadist movements and causes is not their socioeconomic level, but rather
their displaced status as a result of cultural globalization. Like the hijackers
of September 11, these men's trajectories all point to a kind of nomadism, a
permanent mobility in the countries and cultures of the West. For example,
Mohammed Atta, born in Egypt, studied architecture in Hamburg. He left
for Afghanistan in 1997 and for the United States in 2000. These foot

soldiers of jihad are thus a product of the cultural hybridization that characterizes the global metropolis.

In all these cases, the context of the global city is a crucial factor. The global city is the primary environment for the installation and adaptation of Muslim immigrants within their new national and social contexts. Paris, Berlin, London, New York, and Los Angeles are now centers of the Muslim world by virtue of the large concentration of immigrant Muslims that live there. Multiculturalism is the now ruling ideology of Western cities, not only because it is a way to make sense of these cities, growing hybridization and cultural plurality, but also because it allows cities to put this plurality to economic and political use. A multicultural ideology, however, is not the same thing as the actual capacity of individuals to accept this or that culture. For many Muslims, the permanent contact with other cultures that they experience does not necessarily turn them into cosmopolites. An ability to negotiate different languages and cultural regulations should not be confused with the recognition of the equal dignity of all cultures. The global city encourages a transnational outlook: one based on physical mobility and the possibility of experiencing different contexts and cultures, while at the same time preserving one's own cultural and religious identity. The cosmopolite, on the other hand, is one who interacts easily with other cultures, and develops out of that interaction a synthesized culture in regard to points of intellectual reference as well as social relations.[34] Cosmopolitanism therefore represents a successful synthesis, a form of hybridization among different cultural registers. This is not the case for all groups in the global city. For some, the multiplicity of cultures, combined with personal mobility, leads to an intellectual narrowness and the rejection of what is at once inaccessible and inescapable.

This is especially the case with the European Talibanis, who, transnational though they may be, are very far from being cosmopolites. For them, taking up arms against the West expresses the rejection of what is close, familiar—and, at the same time, inaccessible. Their immersion in Western culture only reinforces their need to preserve the purity of Islam and to limit their interactions with the surrounding environment. Rather than welcoming exchange or acculturation based on a principle of openness to the Other, they are more likely to reject outside contributions in favor of an idealized vision of an Islam or an Islam that is considered superior to all other religions and cultures. Thus, while these young Muslims are undoubtedly transnational and internationally mobile, they are by no means cosmopolitan.

The cultural rootlessness of these soldiers battling a decadent West is also demonstrated by the fact that most are apprentices or novices in Islam. Whether because they converted to Islam or because their family's emigration disrupted the normal transmitting of tradition, their education in Islam begins not in the family but in the fundamentalist groups of the Tabligh or the Salafis. Zaccarias Moussaoui, Richard Reid, Hervé Djamel Loiseau (the French Talibani discovered frozen to death in the Afghan mountains): all of them have in common a background of intense Islamicization through the Tabligh.

The Tabligh is, of course, not directly responsible for anyone's involvement in jihadist movements. Furthermore, most men who join the jihadist movement only do so after leaving the Tabligh structure, becoming a sort of "free agent."[35] A period in Afghanistan and a penchant for the theology of hate, on the other hand, are often determining factors in the choosing of violent means.

Since September 11, two theories have competed to explain the violence of the World Trade Center attacks and the appeal of jihadist violence for young people in the West: the theory of nihilism, championed notably by French scholar André Glucksmann, and the theory of humiliation, argued by Jessica Stern, among others.[36]

Nihilism, a doctrine that advocates the refusal of all value systems and extols individual freedom, has historically translated into the attempt to change social and political conditions through violent means. Without question, the September 11 attacks bear all the marks of a war on existing institutions and culture. But the difference between nihilism and the September 11 attacks is that nihilism aims at the elite, taking as its target leaders and politicians. Furthermore, is the use of violence on its own a sufficient criterion to designate the September 11 attacks as acts of nihilism? Is the violence of Al Qaeda truly based on the negation of existing value systems—or is it, rather, a desperate attempt to set up its own hierarchy of values? For the followers of bin Laden and other preachers of hatred, violence is actually a means of purification, a way to clear the slate and establish a new ethical hierarchy based on principles of Islam.

Could humiliation, in that case, be a more satisfactory explanation for why young people dedicate themselves to the theology of hate? The testimony of individuals who have joined extremist movements certainly bears witness to the experience of daily personal degradation. Exclusion from mainstream culture, as well as a feeling of being illegitimate or unrecognized, is experienced as a betrayal and, translated through a religious sensibility, becomes a kind of spiritual wound or stain.

Humiliation does indeed seem to be a powerful motivating factor in an attraction to militancy—but it, too, is not in itself a sufficient explanation. Not all those who experience humiliation within the global city become terrorists. Rather, it is, the feeling of personal humiliation *added* to a feeling of collective humiliation, and subsequently of powerlessness, that is the catalyst for acts of violence. The inadequacy or failure of most other political ideologies—communism, socialism, and liberalism, their images, utopias, and struggles—and the dearth of new ideas, leaves today's youth feeling as if they face an oppression without meaning. This faceless oppression can give rise to despair when accompanied by daily stigmatization—the stigmatization of the postcolonial subject, of the outcast, of the suspect—*even* if one is born, like Khaled Kelkal or Zaccarias Moussaoui, in the center of the Western world. Adherence to a radical and politicized Islam satisfies the need for collective meaning, and at the same time provides spiritual fulfillment. Religious fanaticism is, by definition, a sort of mystical exstasis. On the personal psychological level, it corresponds to a regression to the state of infantile omnipotence in which it appears as if one can satisfy all desires, at the expense of the "reality principle." This feeling of omnipotence is accompanied by a narcissistic stimulation, the euphoria of imagining that one is chosen by God. This euphoria is a potential cure for the angst of those who have been wounded by life.[37]

The proponents of political violence dream of an idealized community in opposition to the dehumanization of the postmodern world. The *Ummah* is synonymous with solidarity and friendship, in contrast to the cold inhumanity of postmodern society. The binary approach to the world advocated by radical groups encourages radicalization against an enemy: in this case, the West. Cold is opposed to warmth, order to chaos, the individual to the community.

As Malek Chebel notes, "Since the very beginning, the greatest success of the Muslim community has been, going against the individualism of the Bedouins, to portray itself as a universal brotherhood, as one body, unified and harmonious as much in its totality . . . as in each of its constituent elements, so that the whole remains intact and so that the whole will never need to attempt, in a kind of panic, to reestablish this initial cohesion, its safeguard and its meaning."[38] Islam appears as both a system of personal beliefs and as an ideology of resistance to Western oppression. Islam is the antidote to the decline/depravity of the Western world, and a weapon in the fight against an arrogant and meaningless culture.

The transition from this kind of ideology to an armed warfare that takes young people as far as Afghanistan is due to the taste for adventure that city life is not likely to satisfy. The figure of the hero and the idea of resistance are glamorized. Thus David Courtailler, the brother of Jerôme Courtailler and himself charged in 1999 for "associating with malefactors in relation to a terrorist enterprise," describes his involvement in Islam:

I was suffocating; I wanted a change of scenery, to do something, no matter what. My friends told me that in Brighton, in England, I could do something. So I left. That was in 1990. Just like that, without a cent. I even hitchhiked . . . I went to a mosque for the first time with some Muslim friends. It was really something, all those people praying. There was just this serenity streaming from their faces. The people were nice. I made friends. I learned Arabic. Then one day I made the leap: I converted. . . . Some friends had spoken to me about Afghanistan, Pakistan. I was curious, and besides, I had never really traveled anywhere. I thought it would be great to go over there. So I went. They totally took care of everything.[39]

As this testimony shows, personal, individual humiliation can culminate in violence by way of a series of mediating steps. The ideologues of hate enter on the stage as the heads of Europe- or U.S.-based movements such as Hizb al Tahir and the Muhajiroun; thus it is in the countries of the West that jihadism takes its most virulent form.

The Ideologues of Hate
These ideologues of hate are often public figures who have faced censure and repression in Muslim countries. They find in the West a liberal environment propitious to the development of their ideas. Up until September 11, Britain was a particularly favorable environment for these ideologues, due to an explicit policy of nonrepression (so long as movements did not directly attack British institutions). Because of this provision, London was home to branches of almost all the national jihadist movements, including Hamas in Palestine, GIA in Algeria, the Taliban in Afghanistan, and Jamaat al-Islamiyya in Egypt. It was also the home of transnational jihadist movements, who focused more on the spreading of propaganda than on direct military action. It seems that antiterrorist measures have put an end to this English tolerance, however, as the police raid on January 21, 2003 of the Finsbury Park mosque demonstrates. Not incidentally, the mosque is well known for the inflammatory sermons of its chief imam, Abu Hamza Al-Masri.

Mustapha Kamel, better known under the name Abu Hamza Al-Masri, was born in Alexandria, Egypt. From the Finsbury Park mosque in the north of London, he directs the organization Ansar Al Shari'a (Partisans of *Shari'a*). He came to London in the 1980s for his studies, and gained British citizenship by marrying an Englishwoman, whom he later divorced. His contact with visiting Afghani Mujahedin led to his transition to radical Islam. In 1990, he moved to Afghanistan with his family to fight alongside the Mujahedin, eventually losing both hands and an eye in a landmine explosion. Upon his return to London, he founded the Partisans of Shari'a. From his London residence, he gave financial and logistical support to the Islamicist army of Aden-Abyan. Yemeni authorities have documented a history of involvement in plots to destabilize the government of Yemen, most notably a 1998 assassination attempt against President Ali Abudllah Saleh, but also including several bomb attacks and the kidnapping of tourists. This political activism in Yemen is only one part of Al-Masri's vision of worldwide destabilization through Islam. Al-Masri lends his support to a number of terrorist organizations throughout the world, and conducts efforts to recruit and train British Muslims in the ways of jihad. In December of 1998, the Partisans' Internet site announced the creation of an Islamic camp, "hosted by the mosque December 24–26 1998," offering to members a military training that would distract them from the influence of television and the blasphemies of Christmas.[40] According to the September 13, 2001 issue of *La Republica*, the Italian Secret Service (SISDE) would have been able to discover the existence of a plot against the president of the United States during the G-8 Summit in Geno. The SISDE report cited a meeting held at the Finsbury Park mosque on June 29, 2001, which was attended by Abu Hamza and representatives of Al Qaeda.[41] As a consequence of the September 11 attacks, the British government decided to punish Abu Hamza in several stages: on January 20, 2003, the police barricaded the Finsbury Park mosque; in February of 2004, Al Masri was stripped of his position as imam; finally, on April 5, 2004, his British citizenship was revoked.[42] He is currently subject to possible extradition by the Yemeni government for his alleged involvement in terrorist activity.

Omar Bakri is another leader of the jihadist movement in the West. Born in Syria in 1958, he entered into politics at a very young age, in the ranks of the Muslim Brothers, who at the time were fighting the installation of Hafez Al Assad's Ba'athist regime. In exile in Beirut, Bakri joined the local branch of Hizb Al Tahrir[43] (Liberation Party). In 1983, he settled in Jeddah, where he created Al Muhajirun (The Immigrants) as a front group for Hizb Al Tahrir. Sent into exile a second time, he went to London, where in 1996 he applied for British citizenship. Currently, Al-Muhajirun has branches in Great Britain, the United States, France, Germany, and Pakistan. In 1998. Omar Bakri was among the men who received Osama bin Laden's letter calling for jihad, and he represents himself as one of the London representatives of Al Qaeda.[44] He has stated on several occasions that he came to England for the express purpose of recruiting fighters for Kashmir, Afghanistan, and Chechnya.[45] Al Muhajirun is known for its intolerance toward homosexuals, Sikhs, Hindus, and Jews, as well as for its calls for the assassination of certain politicians, including British Prime Minister John Major in February 1991.

It is very active on college campuses, and promotes its message through educational groups and professional associations. In August 1997, the Muhajirun organized a protest march against oppression, announced worldwide via the Internet. The march was supposed to have taken place simultaneously in the United States, France, Pakistan, Turkey, and Great Britain; but only the London march, in Trafalgar Square, was successful. The number of participants was estimated at around 700, a figure that betrays just how marginal this movement is even among European Muslims.[46]

Puritanism Within Radical Islam

The actual doctrinal content of the ideology of hate is fairly poor. It reacts to the identity that has been imposed upon Muslims by transforming the stigma of Islam into anti-Western rhetoric: a rhetoric which is based, incidentally, on an essentializing of the West that is the analogue of Western orientalist essentializing. For the apologists of violence, there is indeed a "Clash of Civilizations," in which Islam and the West face off in a constant pitiless battle. The prize is the complete and total dominance of one system of values over the other.

The West is the irreligious, depraved, and arrogant force destroying the soul of Muslims. One must therefore reject it in all its forms, be they cultural, moral, religious, or economic. The seven deadly sins of the decadent West, according to this view, are: pedophilia, bestiality, homosexuality, sodomy, lesbianism, adultery, and fornication.[47] The West's political principles, culture, and sexual customs particularly come under fire. The Western educational system is accused of polluting and corrupting the souls of Muslim children through its teaching of ideas and behaviors incompatible with Islamic values.[48] Any relation to the Other is solely one of proselytism: "After realizing that Islam is the Deen of Haqq [religion of truth] which will dominate other ways of life, we should go out and offer it to non-Muslims. This does not mean that we have to get involved in the current format of interfaith dialogue. Such dialogues are designed to create 'better' understanding of each other's faiths. This assumes that the Qu'ran did not provide us with the 'best understanding.'"[49]

On September 16, 2001, Omar Bakri published a fatwa on the subject of Muslims who assist the United States in its war against Afghanistan: "The punishment of those who wage war against Allah and his Apostle and strive to make mischief in the land is only this: they should be murdered or crucified or their hands and their feet should be cut off on opposite sides or they should be imprisoned, this shall be a disgrace for them in this world, and in the hereafter they shall have a grievous chastisement" (EMQ 5.33).[50]

This kind of extremist outlook is still certainly a minority one among Muslims; nonetheless, the appeal of the theology of hate is a sort of fun-house mirror for certain attitudes and ideologies of Western Muslims. In the theology of hate, the institutional intolerance of conservative and puritanical movements finds itself magnified larger than life.

There are other discourses and practices among Western Muslims, however, that seek to reconcile the space-time of the West with the space-time of global Islam. One manifestation of this (examined in chapter 6) is the emergence of various nontraditional groups and practices in the "third space" of virtual Islam.

CHAPTER 6

The Virtual Community

The primary producers and consumers of Internet-based Islam are Muslims living in the United States. Exact statistics are always difficult to come by in anything having to do with the World Wide Web; nonetheless, a 2001 report by the United Nations estimates that less than 1 percent of the Arab-Muslim world uses the Internet, whereas over 50 percent of the population in the United States and Europe go on-line.[1] This statistic indicates that Western Muslims are the primary producers and consumers of what can be termed "Virtual Islam." The development of virtual Islam is closely tied to a specific socio-professional milieu of technicians and software engineers. These members of the educated classes are the primary producers and consumers of Islamic websites. The virtual *Ummah* of the Internet, therefore, is largely restricted to a group of people possessed of cultural capital and technological knowledge, bound together by a class-based solidarity that transcends countries and cultures.

Along with Saudis, Muslim-Americans are the primary creators of Islam-themed websites, which are for the most part published in English or in both English and Arabic. This dominance of the English language, even among the creators of websites in Muslim countries, attests to the willingness to adapt this new medium to the conditions of the Muslim diaspora, in which individuals often have little or no knowledge of Arabic.

If it is true that the number of Islam-related websites has increased in the past decade, it is also true that not all of them fulfill the same purpose. In other words, there is a difference between Islam *on* the Internet and Islam *of* the Internet. In the case of the former, the Internet is a tool that serves to spread information, which is also accessible outside the web. In the case of the latter, the Internet becomes an environment unto itself: that is, it is a place in which certain forms of religious practice or discourse are possible which could not exist in any other medium.[2]

This distinction helps to clarify the gradual influence of the media on the transformation of Islamic thought and practice. Just how influential the Internet is depends on whether one is talking about the transmitter or the recipient of Internet-based information. The transformative capacity of the Internet has very little effect in terms of the transmitters of information. Most Islamic websites are in no danger of taking part in any innovating or liberalizing trends in Islamic thought. There is an obervable change, however, on the side of the recipient of information, who increasingly exercises his or her freedom to choose in matters of religion. For example, an individual can now study or pray on-line—and thus can also choose at any moment to begin or end the ritual, without the constraints associated with participation in a group. The provider's role usually partakes of one of two main goals: to inform, or to influence. Most websites are primarily concerned with providing information; others, however, seek to influence and educate their audience through a variety of means. From the recipient's point of view, of course, this distinction between information and influence is somewhat artificial: any information, effectively presented, has the the power to change opinions. Nonetheless, we will retain this distinction insofar as it is helpful in clarifying differences among the creators of Internet Islam.

Informational Websites

The majority of Islam-related websites, by far, are those which seek to inform. For this reason in particular, most studies of virtual Islam amount to little more than a list of resources on Islamic religion and the various Islam-themed websites on the net, whose constant growth does indeed necessitate their perpetual reassessment.[3]

Informational websites generally fall under one of two categories: academic and denominational.[4] The former refers to websites that provide objective information on Islam: sites posted by research institutes, universities, think tanks, and international organizations. Some examples include the websites of MAPS (Muslims in the American Public Sphere), a research program Georgetown University; the opinion surveys on Islam and Muslims presented by the Charles Zogby Institute as well as various Islamic Studies departments at universities such as Oxford; and "Orient," a comprehensive website on the history of world religions, based in Strasbourg.[5]

Denominational Islam, on the other hand, refers to sites put up by all the national, ideological, or religious subcategories of Islam. The various denominations of Islam can be based on criteria of nationality (such as www.pakistanlink.com), as well as of religious or ideological orientation, as in the case of Wahhabism, Shi'a, Sufism, and sectarian movements. Denominational Islam also includes local and national Islamic associations, such as the Zentralrat in Germany, the Young Muslim Organization in England, and Islamic lobby groups like the European Muslim League, Council of American-Islamic Relations (CAIR), FAIR (Forum Against Islamophobia and Racism), AMC (American Muslim Council), UCOI (Unione delle Comunita e Organizzazioni Islamiche), and so on. It can also include official institutions such as the Executive Council of Belgian Muslims.

All these Islamic groups or movements make use of the Internet in order to proselytize, as well as to provide general information: the history of this or that movement, contact information, and so on. The Internet is also used to reinforce the internal cohesion of the community through the publication of religious texts, doctrines, manifestoes, and fatwas, and through the sale of various materials associated with the spread and the development of religious information.

The electronic *Ummah* is based on the diffusion of knowledge: How does one pray? What are the Five Pillars? What is the Life of the Prophet? IslamCity.com is perhaps the largest source of information on the Internet about the religious and cultural life of Islam. More specialized are sites such as Ramadhan.Website, Al Hajj, Umrah Information and Resource site, and Islam 101 (www.islam101.com). There are also sites devoted to ethical questions or questions of interpretation on controversial subjects such as extramarital sex, suicide, and apostasy. The e-journal Albalagh[6] is an extensive source of information of this kind. Most of the articles on Albalbagh are written by Khalid Baig, a doctor living in the Chicago area. Some of the main subheadings of the journal are: Islamic Economy, Education, and Women in Islam.

The goal of these and other websites is to provide both information and an "inside view," for Muslims living in the West. The sites hope to give Western Muslims the resources to resist an outside environment seen as corrosive and dangerous.

The Propaganda War

The second facet of virtual Islam, the Islam *of* the Internet, remains largely unexplored despite a number of pioneering works on the subject.[7] Since September 11, 2001, the study of Internet Islam has primarily concerned itself with the study of Islam-oriented activism. One of the aspects of Islamic political life on the web is the idea of cyber-war or cyber-jihad. This web-waged war is a war of ideas, consisting primarily of increasing instances of agitation and propaganda in order to manipulate the thinking of the community. But Muslims also use the internet more neutrally, as a way to disseminate information and share resources. One of the most important examples of this phenomenon is the U.S. website MSAnews (Muslim Students Association News), based at the University of Ohio. This site was started in 1991 as a student group, and has gone on to become one of the most effective sites for the dissemination of information and commentary from every school of thought of the Muslim world, as well as from experts on Islam and the western media.[8] It was very active in the days after September 11, and proved to be an invaluable resource, cataloguing commentaries and facts on the attacks, even including rumors such as the one holding Israel responsible for the destruction of the World Trade Center towers.[9] (Each page was accompanied by a disclaimer announcing that the opinions expressed on MSAnews did not necessarily reflect the opinions of the site's editors.) By 2003, however, the site's activity had dropped off, and by 2004 it has all but disappeared.

"Cyberjihad" also consists in the attempt to sabotage the structures of computer-based communication as they are used by the enemy. It should be noted that cyberjihad is rarely a product of the Islamic diaspora: it is more often led by the initiative of activist groups within the Muslim countries. In his book *Virtually Islamic: Islam in the Digital Age* (published in 2003), the British sociologist Gary Bunt describes several acts of cyberjihad and electronic war between U.S. or Israeli secret services and Islamic jihadist groups. These attacks include the rerouting or destruction of information contained on the site, and even the disabling of the sites themselves. Bunt cites the example of Gforce, a Pakistani hacker group and one of the most effective in carrying out electronic attacks on U.S. government agencies. In the same category are Doctor Nuker and the Pakistan Hackerz Club (PHC). The latter began by attacking Indian websites dealing with Kashmir; it then moved on to the website of the American Israel Public Affairs Committee (AIPAC), hacking into their email database and their financial information. The PHC is said to be responsible for rerouting or damaging more than 47 American and Israeli websites between 1999 and 2001.[10] Another example of cyberjihad is the pro-Israeli hacker group "m0sad," which in 2001 claimed responsibility for defacing the Internet sites of Hezbollah and Hamas. These attacks primarily consisted in disabling the sites' servers, sometimes programming the sites so that anyone who attempted to enter them was automatically linked to pornographic web pages. There have also been cases of cyberjihad from the Western Muslim population, as in the example of the website (now defunct) Azzam.com.[11] Azzam.com had been of particular concern to

American authorities, who suspected it of containing secret codes and instructions for militants, including members of Al Qaeda. According to a Newsweek article of December 10, 2001, British and American intelligence had believed that certain photographs and graphics on the site contained extremely sophisticated coded messages. Azzam.com was managed by the group Azzam Publications named for Abdullah Azzam, a Palestinian militant killed in a bomb attack in Pakistan in 1989. The group operated out of a London post office box and described itself as independent media providing authentic information and news about jihad and mujaheddin foreigners everywhere. In a violently anti-American and anti-western open letter addressed to American president George W. Bush published on the Azzam.com website on 24 September 2001, Azzam Publications openly called for martyrs for a worldwide jihad, and denied that Muslims were in any way involved in the September 11th attacks.

The Lure of New Online Religious Authorities

The more interesting question for this inquiry, however, is how the Internet works to transform religious observance and the concept of religious authority. Without question, the Internet does result in a certain equalizing of religious discourse. Any posted text appears equal in status to the proclamations issued by the custodians of Islamic orthodoxy. In other words, anyone with a bit of technical expertise can express himself on the Internet as much as a graduate of Al Azhar or Medina. But this proliferation of interpreters—or, at least, of voices—of Islam does not necessarily mean that new structures of authority are being created. Most scholars who study this aspect of Islam, such as Gary Bunt, fail to differentiate between the proliferation of voices on the Internet and the emergence of true new religious authorities. It is, in fact, fairly rare that anyone becomes an authority or a recognized voice for Islam *a priori*, simply by setting up a website. To truly achieve the status of "religious authority" in Islam, one must be acknowledged as such in various sociological milieus and by different age groups; this usually requires a method of communication that goes through either transnational networks, political institutions, or local community structures, as chapter 7 discusses. These factors, just as much as the Internet, are essential to understand the structures of Islamic legitimacy and authority.

Furthermore, even if these interpreters are new insofar as their sociological status is not the same as an imam (they are instead doctors, engineers, technicians, etc.) they are often far from being new or innovative in their theology. Our own research on Internet-based Islamic discourse shows, rather, that conservative and Salafi interpretations tend to predominate. There are at least a dozen sites based in the United States and Europe devoted to the issuing of fatwas. Most of these are written in American English, with a few in French and German. In general, these sites are either official sites of Wahhabi doctrine aimed at an English-speaking public (such as Fatwas Online), or else sites reproducing Wahhabi doctrine (such as the French-language version of Fatwas Online). It is also European and American Muslims who ask the majority of questions on the various Wahhabi-oriented question-and-answer sites from the Muslim world. One example of this kind of site is Islam Q&A (www.islam-qa.com), which also posts the fatwas of Sheikh Muhammed Salih Al Munajjid.

A sign of belonging to a minority religion, questions regarding proper belief and practice are by far the most popular: Is it permitted to listen to music? Is it allowed to pray for one's non-Muslim parents? To go to their funeral? Two of the most popular topics of such questioning are questions about the status of women and issues relating to sexuality. The answers given act as a kind of litmus test for distinguishing between those groups with merely conservative tendencies and groups with more extremist points of view. We should point out the distinction between "enlightened orthodox" or conservative answers, and answers given from the Wahabi or Salafi perspective (described in the previous chapter), which are generally more restrictive in matters of orthopraxis. The wearing of *hijab*, for example, is rarely discussed by either conservative groups or more reactionary Salafi/Wahabi movements. The Wahabis, however, go even further and declare themselves against the wearing of pants for women (Fatwa-Online), while sites from conservative groups such as ISNA[12] permit them so long as they are loose-fitting;

"In one *Hadith*," the ISNA's site declares,

> it is reported that the Prophet—peace be upon him—cursed men who imitate women and women who imitate men. It seems to me that what is meant here by imitation is fraud, deception and hiding of one's personality. If there is a dress that conceals a man's identity as man and a woman's identity as woman then it is *haram* to wear that type of dress. However, there are many dresses that are common to men and women. For example in India and Pakistan men and women both wear "shalwar." There is not much difference between the shalwar of men and the shalwar of women. Similarly men and women both wear jeans and pants. Actually there are special jeans and pants for men and women. They cover very well the parts of the body that must be covered. So like wearing the shalwar for men or women, I do not see any thing wrong in jeans and pants. Muslim men and women, however, should not wear very tight jeans and pants.[13]

By the same token, a conservative interpretation of Islam will generally also accept women in professional roles. It will even allow a woman to serve as a religious leader, under the condition that she performs her religious function only for other women and does not neglect her duties as a mother and wife in the process.[14] This view is in contrast to Salafi interpretation, which rejects the possibility of any public role for women. Conservatives also tolerate mixed-sex interaction in professional settings under certain conditions, whereas for Salafis and Wahabis this is forbidden.

Generally speaking, the difference between a conservative and a more radical interpretation is their respective attitudes toward practices that are not discussed in the Qu'ran or the *Hadith*. For Wahabi and Salafi branches, such practices are deemed innovations, and are therefore prohibited.

In contrast, an example of a website with a primarily conservative outlook is the U.S.-based Islam Online. To the question of whether or not women should be allowed to work in mixed-sex environments, for example, the site provides the following response: "It is allowed for women to have a job, if she needs to work, especially in nursing and teaching. But the first and essential role for women is to take care about her family, husband and children . . . Thus, if you are a working woman, then you should strike a balance between your job and marital duties. And you can benefit from the facilities available like having a part-time job or avoid being on call."[15]

Unlike Salafi Muslims, conservative Muslims deny that men are inherently superior to women. Again, as Islam Online comments, "It is really sad that some men in our Islamic countries consider women as second class citizens or treat them in a bad way. However this problem is caused by lack of knowledge and understanding of Islamic texts."

On the same website, Muzammil H. Siddiqi, responding to a similar question, provides a commentary on Verse 34 of the Sura *An-Nisaa*': "Men are the protectors and maintainers of women, because Allah has given the one more [strength] than the other."[16] Says Siddiqui, "The aforementioned verse is not about the absolute excellence of all men over all women. It is talking only about the family organization where the husband has the responsibility to take care of his wife and children. It is not saying that every man is a caretaker of every woman."

One of the rare websites that follows neither the orthodox nor the Salafi interpretation is that of the Progressive Muslims Network, at www.free-mind.org. Relying on an interpretation of revealed Text that attempts to harmonize scripture with present-day concerns, the authors of the site argue that while the Qu'ran does indeed insist on the modesty and virtue of women and the necessity for them to cover their chests, the term *hijab* itself only appears seven times in the Qu'ran, each time to designate a veil, a screen, a curtain or a barrier. Thus the meaning that the term as been given today—*hijab* as a specific article or type of clothing—is not the same meaning as the one it has in the Qu'ran. The website merely states:

> God the Most Merciful gave us three basic rules for the Dress Code of Women in Islam (submission):
>
> - The BEST garment is the garment of righteousness
> - Whenever you dress, cover your chest (bosoms)
> - Lengthen your garment[17]

The Gradual Postmodernization of Islam

Again, it is difficult to determine just how influencial this virtual Islam is on the daily life of Muslims—only a minority of whom, moreover, have access to this on-line community. Nevertheless, it is a significant fact that the electronic *Ummah* is largely a conservative or Salafi *Ummah*. Paradoxical though this may seem, it actually is consistent with the general pattern of religion in the age of globalization.[18]

Desacralization, Personalization and Deterritorialization

On a more general note, we may ask whether the Internet has at all changed the nature of Islamic religiosity. With the Internet, the observant Muslim now has the possibility of fulfilling his or her obligation to pray in a virtual mosque, with actual calls to prayer, a schedule of daily prayers, and a description of ritual.[19] Until very recently, however, on-line ritual practice has been in no danger of supplanting the live observance of rituals, whether in groups or in the mosque.[20] In other words, the cybermosque has not yet succeeded in replacing the neighborhood mosque.[21] Instead, these sites serve more as vehicles for education about the pillars of Islam and proper ritual procedure than as actual substitutes for places of worship.

The long-term consequences of the Internet for ritual practice seem to have more to do with the growth, in number and popularity, of various syncretic practices. Given the amount of information available on the web, the possibilities for picking and choosing from different versions of religion are almost infinite. The use made of the Internet by certain Sufi orders typical of Western mysticism is one example of this phenomenon.[22] The Sufi order Halveti-Jerrahi, for instance, a descendent of the orders of the Whirling Dervishes originally from Turkey,[23] is now established in both North and South America as well as Spain and Italy. Their site is in English and Spanish and makes no reference to the home branch in Turkey. They define themselves as both Sufis and Muslims, emphasizing the multiethnic and multinational character of the order. They also preach the nonsegregation of men and women in the performing of *dikhr*, contrary to their order's practice in Turkey. They also emphasize the range of their charitable activities both in the United States and throughout the world.[24]

If this version of the order can be classified as hybrid, according to Marcia Hermansen's definition, its sister branch, Nur Ashki Jerrahi, is better described as a *perennial*[25] movement. In Askhi Jerrahi, for example, women are accepted as sheikhas, and their website contains all the workshops and sermons of Sheikha Fariha, the head of the American branch.[26]

Besides the practice of ritual, Islamic religiosity is influenced by the Internet through a threefold process: desacralization, individualization, and delocalization. In other words: the rapid growth of sites devoted entirely to the Qu'ran and the on-line posting of the revealed Text, as well as the translating of the Qu'ran into English or other vernacular languages, all change the status of the Text itself.[27]

The Qu'ran thus no longer belongs solely to the space-time of the sacred. It becomes a religious commodity and, increasingly, a normal part of day-to-day living, on the same level as the amulets, rosaries, and other religious objects that fill up the daily life of Muslims. In short, the Internet blurs the dividing line between the sacred and the profane, removing the Qu'ran from its traditional status as something one reads only at designated times, and under the guidance of Islamic scholars. In dramatic contrast to the traditional *madrasa*, where knowledge is passed down from teacher to student, today even a non-Muslim with no knowledge of Arabic can have access to a reading of the Qu'ran in English, French, or German.

Despite these developments, it is difficult to claim, with John B. Thompson,[28] that such easy access to religious texts and rite destroys their integrity. What actually happens is that rite becomes more and more a part of everyday life. The sacred object becomes an object of everyday consumption, a transformation that now influences even global Islamic movements.[29] Thus, rather than thinking of virtual Islam merely as a desecration of ritual or sacred objects, one must also recognize its dialectical function in giving daily life a heightened religious character.

Thompson's theory is that these new modes of religious communication and transmission depersonalize the content of the religious message. The truth is rather to the contrary: the Internet encourages the *re*-personalization—even to the point of total subjectivity—of religious belief and practice. The Internet actually reinforces a postmodern view of religion; that is, it promotes a relativism of beliefs and values even within the religious context. The

Islam of the Internet is an Islam of various forms of identification. Personal testimony replaces interpretation, and often confers the illusion of authority. The trajectory of Muqtedar Khan is an example of the Internet's ability to display and highlight certain opinions. Khan created his website, ijtihad.org, while studying for his doctorate at Georgetown University. Through the site, he became known for his positions in favor of taking American citizenship, as well as his critique of the Muslim establishment for giving the cold shoulder to an American form of Islam, independent of both the contingencies of international politics and ethnic allegiance.

After September 11, Khan achieved true notoriety with a memo addressed to his Muslim brothers, posted on his website on October 7, 2001, and subsequently reprinted several times in the press. In his memo, Khan exhorts his fellow Muslims to put an end to their apologist tendencies and to adopt a critical stance toward Islamic extremists. Entitled "Memo to American Muslims," Khan's text reads: "The worst exhibition of Islam happened on our turf. We must take first responsibility to undo the evil it has manifest. This is our mandate, our burden and also our opportunity. It is time for soul searching. How can the message of Muhammad (pbuh) who was sent as mercy to mankind become a source of horror and fear? How can Islam inspire thousands of youth to dedicate their lives to killing others? We are supposed to invite people to Islam not murder them."

The proliferation of public intellectuals with their own web pages (Tariq Ramadan, Abdolkarim Soroush, Farid Esack, and others described in detail in chapter 9) testifies to what extent Islam is becoming "postmodernized" on the Internet.[30] The postmodern quality of these websites has less to do with the sites' audience, however, than with the sites' interpretation of Islam as an integral part of the authors' personal histories. The postmodernization of Islam is characterized by a preponderance of personal testimony, of individual experience, of the ability to express one's identity through religious discourse. The idea of a personal Islamic identity is reinforced by the hundreds of confessions, repentances, stories, and so on posted on the Internet, such as "How Emily Became a Muslim" (published in 2003 on Islam Q & A), which tells the story of the conversion of a Filipina servant in Saudi Arabia.[31] Similarly, in a story posted in 2003 on the French website saphir.com, a young woman relates how she became a good Muslim woman during the month of Ramadan.[32]

A New Visibility of Marginalized Muslims

Last but not least, the Internet is also an important factor in making it possible for Islamic groups considered marginal or deviant to express themselves. The Internet is a nonhierarchical environment: all points of view, in other words—from the most orthodox to the most atypical of heretical—appear in exactly the same manner on the computer scree. In this sense, the Internet does indeed expand the boundaries of what can be considered legitimate in Islam. The visions of Islam held by groups or sects that have historically been seen as deviant by orthodox Islam are today accessible to all, Muslim and non-Muslim alike, without risk of censorship or suppression. The Internet grants a space and a visibility to Muslims of the margins such as Sufi groups and sects such as the Nation of Islam and Ahmadiyya. Ahmadiyya, for its part, has become a truly global movement, currently claiming more than 10 million members in over 174 countries.[33]

More than any other group, it is the homosexual and transsexual minority in Islam that finds in the Internet more than just an efficient vehicle for expression. The Internet gives these minorities within a minority the means to exist at all, in a way that the physical Islamic communities of Berlin or Los Angeles—not to even mention Cairo or Rabat—do not allow. There are, of course, similar sites within the Muslim world (such as Gay Egypt), but as a general rule they are frequently subject to censorship and repression. The creators of Gay Egypt were imprisoned by the Egyptian government in February 2001 for having designed their website.[34] In May that same year, 52 men were arrested and charged with perversion on a cruise ship on the Nile. This event elicited much international protest: particularly in the United States, where 35 U.S. senators signed a letter to Egyptian president Mubarak condemning the arrest and warning the president of the negative consequences of such repression for U.S.–Egypt relations.[35] Only those sites that are based in the West enjoy an unmolested existence and net access. Thus Gay Egypt has been able to survive, for example, because the server of the site is actually located in London.

The U.S.-based Al Fatiha Foundation (www.al-fatiha.net), devoted to issues concerning gay, lesbian, and transsexual Muslims, is one such space. Founded in 1988, its objective is to promote spirituality within the homosexual Muslim community and to reconcile homosexuality with Islamic faith. The foundation also includes the only openly gay imam. In 1997, its founder, Faisal Al-Asam, created a listserv for the organization: at the time of this writing the listserv claims over 275 member organizations in more than 20 countries.

Virtual Islam helps the Islamic community to come together in spite of geographic distances—the same kind of delocalization, let us recall, that is the basis of Muslim identification with the *Ummah*. The sense of community in Islam is, in essence, not merely physical and regional, but also transregional and transtemporal. The Internet helps to actualize this ideal by bringing people together across geographic space. In addition, it introduces into the

Ummah those aspects of Islam otherwise considered marginal, or even deviant, by orthodox doctrine.

After this overview of the new imagined or virtual forms of the Ummah, it becomes clear that fundamentalism has emerged as the dominant religious tendency. It is not, however, the only one. Most scholarly interpretations seem to agree that cultural globalization does indeed privilege fundamentalist identification among Muslims.[36] For certain theoreticians of postmodernity, Muslims' search for an authentic Islamic identity is one sign of the definitive decline of Western civilization. In this interpretation, the anticonsumerist bent of contemporary Islamic ideology is a reaction to the relentless consumerism of postmodern culture. In response, the isolationist tendencies of certain groups in the Muslim world begin to take the form of a rigid fundamentalism, which comes to color all aspects of life, from the individual level to the social and the political.[37] But on closer inspection, one finds that, though Islamic fundamentalist movements are certainly puritanical, they are far from being universally anticonsumerist. Indeed, for groups such as the Wahabis, wealth and prosperity are objects of praise, and the capitalist system is unchallenged.

But the primary weakness of the above works is that they fail to take into account those forms of globalized Islam that are neither defensive nor fundamentalist. These forms may be in the minority, but they nonetheless point to a significant evolution in Islamic thought and practice. This situation of Western Muslims, in particular, demonstrates that a unilateral interpretation is overly simplistic. The interpretation of Islamic fundamentalism as direct reaction to Western excess fails to take into account the emergence of a hybrid Islamic culture, created through the interaction between the message of Islam and the Western contexts in which they are placed, as chapter 7 shows. The imagined *Ummah*, then, is not merely the desire to recreate the past; it is also an *Ummah* reconstructed for the future.

PART III

The Reinvented Community: New Figures of Islamic Authority in the West

P ublic education programs, as well as the development of new communication technologies—telephone, radio, television, and of course the Internet—have all contributed to the transformation of religious authority in the Muslim world. Authority was traditionally conferred by one's theological knowledge and mastery of the methodologies by which to interpret this knowledge. The dividing line was between knowledge and ignorance; only those who possessed knowledge that had been passed down through a chain of authorities or a line of recognized masters could claim legitimacy as religious leaders.[1] This method of transmitting religious authority was not necessarily a matter of formal education, particularly if the knowledge passed down was esoteric in nature, as in the case of the Sufi masters.

These forms of traditional authority are now facing competition, however, by Muslims exercising their right to interpret the religious message outside of traditional structures. Established religious figures like the sheikhs of Al Azhar or Medina and other established imams are increasingly supplanted by the engineer, the student, the businessman, and the autodidact, who mobilize the masses and speak for Islam in arenas, in stadiums, on the radio. The most notorious of these spokesmen are those with explicitly political messages, such as Ali bin Hadj or Osama bin Laden. But there are also those who simply espouse their own alternatives to traditional Azhari interpretations or to Sufi interpretations: for example, Syrian Mohammed Shahrour.[2] The increased availability of communication technology, such as magazines, cassette tapes, and, most recently, Internet sites, aids in this multiplication of Islamic voices.

In Europe and the United States, the traditional modes of conferring religious authority are definitively losing their influence. The institutional structures of the Muslim world cannot be simply duplicated in the host countries. Muslims are thus in the process of creating new institutions and forms of authority appropriate to their new environment.

Community and local ties are particularly important in the reinvention of authority. It is now often neighborhood religious communities, not the State, that have the power to grant legitimacy to religious authorities. The rise of the small community comes out of an unprecedented democratization of authority in Islam. It also acts in combination with other sources of legitimacy, including membership in national or international religious institutions, participation in transnational religious movements, or personal charisma.

There are four types of religious authority that emerge in this context: (1) the bureaucratic leader, who works on behalf of institutions originating from the Muslim countries; (2) the community or "parochial" leader, whose activity is concentrated in the mosque or Islamic association of a particular neighborhood or city; (3) the globalized leader, whose activities are focused on transnational Islamic movements, whether they be Salafi groups or Sufi brotherhoods; and, lastly, (4) the preacher or public speaker. The roles taken on by any one individual can change or be combined. The globalized leader, in particular, benefits from establishment in a local community, which enables him to ground his international activity, so to speak, in a specific place. Many leaders of the Tabligh movement follow this model. Personal charisma can come into play in any of these types, and often makes all the difference in terms of a leader's influence and self-presentation. The celebrity preachers and public speakers of Islam may not necessarily have local ties, and generally tend to follow the model of the globalized leader. We should also mention that women are still absent from most positions of leadership, although since the year 2000 they have made a spectacular entry into religious debates and dialogue (not to mention mosques) in the United States.

CHAPTER 7

Bureaucratic and Parochial Leaders

The Bureaucratic Leader

Bureaucratic leaders in Islam are leaders paid by or otherwise associated with the Islamic institutions of influential Muslim countries. In Europe, this influence was exerted throughout the 1960s via national associations or other secular groups. Since the 1980s, however, religious organizations have become the primary means of keeping control over expatriate Muslim populations. This influence is exerted by countries such as Algeria, Morocco, and Turkey, and Saudi Arabia, through associations like the World Islamic League. Paris, Madrid, Milan, Brussels, and Geneva are all home to large mosques controlled by the governments of Algeria, Morocco, or Saudi Arabia. One of the most recent of these is the mosque of Berlin, which opened its doors on December 5, 2003. This mosque is run by the DITIB (Islamic Union of Turkish Religious Affairs), the religious arm of the Turkish State in Germany.

Dalil Boubakeur, rector of the great Mosque of Paris and president of the French Council of Islam since May 2003, is a prime example of the bureaucratic Islamic leader. The son of the late Sheikh Hamza Boubakeur (former rector of the mosque, under whose leadership it gradually passed from French to Algerian control), Dalil Boubakeur is a member of the Algerian elite, equally knowledgeable about Islamic and French culture: his post at the mosque in Paris is subsidized by the Algerian government.

These bureaucratic leaders, the spokesmen for nationalized versions of Islam, have the task of supervising immigrant populations and facilitating communication between them and the country of origin. The Muslim States, for their part—in addition to their various strategies for gaining a monopoly over the official image of Islam—also attempt to control mosques on the local level by choosing and exporting imams. Thus one can find imams affiliated with the DITIB, the Mosque of Paris, or the King of Morocco throughout Europe.[3] These imams often face criticisms from younger generations for their inability to understand the particularities of European Islam, as well as for their poor command of the language of the host country.

Bureaucratic imams also exist in the United States, even if their influence relative to Europe is appreciably less.[4] In 1999, we met with Sheikh Shamsi Ali, the imam of an Indonesian Islamic center in New York. Born in a small village in Indonesia, Ali was enrolled by his family in an Islamic school when he was still very young. From there, he was chosen to study at an Islamic university in Pakistan. His first position with the Islamic Foundation was in Jeddah, as an administrator of education. As a result of his connections in the Indonesian government, he was sent to the United States in 1996.

The center in which Ali works was created by a small group of Indonesian businessmen and diplomats. It was built in 1995 thanks to a donation from President Suhartu and the help of the Indonesian Minister of Religious Affairs: "Yes, he [Suhartu] came here to the United Nations and it happened that the head of the community at that time [was able] to meet him and explain about the intention of the Muslims here to build a *masjid*. So, he donated around 150 thousand dollars . . . boy, that was a big donation there . . . and our minister of religion of affairs contacted some rich people from our community. They donated also."[5]

In Shiite communities, the bureaucratic leader is the most common type of religious figure. In the hierarchical structure of Shi'a, each mosque is directed by a *marja*, a learned Muslim chosen through the hierarchy of religious leaders and subsidized in part by the local congregation. Because of the differences between the Duodecimial and Ismaili sects of Shiite Islam—which are exacerbated still further by political divisions and ethnic diversity—the degree of fragmentation in Shi'a is fairly high. The Al Bayt Federation of America, created in 1996, has nonetheless attempted to provide a measure of unity for the different branches of Shiite Islam.

In New York in 2000, we spoke to Sheikh Al Shalani, a representative of the Al Khuai Foundation and the spokesman for the Shi'ite Muslim Scholars of North America.[6] Iraqi-born, Al Shalani studied at the Islamic seminary in Najaf and at Kullyyat Al-Fiqh, a university specializing in the study of jurisprudence, and received his master's degree in Islamic studies from Cairo. He describes the beginnings of his organization:

Bism Allah Al-Rahman Al-Rahim. I have been here for about eleven years now, working with the Al-Khuai benevolent foundation. This foundation was established almost twelve years or eleven years ago by the great Ayatu Allah Al-Sayed Abu Al-Qasim Al-Khuai. Its main headquarters are in London. We also have branches in the United States, Canada, France, Thailand, India, and Pakistan, plus some other branches here and there. The aim of this foundation is to serve the Muslim community in general and the Shi'a community in particular, [as well as] to give the right image of Islam and Muslims to Western society . . . . The foundation started almost at the end of the war between Iran and Iraq. During that period of time, Iran was [portrayed] by western society [as] terrorists [and people who] have no respect for other religions, no respect for human beings, etc.—which is, we believe, propaganda coming especially from America, because Iran was so against them. [We wanted] to [get away from] politics, because whatever happened between Iran and western society, specifically the United States, had to do with politics. It had nothing to do with religion. We try to [teach] the non-Muslim society that Muslims, and especially Shi'a, do all follow the Republic of Iran in every aspect and that whatever is going on is [just] politics, [and has] nothing to do with religion.[7]

Although they still retain a presence in the United States and in Europe, bureaucratic leaders, tied directly to the institutions and governments of the Muslim world, have since the 1980s been largely shut out by local community, or "parochial" leaders. These latter are similar to Catholic priests or Protestant pastors, who have traditionally derived their authority from the local parish. We should also note that in the United States, parochial leaders have always been dominant, particularly in the African American Muslim community.

Local Authority: The Congregational Model

In Europe and the United States, the hierarchies and clerical dynasties of the Muslim world symply cease to apply. Instead, the mobilization of ordinary Muslims is the deciding factor for the new forms of authority. This mobilization is seen, for example, in the development of mosques and Islamic centers throughout the Western world. Over 1,500 Islamic centers have been built in the United States since 1980, and more than 6,000 in Western Europe in the past three decades. Such rapid growth in the number of Islamic centers—not to mention the increase in Muslim funeral parlors, *halal* butcher shops, Islamic schools, and so on—is a striking indication of how well Islam has adapted to its democratic and secularized context. This adaptation takes the form of what is understood in America by the term "congregation." The term designates a kind of religious activism based on principles of (a) voluntarism, (b) management of the congregation by the congregants themselves, and (c) the organization of social and cultural activities as an integral part of the congregation's social function.

These three aspects of the congregational model contribute to the changing nature of Islam in American and European society. In Muslim countries, Islam is an official institution of the State. To be Muslim in a Muslim country is an aspect of social and cultural convention. But in Europe and the United States, on the other hand, there is little societal pressure to belong to a religious group of any kind. To belong to or leave a religious group is, therefore, an act of personal choice and a result of the voluntarism that characterizes religious life in contemporary society. Thus the creation of new Islamic centers is due, more than anything, to mobilization on the part of the Muslim community itself. That is, the construction, administration, and development of Islamic centers are all the result of voluntarism, the daily involvement of its members, who donate their time, ability, and money so that these places can exist.

Second, in Muslim countries, the people are not empowered to run prayer rooms and mosques. These places of worship are public property and are consequently created, run, and maintained by the State. Because this kind of management by State power is largely impossible in Europe,[8] and even less likely in the United States, it is the congregants themselves who take over the management of places of worship.

The third important role played by the congregation is in the creation and implementation of social activities. In both Europe and the United States, the mosque is the center of community life. In other words, the mosque is not just a place one goes to pray, but a true "community center," toward which preexisting networks of solidarity are redirected. This means, that the various activities that set the rhythm of religious life—marriage rites, circumcision, funerals—take place in the mosque itself more and more often. Moreover, Islamic centers now also provide such activities as courses on the Qu'ran for children and adults, conference series and seminars, courses for new converts (primarily in the United States) assistance with funeral rites, recreational activities for children and women, social assistance, and even psychological counseling.

Education is by far the mosque's most important function, in both Europe and America. In almost every mosque, adjacent to the prayer room, is a room reserved for religious training. This training usually consists of lessons on the life of the Prophet, the fundamentals of Qu'ran and *Hadith*, and basic Arabic. These educational programs achieve a dual purpose: not only the transmission of religious and cultural tradition, but also the socialization of children in Islamic culture, so that they may avoid the "temptations" presented by a Western environment. Islamic education can also take the form of intensive seminars for teenagers and women, conferences, or cultural programs.

In contrast to the simple place of worship—whose activities are limited to the observance of ritual practice, and in which the cleric or religious leader plays the dominant role—the congregation is characterized by the active involvement of its congregants in the creation and administration of the religious space—sometimes even including the direction of religious activity itself. This model applies not just to Islam, but to all religious groups in the United States. It is a striking factor of American religious life how rapidly almost all recent arrivals, including Buddhists and Sikhs, adapt to the congregational model. Islam's integration into the different societies of Europe also reflects this developing congregationalism, even if the term itself is never really used.

It should be noted, however, that in contrast to other immigrant groups, Muslim immigrants to the United States after 1965 never assimilated to the point of modeling their rituals on those of Protestant congregations: adopting Sunday as the primary day of religious observance, for example, or English as the language of prayer. Prayers continue to be said in Arabic, although sermons are delivered in English with increasing frequency. The same trend applies in Europe, although the use of vernacular languages in the mosque has frequently encountered hostility on the part of first-generation immigrants from Turkey and North Africa.

Ebaugh and Yang[9] note the centrality of the imam's role as another aspect of adaptation to the mainstream Protestant model of religion. However, as the same evolution is occurring in Europe—where the Protestant congregational model is far from the mainstream—we maintain that the so-called Protestant model is more accurately described as the adaptation of religious authority figures to the constraints of postmodern pluralism and relativism.

The aforementioned structural changes in the structure of Islam in the West particularly affect the status of religious leaders. In the West, the imam acquires a centrality unheard of in the Muslim world. We should recall that in countries where Islam is the official state religion, it is organized as a rigid hierarchy with a strict division of religious roles. The principal figures—the *cadi* and the *mufti*—have the status of civil servants. The mufti's role within the religious hierarchy is to decide questions of religion; the cadi is qualified to decide legal issues (marriage, divorce, etc.). The imam, for his part, is responsible for leading prayer and delivering sermons. He defers to the mufti and the cadi, and sometimes (in cases where the mosque-goers have a need that is beyond the imam's power to address), to other specialists.

In Europe and in the United States, on the other hand, the imam's sphere of activity is not nearly so circumscribed. The person who leads the prayer service is usually the most highly educated or the most respected member of the community (though this still does not necessarily mean that he has a degree in religion). Because there is no true institutional structure, he is imam, cadi, mufti, and teacher all at once; he presides over burials, represents the community in official ceremonies, and so on. The list of his roles both within and without the religious community is potentially endless.

The challenge of this kind of expansion of the imam's duties within the community is not merely one of religious competence: it is also and especially one of cultural and psychological skill. The Muslim community can be extremely diverse—particularly in the United States, where characteristics such as country of origin, ethnicity, socio-economic level, generation, and so on, vary widely, and Pakistani communities live side by side with Lebanese and Turkish groups. The African American mosques of the inner city are perhaps the only non-multiethnic Islamic communities existing the United States. Farouque Khan, the president of the Long Island Islamic Center describes the creation and the expansion of his mosque:

> This group of fifteen families would meet in church basements, in houses on Sundays and try to educate the children. That was the beginning of this community. And in 1984, this property became available—835 Rush Hollow—a property with a nice piece of land in front. The place where we are now was the house on sale. So we purchased this house, along with the land, in 1984. And to give you an idea, in 1984 when we prayed here for the first time for Friday, there were three of us. And now we have six to seven hundred people praying on Fridays here . . . Six to seven hundred people. So that was the beginning. We then started the Sunday school, and the community started growing. We started designs for the mosque in 1989. We laid the foundation stone and started actively fundraising, and as the money became available, we proceeded with the construction. And I think [it was in] 1991 [that] we inaugurated the mosque which you see right in front of you here. Now the community has grown to where we have over four hundred children coming to the Sunday school. We have had to have two shifts. We have an adult [education] program. We have special programs—every day basically—for Qu'ranic recitation. Different groups meet on different days in the

Center. So it has become a very active community. And on our mailing list we have almost three thousand individuals. So they are basically the supporters of the Center. . . . The fifteen families who started the center were mostly from South Asia. Most of the people who were together at that time were from Pakistan, India, Kashmir, with a few from the Middle East, not many, [but a] few. Now it's everybody. Everybody. As we developed by-laws for the institution, some rules and regulations, we made sure that this place was kept open for anyone who wanted to come, whether they are Shi'a, Sunni, Hanafi, [or] Wahabi.[10]

In Europe, on the other hand, the neighborhood mosque tends to be much less ethnically diverse. Whether in Paris or Berlin, Amsterdam or Madrid, local mosques remain fairly homogenous, both in their leadership and in their congregants. It is not at all surprising, therefore, that local mosques tend overwhelmingly to be North African in the suburbs of France, Pakistani or Bangladeshi in English cities, and Turkish in Germany.

Negotiating the Building of Mosques

The other challenge posed to the imam by the Western environment relates to the necessity of communicating with non-Muslim society. The changes in the nature of the mosque in Europe testify to a growing need for dialogue between Muslims and Western governments. The extent to which Islamic community life has established itself in the cities of the West can be seen in the transition from the prayer room, often invisible and anonymous, as a place of Muslim worship, to the public space of the mosque. The difference between these two spaces is not a matter of building area or size. The difference is in how visible the mosque is as a locus of Islamic activity within the city as opposed to the private space of the prayer room, (often simply an apartment or the back room of a shop).

If the prayer room goes unnoticed by the non-Muslim community almost by definition, the same can hardly be said of the mosque. Every project for the building of a mosque entails discussion and negotiation between the different protagonists in the urban context. The mosque transforms Islam from being invisible to being unwanted.

Wherever Islam seeks to establish itself within the urban environment, it encounters resistance from the very outset. No matter what the actual content of the demand made by Muslims regarding the proposed mosque, the first stage of dialogue is often a veiled or explicit refusal on the part of the municipal or local (i.e., neighborhood association) negotiating partners.[11]

The strength of this refusal is in indirect proportion to the degree of acceptance enjoyed by Islam in its respective national and local contexts. In countries with a long-standing history of immigration, such as France or Great Britain, the *a priori* resistance to mosques is losing its force. Some mosques have already been built (Lyon, Evry, Mantes la Jolie), others are in progress, but regardless, the construction of a mosque inevitably entails a process of negotiation with the municipality and local organizations. The projects at Marseille and Toulouse provide two examples of resistance to mosque construction in which it is no longer the resistance of local authorities that creates the problem; the delay in construction is due mostly to competition between different Muslim organizations, to such an extent that on June 17, 2004, the mayor of Marseille announced the cancellation of plans for a Grand Mosque in favor of several smaller local mosques. Even the Paris city council's long-standing refusal to grant a building permit to the expansion project of the Addawa mosque, in the nineteenth Arrondissement, was resolved in 2001 after the election of a new mayor.

One of reasons why this kind of resistance is losing strength in Europe is that at least some of the mosques constructed in the past ten years have proven themselves to be good neighbors in the religious environment of their respective communities. The mosque of Lyon, established in 1994, almost did not come to be, due in part to the explicit hostility of certain local community preservation associations, but also and especially to the first Gulf War and the accompanying outburst of anti-Islamic sentiment. These two factors were nearly fatal to the mosque project. Today, however, this mosque—officially inaugurated in September of 1994 in the presence of the Minister of the Interior—is a favored negotiating partner in local politics. Similarly, in Evry and Lille, mosque representatives and municipal authorities continue to work together. Another reason for this change of heart on the part of local authorities is the realization—particularly after the 1989 controversy over the wearing of headscarves—that Islam is no longer solely a matter of isolated migrant workers, but also of new and established generations. Municipalities thus have a vested interest in bringing Islam out of the shadows and releasing it from its status as a religion on the margins. Governments are now banking on a strategy of official recognition for Islam. With this strategy, they hope to forestall the threat of fundamentalism raised by the Paris Métro bombings of 1995 and other attacks by imitators of Khaled Kelkal.[12]

In England, as well, the construction of mosques and their establishment within the urban environment has become fairly noncontroversial. Of the more than 1,200 Muslim associations in Great Britain, almost all have officially recognized status in religious matters (the ritual slaughter of animals, burial rites).[13] In some cities, these associations have banded together in coalition to maintain a permanent dialogue with the municipal authorities. The Council of Mosques of Bradford and the Federation of Islamic Associations of Leicester are two notable examples. According to Sean McLoughlin, one of the reasons for this lack of controversy is the demographic concentration of Muslim populations in cities like Bradford.[14] In all of these cases, the lack of controversy over proposals for the building of mosques is due to good communication between the local community, municipal authorities, and Islamic representatives. The emergence of a new generation of educated and middle-class Muslims at the head of these associations has meant a greater skill in conducting negotiations compared to that of first-generation immigrants.

In countries such as Spain or Italy, however, where Muslim immigration is a relatively recent phenomenon, proposals for the construction of mosques continue to encounter heavy resistance. A project to build a mosque in Lodi, for example, provoked a resistance, in 2000, on the part of both the general population and the local authorities that serves as a sort of model for resistance to mosque construction throughout Italy.[15] Similarly, in Germany—where recognition of the definitive nature of Turkish immigration is relatively recent, despite the fact that Turkish immigration itself is hardly new—proposals for mosques continue to encounter significant obstacles.

The Emergence of a New Generation of Local Leaders in Europe

The ability to communicate with the non-Muslim community and to conduct negotiations with political authorities is crucial for local religious leadership. Many first-generation immigrant imams in Europe have confined themselves to their ethnic community, be it Turkish, North African, or Middle Eastern. In most cases, the initiative to build a mosque is taken by Muslims from the same country or region and who live near one another in a particular city or neighborhood. In France, for example, the first mosques and prayer rooms of the 1980s were almost exclusively created by immigrants from the Maghreb. In England, it was the *Babas*—an Urdu word that translates as Daddies and refers to first-generation immigrants from the Indian subcontinent—who both built and retained control of the first mosques. The "Babas" hegemony has led to conflicts between the different prayer rooms that correspond, in turn, to the regional and religious divisions of the country of origin: Punjabi, Gujrati, Barelvi, Deobandi, and so on.

For the most part, the imams of the first mosques received no formal religious training, or else a training that limited the possibility of spreading the religious message in a Western context, as shown by Daniel Rivet's report on French imams presented to the National Ministry of Education in June 2003.[16] According to this report, the majority of French imams are foreign-born—primarily Turkish and North African—and lack proficiency in the French language. But as the new, European-born or educated generation come to take the helm of Muslim congregations, the spectrum of activities for which the imam is responsible continues to expand, as does the interaction between the Muslim community and the outside environment. It is often the case nowadays that the position of imam and director of the mosque are combined. Mamadou Daffé, for example, a director of research and expert in pharmacology at the Centre National de la Recherche Scientifique (CNRS, National Science Research Center), is the "charismatic" imam of the Mirail neighborhood in Toulouse. As of 2004, he leads evening prayer in the Al-Houciene mosque, the only religious institution in Toulouse where the *khotba* (sermon) is given in French. Daffé is the prototype of the local leader. A self-described "imam-researcher," he came to France from Mali in 1975. He currently lives with his family in a housing project in the Empalot quarter, and in the space of only a few years, has become the spiritual guide to many of Toulouse's young Muslims.

Larbi Kechat, the director and imam of the Addawa mosque, located on the Rue de Tanger, is another local religious leader who, since the mid-1980s, has contributed to the new openness of the mosque. Kechat, a graduate of the Sorbonne, has kept somewhat apart from the French Islamic world. Refusing to participate in the national competition for institutional leadership, he achieved his position instead through the development of social and cultural activities within the mosque. His mosque has gained popularity among Muslim youth largely because of his determination to situate it in a non muslim environment. His reputation as "a martyr" also contributed to his attractiveness to the younger generations: in 1994, he was unjustly arrested and sentenced to house arrest on suspicion of having supported the Algerian radical group GIA (Groupe Islamique Arme, or Armed Islamic Group).[17] He delivers his sermons in French, and has organized a number of colloquia and seminars, inviting religious, intellectual, and political figures to discuss subjects on such varied topics as secularization, modernization, and women's rights. The Addawa mosque is located in a former textiles warehouse, transformed into a religious center in 1967. After more than 20 years of legal battles with the Paris City Hall, Kechat finally obtained permission in 2001 to build a real mosque—which, once it is completed, will be one of the largest in Europe.[18]

In Germany, the emergence of a new generation—represented, for example, by the Islamic Federation of Berlin—also permitted negotiations to be opened with government authorities in 2002 on a proposal for a mosque in the Kreutzberg district of Berlin. The Islamic Federation of Berlin[19]—made up of high school and college students and lawyers, all Turkish in origin—represents the new face of German Islam, which is just beginning to come out of isolation. This new generation is more likely than previous ones to engage in discussion with German authorities, as well as with other segments of German society, such as churches and political parties.[20] This fact, however, does not mean that the dialogue between Muslim groups and the outside world is always easy.

Even in England, a new generation of leaders are beginning to emerge from within the Muslim community. While these leaders are still primarily known for their family positions and their roles as providers of traditional education, they are at the same time developing connections with local governments and non-Muslim organizations. One of these new leaders is Ibrahim Mogra, imam of the Umar mosque in Leicester. Born in England, he is a recognized figure within the Deobandi community that dominates Islamic life in Leicester. At the same time, he is involved in a variety of interfaith dialogues and communication efforts with the non-Muslim world around him. "If we want to change the perception people have of us," he says, "we must take the initiative, we must build relational networks and friendships."[21]

The Growing Integration of American Mosques

Most religious leaders in the United States establish relations with the non-Muslim world as a matter of course, with the exception of leaders from Salafi and Tablighi groups. Resistance from the non-Muslim world to the building of Islamic centers, is much less pronounced than in Europe—or at least it was before September 2001—largely because religious freedom and the social role of religion is seen as one of the cornerstones of American society. Muslim dialogue in America also tends to be more inclusive than in Europe, encompassing not only local authorities but also the media, the schools, social services, and the churches. Talal Eid has been the imam and director of religious affairs at the New England Islamic Center of Quincy and Sharon since 1982. At a meeting held on November 2003, he insisted on the necessity of communication with non-Muslims in the post–September 11 context. "We have to educate people about key concepts like *jihad* and *kafir*," he stated, "and also explain certain rules like *hijab* and the prohibition against mixed-sex relations."

The New England Islamic Center is one of the oldest Islamic centers in the United States. It began in the 1920s as a permanent space for Lebanese immigrants to gather. The religious differences between Christians and Muslims were minimized in order to concentrate on the preservation of Arab language and culture. With the passing of the years, the religious activities of the center came to be modeled on those of Protestant congregations, including the adoption of mixed-sex religious services and the copying of Christian almsgiving practices in the *zakat*. The arrival of immigrants who were more strict in their observance of Islam after 1965 changed the character of the center. Muzammil H. Siddiqi, who served as president of the ISNA from 1996 to 2000, was the imam responsible for turning the center toward a more orthodox orientation.[22]

Originally from Lebanon, Talal Eid holds a degree from the University of Al Azhar, as well as master's degree in Theology from Harvard Divinity School. Since 1993, he has been studying for his doctorate at Harvard. Before coming to the United States, Eid was the imam of the An-Nasir mosque in Tripoli. His current post is partially subsidized by the World Islamic League. The community has grown dramatically since the 1980s, and the center now has two locations, Quincy and Sharon, Massachusetts. The center's activities attract hundreds of families every year. Among its most popular are a full-time elementary school, seminars for adults, and a summer camp.

The dual challenge for Islam—"To explain America to Muslims and Islam to Americans," in the words of Imam Talal—is made more difficult by the majority of imams' failure to adapt to their new context. The first generation of Muslim immigrants to Europe was often poorly educated in Islamic theology, or educated in such a way that limits their ability to teach in a Western setting (as the Rivet report on French imams, presented to the Minister of the Interior in May 2003, demonstrates[23]). The fact that many foreign-born imams are brought to the West on the initiative of institutions in the country of origin—or even, in the United States, of the congregants themselves—further reinforces this situation. Communication between imams and their congregants is often difficult. Problems have arisen in almost every mosque: either because the imam is too strict, or because he has political aspirations, or because he does not sufficiently address the particularities of the environment in his sermons or even in his everyday speech.

This failure to adapt on the part of the imam is often "counterbalanced," especially in the United States, by the role played by the president of the mosque or organization. According to a 2001 survey on American mosques (1209 total surveyed), sponsored by CAIR, 81 percent of American mosques have an imam. In half of these, the office of imam and the office of president are filled by two different people.[24] Most large American mosques tend to be organized in a fairly systematic fashion, with the president elected by an executive council and the imam hired as an employee. This is the case, for example, of the Islamic Center of Long Island, run by an executive committee of 25 members (including two women) and a committee of sponsors. The president is elected by the committee. The imam is an employee of the center.

This is how the president of the center describes the process by which their imam was hired:

What we have avoided is a single person coming and telling us what's right and what's wrong. Many years ago, we went looking for imam. We put together a job description. What does the imam have to do? Well, he's got to lead the prayers. He's got to ask—to deal with non-Muslims, okay. He's got to deal with the youth, he's got to deal with the women. Major issues. So we interviewed a whole bunch of candidates. We advertised and a lot of people came through. We could not find one person who could do all this. So we divided up the responsibilities and the job. . . .

Well, the imam, Hafez, he leads the prayers, okay, he's good at it. He does that. [But] if a question comes from the community which is sensitive, they refer it to me. I am the spokesperson. So we divided up the job. We said, we do not have anybody at this time with whom we feel comfortable that he can do all these things. So let us do it bit by bit and do it well. And it's worked out very well . . . As far as I know—in terms of Islamic history, I mean—the job description for an imam was never someone who did everything. You know, the Prophet in Islam himself did not do everything. And unfortunately, [there are] a lot of people who do come here to go to the States, or come from, you know, very reputable institutions, Al Azhar, etc. . . . after they come here and they get a job here as an imam, then suddenly they're autocratic.[25]

According to the CAIR survey mentioned above, the median age for imams who are not also presidents of the mosque is 42; for those who are both imam and president, 48. In cases where the roles of president and of imam are separate, the imam is a full-time employee. Most imams have a university degree, 77 percent of these in Islamic Studies. The percentage of degree-holders is even higher (93 percent) among presidents or directors of mosques who do not serve as imams. Farouqe Khan, the president of the Long Island mosque, came to the United States in 1967 to conduct post-doctoral research. A doctor who took his early training in Kashmir, he is also the head of a cardiology unit in a large New York hospital.

It is within the African American community that the function of imam and director are most often combined. The level of Islamic education of these imam-directors also tends to be lower than the average. Imam Siraj Wahaj has been the imam of the Taqwa mosque in Brooklyn since its creation in 1981. Born Jeffrey Kearse, he was raised Baptist, and converted to Islam while still a young man. When Martin Luther King Jr. was assassinated, Kearse was 18 years old: "When they killed Martin Luther King," he says, "they killed the dream. After that, we became more militant and more radical."[26] As a student at New York University, he was attracted to both the Nation of Islam and the Black Panthers. He eventually joined the Nation of Islam in 1969. Upon the death of Elijah Muhammed in 1975, the founder of the movement, he followed the path set out by Warith Deen Mohammed and turned to Sunni Islam. Self-taught in both Arabic and Islam, Wahaj, along with 50 of his core-ligionists, took an intensive 40-day course in Islam sponsored by the government of Saudi Arabia. He subsequently decided to build on this foundation with a four-month course in Mecca. In 1981, with the help of some friends, he founded his own mosque, located in a Brooklyn apartment. His next step was to purchase a former clothing store at public auction, for a sum of $30,000, and convert it to an Islamic center. Sixty percent of Wahaj's congregants are black immigrants from Africa. As both imam and president of the mosque, Wahaj is, in his own words, "in charge of everything."

The fight against drug use has been one of Wahaj's primary "missions" in the Taqwa mosque. In an unprecedented move for the time, he formed an alliance with the police in order to find and prosecute drug dealers, and eventually succeeded in eradicating drug traffic in the mosque's immediate neighborhood. "In '89," Wahaj recounts,

we had a 40-day anti-drug campaign, where we were able to close down fifteen drug houses in this particular area. We know that in order for our congregants to be saved, we had to get rid of the drugs in the area. So, we literally closed them down. We had a big rally. It was on January 21, I think in '89 or '88, something like that. And the police came and they raided all those fifteen drug houses. And when they raided them and arrested the people, we stood our men in front of them and then a lot of them came back. And so we stood in front of these drug houses. Other brothers walked around the block, others drove around. We did this for 40 days, 24 hours a day. And, in a way, to keep the drugs out. That is why we got a big reputation for that. As you know, it was in the *Times* newspaper. It was in every major media. I mean, they came all over the world: from Germany, from France, from Italy, from Spain, from everywhere, you know, to know, to cover. Because it was major, major news . . . It was *jihad*.[27]

Since September 11, the situation has changed for American mosques. Attacks and acts of vandalism have increased exponentially.[28] More important, the "War on Terror" has resulted in the heightened surveillance of Islamic centers and organizations and a tighter regulation of their activities. The Islamic Society of Boston began in the 1980s as a congregation of MIT students in Cambridge. In the decade that followed, its membership grew in rhythm with successive waves of immigration. The center's membership is primarily Middle Eastern and North African. New branches are currently being constructed in Boston's primarily black Roxbury district, a development that will doubtless change the ethnic balance of the center's membership.

In a November 2003 interview with the author, W., the director of communication for the center, described visits to the center after September 11 by the FBI and the INS, visits that are now the daily lot of all Islamic places of worship. The most delicate political problem in this area concerns the religious or financial sponsorship of certain mosques. Some mosques are tied to associations labeled by the Bush administration as "international terrorist organizations." During the month of October 2003, the Islamic Center of Boston was the object of several articles in the local press after one of its members was arrested for "giving support to a terrorist group involved in Palestinian issues." A further source of controversy was the fact that Sheikh Qaradawi, one of the official sponsors of the center, was also known as a sometime supporter of Hamas.[29]

At the same time, however, such a climate of suspicion requires more than ever an openness to the non-Muslim world and an active solicitation of allies. Thus the leaders of the ISB, following the example of many other Islamic spaces, decided to increase its "open door" programs, to provide proof of the center's transparency and the goodwill of its administration.

Because first-generation immigrants still tend to dominate European mosques, the median age for imams is higher, and the level of education lower, than those of American mosques. Socioeconomic level is the crucial difference here. Most American mosques are financially self-sufficient and in good financial health.[30] The building of a mosque or center is rarely, if ever, described as a problem of finances. In Europe, on the other hand, the financing of both the construction and the day-to-day upkeep of Islamic spaces is constantly presented as both a political and a financial difficulty. The Islamic Federation of Berlin's 2002 negotiations for the construction of a mosque in the Kreutzberg district, for example, were additionally hampered by the Federation's lack of funding.[31]

Within the gradual restructuring of Muslim communities in the West, the emergence of "parochial leaders" constitutes a noteworthy phenomenon. This emergence, however, does not mean that diaspora Muslims are cut off from the larger religious currents, all of them more or less political, which have spread throughout the Muslim world during the course of the twentieth century: first as a form of resistance to colonialism and then as an oppositional stance to secular political regimes. The proof of the connection between Western Islam and the Muslim World is (1) the influence of these movements—the Egyptian Muslim Brothers movement in particular—on local leaders in Europe and the United States; and (2) the role played by particular "transnational" leaders and charismatic speakers within diaspora Islam.

CHAPTER 8

Transnational Leaders and Charismatic Speakers

The West: The New Locus of Muslim Brothers' Influence

Certain religious authorities in Islam are also associated with transnational religious movements. As we have already seen in chapter 5, The Tablighis and Salafis, are two forms of this transnational Islam. Both movements reject their non-Muslim environment and encourage their followers to separate themselves from mainstream society. In contrast, followers of movements such as the Muslim Brothers or the Pakistani Jamaat Islamiyya are much more involved in the recognition of and activity within Western society. Given this fact, these latter movements appear as the primary forces behind the reinvention of the *Ummah* in the West (a preoccupation not universally shared, however, by all "parochial" leaders).

The followers of the Muslim Brothers explicitly try to recreate the spirit of *salafiyya* which emerged in the nineteenth century. The attempt to place modern culture within an Islamic context is not a recent phenomenon. It also formed an integral part of the sweeping reform movements (*islâh*) of the nineteenth century. These reform movements were in large part a response to the renewed confrontation with the Western world triggered by Napoleon Bonaparte's invasion of Egypt. The chief representatives of these movements, collectively known as *salafiyya*, were the Persian Djamal Eddin Afghani (died 1897), the Egyptian Mohammad Abduh (died 1905) and his disciple, Rachid Ridâ, the Syrian Kawakibî, the Algerian Ibn Badis, and the Moroccan Allal Al-Fassi. Confronted with the challenge of modernity, these scholars believed that the Islamic tradition contained the resources

Muslims required. They advocated a return to the faith of the Elders (*salaf*) and the rejection of the compromises and superstitious practices that had obscured the true nature of the Revelation. In contrast to many members of the elite—who saw modernity as the absorption and adaptation of Western methods—the Muslim reformists argued against the strict division of past and present, acknowledging the possible benefits of both modernity and the Muslim tradition. To this end, the Salafi reformists promoted the practice of *ijtihad* (interpretation) to combat the traditionalism that rendered Islam inflexible and hindered its ability to adapt to new circumstances in the areas of society, culture, or politics. The trauma of Islam's contact with the West, therefore, did not originally result in a schism between those who approved of Western culture and those who disapproved of it; rather, it resulted in the intense desire of many Muslims for reform within Islam itself.

In the period between the two world wars, the balance of power shifted in favor of secular modernists. This signified the end of the efforts of the reformists, who had attempted to ground modernity in a foundation of classical Muslim culture, and the beginning of an era in which Islamic thought was removed from any historical or geographical context. This break explains the evolution of Islamic political thinking toward radicalism and antimodernism, as well as how the motivating principle behind these movements came to be not progress, but justice.[1]

The Society of Muslim Brothers was the first translation of *salafiyya* into a concrete organizational structure. The date of its creation, 1928, situates it in a decade that saw the disappearance of the last institutional manifestation of Muslim political unity, with Kemal Ataturk's dissolution, in 1924, of the Ottoman Caliphate. The political vision of the Muslim Brothers also serves as a sort of model: in its 60 years of existence it has encompassed a vast spectrum of modes of action—from socio-educative and medical charity work to electoral politics and even underground activities (against the repression of the Nasser regime)—and has been claimed, if sometimes only temporarily, by almost all other Egyptian, Middle Eastern, or North African Islamist movements.[2] The Muslim Brothers has always distanced itself from the Wahabi doctrines of the Saudi regime, which, as we have discussed in chapter 5, has since the 1980s been in the process of changing the meaning of the term "Salafi." Like the Salafists of today, followers of the Muslim Brothers consider the Salaf—the first generations of Muslims and companions of the Prophet—as their point of reference, and refuse to follow a particular school of jurisprudence. Contrary to Wahabi-inspired Salafists, however, followers of the Muslim Brothers rely on *ijtihad* (the power to interpret the revealed text) as a way to construct a form of jurisprudence adapted to the circumstances of modernity.

In Europe and in the United States, there are a number of different organizations who derive inspiration from the Muslim Brothers. In Europe, the most important of these are the UOIF (Union des Organisations Islamiques de France), the UOIE (Union des Organisations Islamiques d'Europe or Federation of Islamic Organizations in Europe), the Zentralrat in Germany, and in England, the Muslim Council of Britain, and the Islamic Foundation. In the United States, the MSA (Muslim Student Association) and its satellite organizations, of which the ISNA is perhaps the most important, follow the Brothers' model. The leaders of all these organizations display a remarkable social and intellectual homogeneity. The first generation of leadership, all from the urban educated middle class of the Middle East, is the product of opposition movements in Muslim countries. This leadership includes such individuals as Dr. Nadeem Elyas, the Syrian president of the Zentralrat, and the first president of the UOIF, Ahmed Jaballah, who was a member of the Islamist opposition in Tunisia. In the past decade, however, a new, European-born generation, belonging to the educated middle-classes, has come to the fore in organizations such as the Muslim Council of Britain (MCB).

Both generations of leaders are involved in the struggle for official representation of Islam by the respective countries in which they live. The secretary general of the UOIF, Fouad Allaoui, is also one of the two vice presidents of the French Council on Islamic Religion. In 2002, Dr. Elyas drew up a charter in which he demonstrated the compatibility between Islamic principles and German democracy. Since the Rushdie Affair, and even more so after September 11, the MCB has become one of the main negotiating partners with the British government on issues relating to Islam.

Within this new democratic and pluralistic context, the Muslim Brothers have reconnected with their historical origins as an activist movement with a devoutly religious outlook. It bases its conduct on the principle of respect for the institutional and political environment of the host country, hand in hand with the maintenance or restoration of religious and ethical heritage. This "remoralizing" approach is expressed via the organization of various educational, charitable, athletic, and cultural activities.

Many imams, particularly among the young and educated, subscribe to the philosophy of the Muslim Brothers. They are sympathetic to its interpretation of Islamic tradition, or else they admire certain historical figures within the movement. It should also be noted, however, that an attraction to the Muslim Brothers does not necessarily mean affiliation with a particular organization.

Enlightened and Mobilized Orthodoxy

In the United States, the Hathout Brothers are the real "veterans" of this movement. Both are doctors of Egyptian origin, very active in Islamic lobbies. We spoke with Dr. Hassan Hathout in his office in June of 1999. We also visited him at the California Islamic Center, in the heart of Los Angeles. A practicing gynecologist originally from Cairo (his brother is a cardiologist), Dr. Hathout received his Ph.D. from the University of Edinburgh, and emigrated to the United States in 1989. In addition to his medical practice, he has tirelessly devoted himself to the development of Islamic activities. Besides his work as an author and public speaker,[3] his most significant project (in cooperation with his brother) has been the Southern California Islamic Center and the expansion of its activities, which now include conferences, seminars, educational programs,[4] interfaith dialogues, and community programs.[5] He has also had the distinction of being the first Muslim to open a plenary session of Congress.

The New York Islamic Center was built thanks to the financial support of the governments of Kuwait, Libya, and Saudi Arabia, as well as contributions from countries such as Indonesia, Turkey, Morocco, and Algeria. The center was completed in 1991 in midtown Manhattan. Its architecture demonstrates a desire to reconcile Islam and modernity. Its construction alone cost over 20 million dollars. In 2000, we spoke with the Egyptian-born imam of the center, Mohammed Gemeaha, then in charge of religious affairs. A cheerful-looking man of around 40 years, he places himself deliberately in the tradition of Qaradawi, whom he names as one of his models in theological matters, along with Tantawi, at Al Azhar. Himself an alumnus of Al Azhar, Gemeaha worked as a translator for the head imam of this prestigious Islamic university, before being sent to Europe and from there to New York. Talking about Islam in the United States, Gemeaha tends to minimize the restrictions that Muslims face, explaining that it is possible for Muslims to eat the same meat as Christians[6] and to have recourse to civil courts, even in questions of Islamic civil law.

This kind of openness to Western society, however, could not prevent the fallout of September 11. Two weeks after the attack on the World Trade Center, Gemeaha returned with his family to Egypt. In official accounts, his departure was motivated by death threats directed at both him and his family. Another version, however, is that Gemeaha's departure was due to an interview he gave, published on an Arabic-language website[7] (in which he spoke of the attacks as a Zionist plot).

Nonetheless, the Muslim Brothers movement—along with authorities such as Sheikh Qaradawi—continue to attract young educated Muslims throughout the Western world who want to reconcile the exigencies of Islam with secular life without losing their soul. The author of more than 50 works, including *Islamic Awakening between Rejection and Extremism* (1984),[8] Sheikh Qaradawi became famous for his participation in debates televised on Al Jazeera. He is one of the chief figures of the Brothers movement in Europe and the United States. Born in Egypt in 1926, his entire education was focused on Islamic Studies: he received his B.A. from Al Azhar in 1953, and his doctorate from the same institution in 1973. Along with Sheikh Mawlawi of Lebanon, he was one of the first to become interested in the minority condition of Muslims living in the West. In the middle of the 1990 headscarf controversy in France, he took an extremely liberal position, counseling families to give up the headscarf if it was disrupting the life of the family or the young woman concerned. Sheikh Tantawi, of the same persuasion and ideology as Qaradawi, went even further, in 2003 taking a position in support of French government policy to ban headscarves from public schools. Qaradawi is a sponsor of both the UOIF and the UOIE. His book *The Permitted and the Forbidden in Islam*, which has been translated into both French and English, restates his moderate positions on the interpretation of Islamic law. It was nonetheless censored in 1997 by the French Minister of Interior.[9] Qaradawi is currently the president of the European Fatwa Council, of which Sheikh Mawlawi is vice president.

The Muslim Brothers expends its energies in two main areas: theological reflection, based on the principles of *ijtihad*, and intellectual production. The European Council for Fatwa and Research and the Fiqh Council of North America are examples of the first type of activity. Created in London in 1997 on the initiative of the FIOE[10], Federation of Islamic Organizations in Europe, the European Council for Fatwa and Research is composed of 35 members representing the majority of Western European countries. Their fatwas are responses to questions asked by Muslims throughout Europe. The Muslim Brothers distinguish themselves from Salafis or Tablighis by their efforts to situate the interpretation of *fiqh* within a Western context. In spite of this, however, they can by no means be called a liberal or progressive movement. Their philosophy is most accurately described as one of enlightened conservatism. They actively practice *ijtihad*, with the primary aim of allowing Muslims to live devout lives within the European environment. Their rulings attempt to reconcile the requirements of Islamic practice with secular life. The result is a certain strictness in private matters, in combination with an active involvement in civil and political life. In October 1998, they issued a fatwa, for example, advocating political participation for Muslims in the democratic system.[11] At the same time, however, another fatwa prohibits the sale of alcohol in Muslim-owned restaurants and discourages Muslims from working in places that prepare pork. Yet another fatwa recommends against investing any money in order to earn interest. And much ink was spilled over the council's fatwa (issued in 2001, after a process of discussion begun in 1999) regarding a female convert to Islam whose husband remains a Christian.[12] The council ultimately decided that the woman could remain married, but only in the hope that the husband would eventually convert.

This kind of decision, which takes into account the difficulties presented by a Western environment, is also typical of the rulings given on many internet sites, such as Islam-online, discussed in chapter 6, which could be categorized as "enlightened conservatism." Taking the same line as the FIOE, imam Al-Hanooti[13]—a graduate of Al Azhar and proponent of the Muslim Brothers' philosophy who writes for both the ISNA's website and that of the Muslim American Society[14]—issued a fatwa in which he states that a Muslim woman may not marry a non-Muslim man, but she can remain married to her non-Muslim husband if she thinks that he might convert. A question on the website asks, "I am a recent convert to Islam, Alhamdullihah! My problem is I reverted[15] and my husband and children did not. My main frustration is whether I am committing a sin by staying married to my husband since he is not Muslim or whether I should wait and see if he becomes a Muslim and if so for how long? I must also mention that he encourages me to go to the masjid and reminds me of my prayer time, however he will not revert at this time. I need your help as I can not seem to get an answer." Al-Hanooti's answer is: "It is unlawful for you to stay with your husband if he is a non-Muslim, but you can still give him time if you are hopeful that he will accept Islam. If there is no hope, I encourage you to get out of the marriage the moment you can do it."[16]

The most divisive question among religious authorities is to what extent the obligations of *Shari'a* can be fulfilled in the West. In other words, can one consider, with the *Hanafi* school of thought, that as a cultural minority, Muslims may not be able to follow all the obligations of *Shari'a*, even those with a moral dimension such as prohibition against earning interest? The council's various fatwas demonstrate a certain ambivalence in this area. In one fatwa, mentioned above, they prohibit the sale of alcohol by a Muslim, but in another—hotly disputed—fatwa, they allow the use of credit, arguing that in a Western country the Islamic rules prohibiting lending on credit cannot be followed.

The Fiqh Council of North America, presided over by Sheikh Taha Al-Alwani, takes a similarly moderate stance. Born in 1935 in Iraq, Dr. Al-Alwani is a graduate of Al Azhar, where he received a Ph.D. in Islamic Law in 1973. After working for many years in the Arab world's university system, he came to the United States in 1984. He has been active in many of the founding activities of Islam in the United States. He is the first president of the School of Islamic and Social Sciences in Virginia, the president of the Fiqh Council of North America, and a founding member of the International Institute of Islamic Thought (IIIT). Today, he is one of the foremost thinkers on *fiqh* as it relates to minority issues—a subject that elicits a great deal of debate, even among those who subscribe to the Muslim Brothers philosophy.[17] One fatwa of the Fiqh Council that set innumerable pens to writing, for example, declared, in September of 2001, that it was legitimate for American Muslims to fight in the U.S. Army against Afghanistan. This fatwa demonstrates the desire to reconcile Islam with its western context that is characteristic of the Muslim Brothers movement.[18]

The Ambitious Project of Islamicizing Knowledge

In terms of intellectual production, it is the Islamic Foundation—sponsored by Ahmad Kurshid of Pakistan's Jamaat Islamiyya—which constitutes the chief center of research and reflection on questions of Islam in Europe. The Foundation operates through a variety of research and educational programs and publications, including a number of books and magazines like *Encounters: A Journal of Multi-Cultural Perspectives*. According to its mission statement, The Islamic Foundation,

> established in 1973 in the city of Leicester, is a major centre for education, training, research and publication. The Foundation seeks to build bridges between Muslims and others, while promoting the highest standards of academic research and publications. Since its inception, the Foundation has been pursuing the following objectives: to contribute to a better understanding of Islam in the West; to foster better relations between Muslims and members of other faith communities; to promote educational ventures for the intellectual nourishment of the Muslim community; to present Islamic responses to the contemporary challenges in the academic field and enhance a global dialogue of civilizations. The Foundation has established research units on interfaith studies, Islamic economics, Islam in Europe, Muslim educational needs, education and training for new Muslims and non-Muslim professionals and cultural awareness about Islam. The Foundation has published nearly 300 books on a range of subjects related to Islam and the Muslim world and regularly publishes three journals. It houses the largest private Islamic library in Europe, which contains over 36,000 books and around 300 different journals.[19]

One of the foundation's most recent projects is the creation of the Markfield Institute of Higher Education, officially established by Prince Charles in January of 2003. The Institute was created to allow university graduates to study aspects of Islam.

Across the Atlantic, a network of scholars and scientists who all met through the MSA founded the International Institute of Islamic Thought (IIIT) under the sponsorship of Sheikh Al-Alwani and Ismael Faruqi. Their first meeting took place in Lugano, Switzerland, in 1977.[20] In addition to its publications, the Institute holds dozens of colloquia and seminars on both the national and international level, usually in cooperation with the MSA or American academic institutions. Shortly after September 11, we attended a conference on "Conflict and Religion in International Relations", organized jointly by the IIIT and Georgetown University. This conference strongly criticized the lack or inefficiency of communication between Muslims and the different segments of American society on topics relating to Islam. IIIT has branches all over the world: it operates in Egypt, Iraq, Syria, Germany, and, since 2001, in France. As a forum of intellectuals created to promote research, publications, and seminars on the question of Islam in relation to scholarship and modernity in general, the IIIT attempts a critique of Western thought from the standpoint of Islamic thought. Their vast and ambitious project is the "Islamicization of knowledge." Several different interpretations of Islam, not all of them based on *salafiyya*, are represented in this project. Their common conviction, however, is the idea that Western scholarship is in crisis, and that this crisis is, in turn, affecting the *Ummah*. One must find a way out of this crisis by attempting either to discover a kind of properly Islamic scholarship;[21] to create a scholarship that would respect the sacred, in the universal sense; [22] or to somehow reconcile Islamic tradition and Western scholarship.[23]

The School of Social and Islamic Sciences was founded in 1996 in Leesburg, Virginia by Dr Taha Al Alwani. Its mission corresponds to IIIT's project of reconciling Western and Islamic forms of thought, doing so from the standpoint of "enlightened *salafiyya*." Combining the contributions of Western social sciences with Islamic tradition, the school aims to reconnect knowledge to a respect for religious principles and values, and to contribute to the Islamicization of knowledge. The social sciences are thus practiced and imagined in terms of an Islamic vision of life, humankind, and the universe. A knowledge of traditional Islamic scholarship is important, but should itself be looked at critically, in a sort of "intellectual *ijtihad*," which would allow students to develop new methodologies for classical sources. The school grants two types of academic degrees: Master of Islamic Studies and a professional degree for practicing imams. About forty students are enrolled every year in both programs. In 1999, the school was authorized by the State of Virginia to give doctoral degrees in Islamic Studies, making it the first Islamic university in America to receive State recognition. The school's other great success has been to train and grant degrees to Islamic chaplains in the U.S. Army. The number of Muslims serving in the four branches of the U.S. Army is estimated to be between 10,000 and 20,000.[24] The school grants degrees to approximately ten military chaplains per year.

Preachers and Public Speakers

The term "charismatic leader" applies to figures such as Siraj Wahaj, or Sheikh Younous of the Tabligh Al Rahma mosque, located in a Paris suburb. Young, physically appealing, Younous attracts hundreds of young people to his Thursday conferences, making him one of the most popular Muslim leaders in the area. But it should come as no surprise that charisma is a characteristic shared by many preachers and spokespeople in Islam. Charismatic leaders in Islam mostly come from among the community of intellectuals, academics, and scholars. Their success demonstrates the evolution, described by Anderson and Eickelman, of a new kind of legitimacy in Islam that exists alongside traditional authority. In the West, these new authorities have in fact become the norm, not the exception. In general, they are not students of religion, and do not situate themselves within a particular official Islamic tradition. But they have a microphone, a pen, an Internet connection, and the faithful audience they attract with their message is the primary source of their legitimacy.

Didacticism and apologism are two tendencies shared in common by most popular Islamic leaders. Didacticism here refers to a kind of desire to teach Islam that has no equivalent in the Islamic world proper. In an environment where scholarly institutions are few, the spokesperson often has to take on the role of teacher. Conferences often highlight topics dealing with central concepts of the Qu'ran or Islamic tradition, or with issues of faith in general. The apologist tendency has to do with the defense of Islam and with explaining to audiences influenced by a widespread Islamophobia that Islam is not as bad as "they" (Westerners) say. After the events of September 11, 2001—particularly in the United States—this apologist tendency has generally ceded to a more critical attitude towards certain branches or personalities in Islam.

Sayyed Hosein Nasr was born in Teheran in 1933, emigrating to the United States at the age of 12. He was the first Iranian-born graduate of MIT, and received his Ph.D. in history of sciences from Harvard University in 1958. He then returned to Iran, where he enjoyed a brilliant career as a professor until the 1979 Iranian Revolution. In that same year, he returned to the United States. At Temple University, he joined with Ismael Faruqi to develop a program of Islamic Studies. Today, he holds the chair in Islamic Studies at Georgetown University. He has written over 30 works in English, and some in Persian and English.[25] Thanks to his universalist perspective on critiques of knowledge, as well as the inspiration he takes from Persian mysticism, he has become one of the best-known conference-speakers and intellectuals outside Muslim circles. Within Muslim circles, on the other hand, it is his book, *A Young Muslim's Guide to the Modern World*, that has attracted the most attention. The book stresses the necessity of preserving an authentic Islamic identity in the heart of the West.

Jamal Badawi is Canadian. A professor of Islamic Studies and Management at Halifax, he began his studies in Cairo and completed his Ph.D. at the University of Indiana. He is the author of a number of books and articles,[26] and has created more than 300 programs and special reports on Islam. He enjoys a great popularity among North American Muslims, and his conferences, recorded on cassette or video, are bestsellers. His main areas of interest are the economy, women's issues, and interfaith dialogue.

During one of his conferences on women's issues in Islam, he claimed that women's liberation in the West had been due to their struggle against the evil intentions of men; whereas in Islam, women's status came from divine decree and was thus inherently true.[27] In another conference, citing verses from the Qu'ran, he described domestic violence as something to be shunned except in exceptional circumstances, and even those bound by certain limits, such as not striking the face.[28] One of his more noteworthy conferences, held after September 11, was "Islam, World Peace, and September 11." In this conference, he declared the September 11 attacks to be against the principles of Islam, and gave advice to Muslims on how to communicate with non-Muslims regarding the concept of *jihad* and the confusion between it and holy war.

Hamza Yusuf was born in Washington and raised in Northern California. He converted to Islam in 1977, at the age of 17. He then spent ten years in Saudi Arabia, Algeria, Morocco, and Mauritania studying Islam under a variety of ulemas and sheikhs. Upon his return to the States, he began a double major in Paramedics and Religious Studies at San Jose State University. He is a primary cofounder of the Zaytuna Institute, where he promotes the reinstatement of traditional methods for the teaching of Islam.

We should additionally mention Mokhtar Maghraoui, an Algerian American professor of Physics at the University of Syracuse, who serves as a member of the ICNA's Council of Imams; Dr. Ahmed Sakr, professor of Education at the University of Illinois, who specializes in family and economy. Sherman Jackson, professor of Islamic Studies at the University of Michigan and an expert on Islamic law; and imam Siraj Wahaj, mentioned above, are African American Muslims who have also achieved prominence within the general Muslim community.

Turning to Europe, let us mention Sheikh Ahmad Ali. Ali came to England from Pakistan at a very young age. He studied both secular and Islamic subjects at school, and eventually founded Al Mahad al-Islam, a Bradford-based institution that provides information and education on Islam for high school- and college-age students. His conferences focus on the system of beliefs in Islam, Islamic law, Hadith, and the interpretation of texts.

Tariq Ramadan: A Leading Spokesman for Islam

During the 1990's, France saw the emergence of a new generation of local preachers and speakers born and raised on its soil. The growing popularity of these preachers among the children of immigrants attracted the attention of social workers, who were taken off guard by this singular act of "integration," as Dounia Bouzar's pioneering survey demonstrates.[29]

But it is Tariq Ramadan who has emerged as the most popular preacher among European Muslims. As the son of Saïd Ramadan[30] and the grandson of Hassan El-Banna, the founder of the Muslim Brothers, he enjoys a special cachet among European Muslim youth. The author of numerous publications, he has been the main intellectual figure of the European Muslim world since 1990, particularly among Maghrebi communities. His position as professor of Islamic Studies at the University of Fribourg in Switzerland further confirms his status as a model for young Muslims in search of their spirituality. His brother Hani, the current president of the Geneva Islamic Center, has also achieved a certain renown, albeit along more fundamentalist lines. Hani's article, which appeared in the September 10, 2003, Le Monde, advocating stoning as a punishment for adulterous women, cost him his teaching position.

Tariq Ramadan, for his part, is one of the most listened-to and respected figures in the French-speaking Muslim world, a fact proven by the number of young people his conferences attract. He can also cite the immense support he received from the community when, between November 1995 and May 1996, he was forbidden entry into France, for reasons that were eventually proven baseless. His popularity is largely due to his understanding of how to address the hopes and needs of French Muslim youth. His language is strict but enlightened, promoting respect and understanding between the fundamental values of the host country and the values of Islam. "A young Muslim," he states, "is someone who is both French and Muslim and must find ways in which he can figure out how he is French and Muslim at the same time. It is a kind of realization, but one which requires a long process. The true Muslim comes to understand himself in the rigorousness of his conversation with God, and in the Muslim community by initiating dialogue with those who think differently from him."[31]

A further reason for Ramadan's popularity is that he has managed to keep himself out of the internal conflicts and rivalries between Muslim organizations for the privilege of representing Islam in France. There are some Islamic leaders who choose a representative role, and others who choose to focus on education and the spreading of the Islamic message. Ramadan situates himself among the latter. Since 1997, he has organized traveling conferences in Nîmes, Paris, Lyon, Strasbourg, Toulouse, Nantes, Geneva, and Brussels. These conferences cover a variety topics associated with Muslim tradition (*Tafsir*[32], the life of the Prophet, mysticism, etc.) through a monthly cycle of workshops. The conferences regularly attract between 1,000 and 2,000 young people, depending on the city. Muslim Presence (Présence musulmane), a coalition bringing together various youth associations in each city, is the main support of this traveling school.

The other facet of Ramadan's vocation as preacher is a tireless effort to explain to the media and to intellectuals what Islam is. In numerous interviews and publications, Ramadan has solidified his reputation as a central figure in public debate about Islam, at least among the French public. His article, "Criticism of the (new) communitarian intellectuals," published in October 2003 on the website Oumma.com—in which Ramadan accused certain Jewish journalists and intellectuals of lacking objectivity in the Israeli–Palestinian conflict—caused a veritable uproar. Thus, accused of anti-Semitism by some, victim of mainstream Islamophobia according to others, Ramadan has divided both public opinion and the French intellectual world into two camps. The pro-Ramadan camp includes a number of old leftists, today remobilized in the fight against globalization. The anti-Ramadan camp claims a number of highly prominent figures such as Bernard-Henri Lévy, André Glucksmann, and Bernard Kouchner (who once called Ramadan an "Intellectual crook").[33] The controversy surrounding Ramadan guarantees that he will remain a prominent figure from now on, not only for Muslims but also for many segments of French intellectual and political life that are marginalized in official political circles.[34]

But it is in the United States, without question, that the status of preacher in Islam is undergoing the most profound change. The criticisms of American policy or society that formed the content of some Islamic discourse before September 11 have largely disappeared. In Talal Eid's coinage, an "Islamically correct" discourse now prevails in Friday sermons, widely understood to be under high surveillance, and imams and speakers specifically instruct Muslims to no longer use words like "diabolic" to describe the United States.

Imam Anwar Al-Awlkai, from the Al Hijra mosque in Virginia, explains: "in the past, people made inflammatory statements, and we thought that they were just words. Now we know that these words should be taken seriously and that they can have serious consequences."[35]

In contrast to European Muslims, Muslims in America have displayed an increasing willingness to criticize aspects of their community. Two days before September 11, Hamza Yusuf predicted that America was about to go through a period of crisis. Shortly after the attacks, Yusuf made a public statement that he regretted his language, which, he said, could be easily misinterpreted. He has since become one of the most fervent advocates for change in Muslim leadership in the United States. "Islam has been taken hostage," was his response to the World Trade Center hijackers. He has also publicly criticized the training and education of the religious authorities in America, who, according to him, are insufficiently trained in the humanist elements of Islamic tradition.

Let us note, finally, that in this still very closed world of Islamic religious authority, it is as speakers and workshop leaders that women are beginning to come to the fore. The woman's voice in Islam is still very much a North American phenomenon, but we should mention the examples of Azizah al-Hibri and Ingrid Mattson in this context. El-Hibri is a professor of Law at the University of Richmond and president of Karama, an organization of Muslim women lawyers and human rights specialists. Mattson is professor of Islamic Studies at Hartford Seminary in Connecticut and vice president of the ISNA, the largest Islamic organization in America. Despite this progress, there are still no women imams who lead prayers in mixed-gender congregation, though this has begun to be a subject of debate in some communities since early 2000.

Conservatism and the Democratization of Religious Authority

To conclude this look at the democratization of Islamic authority in the United States and Europe, we should note some characteristics that all these groups and types of leaders share, and which make up the particular character of Islamic transmission in the West.[36] The problem of religious authority is how to transfer legitimacy from the Muslim world to the West. There is no longer any one person or movement who can claim sole jurisdiction on Islam. This lack of monopoly is as much an issue within the Muslim world as it is in the West. Nonetheless, the minority status of Muslims in the West means that institutions with a guaranted legitimacy and authority disappear completely. This, in turn, exacerbates the current global crisis.

In the West, therefore, even more than in the Muslim world, criteria for legitimacy in matters of religious authority tend to be relaxed. It is no longer a requirement, for example, to be a disciple in a long line of religious masters. The hiring criteria for both the Fiqh Council of North America and the European Council for Fatwa and Research are much less stringent than those of the traditional *ijaza* (license). The Councils' hiring criteria are: residence in the United States or Europe, respectively; a degree in Islamic Studies; and the recognition that the candidate is faithful to the values of Islam. Such flexibility has allowed for the inclusion of scholars such as Jamal Badawi, Sherman Jackson, Khaled Abou El-Fadl, and Moktar Maghraoui, as well as of women such as Azizah al-Hibri.

Once again, however, the greatest problem is how to transfer theology from the Muslim to the Western world. The Salafi interpretation tends to take primacy over all others, eventually becoming recognized as the "orthodox" version of Islam, which one can either adhere to or abjure. The widespread tendency in contemporary Islam to categorize everything as either *haram* or *halal* is one consequence of Salafi dominance. This binary opposition precludes the options of the possible, the neutral, the recommended and discouraged, which are equally valid within Islamic tradition.

The uncertainty surrounding the teaching of Islam also results in the fact that schools of jurisprudence[37] are often regarded with suspicion, and sometimes even wholly rejected. Most schools continue to have representation in the West—Maleki, Hanafi, and Shafi in Europe; Hanbali, Hanafi, and Maleki in the United States—but very few religious authorities, including many bureaucratic leaders, follow a specific school. Thus Sheikh Shamsi Ali, from the Indonesian Islamic center in New York, describes his position: "Most Indonesians are Shafi, but in my teaching methods, I don't subscribe to any school in particular. I use them all. If we can practice *ijtihad*, why not? That's what Islam wants. The Qu'ran has been interpreted in terms of the understanding of the Arabs and the conditions in which they live. We have to interpret the Qu'ran in terms of these changes: for example, regarding usury and how the prohibition is understood differently in the American context."

There are, of course, exceptions to this rule. From his Zaytuna Institute, located in the San Francisco Bay area, Hamza Yusuf specifically promotes Maleki rite. Abdulaah Adhami, an imam and teacher at an Islamic school in New York, provides another counterexample. His father was a Syrian diplomat, and he himself was born in the United States but spent his childhood in Damascus. In a 2000 interview, he recounted:

I began training in the traditional Islamic discipline [when I was a child], on the authority of my maternal grandfather. He was *naqeeb Al-Ashraf*, or the head of those who have documented lineage back to the Prophet, peace be upon him. And in narration, in the first *Isnad* would be the family one, of course, on his authority back to the Prophet, peace be upon him, and of course back to the narrators of *Hadith*. I am honored to have earned a license to narrate over fifty collections, documenting the prophetic tradition of the Prophet, peace be upon him. This is called *Hadith Ijazah*, or a license to narrate. And my training still continues, it's still continuing. . . . I've heard from other *shuyoukh* [sheikhs] and studied for about four years with various *shuyoukh* in Damascus before I came back here. That was my initial base in the tradition or discipline. The rest of it was supervised study. When I was here on my own . . . [it was] a very alienating environment, because obviously it's nothing parallel to being under the care of the masters, the *shuyoukh* in Damascus. There is no comparison. . . . And that environment is really unparalleled in modern times; it's not the same, now, because of various circumstances. And because the *shuyoukh* are older now. They don't have the same level of energy in giving. So, I consider myself extremely blessed to have been in Damascus during a most right period of religious development and learning. And that continues to this day.[38]

Another consequence of the minority condition, particularly in the United States, is that the differences between Sunni and Shiite Islam tend to be minimized. In mosque attendance as well as interpersonal relationships, the divergence between the two branches of Islam appears as less and less of a determining factor. Nonetheless, the preeminence of Shiite clerics appears undiminished, largely due to the continued influence of international movements linked to Shi'a governments or to the religious institutions of Iran, Lebanon and Iraq.

But despite all these changes and pressures—and contrary to much received opinion—Islamic thought is in no danger of becoming a force for innovation or critique. At most, it is tailoring its moralistic stance to better take into account a changing outside environment. As we have already noted in our examination of virtual Islam, the democratization of Islamic religious authority does not necessarily imply its liberalization.

Diasporic Islam and the Challenge of Universal Democratic Principles

In conclusion, an investigation into the world of the mosque shows an adaptation to the European or American environment. We have described this adaptation in terms of the adoption of the congregational model, particularly in the changing relationship between ordinary Muslims and figures of religious authority. In this sense, the community's increased access to aspects of religion and religious teaching, as well as its greater involvement in the day-to-day running of religious spaces and functions, does indeed constitute a kind of democratic progress. Nonetheless, this democratization of religious life should not be confused with an enthusiastic embrace of liberal democratic norms and values. Two mistakes in thinking must be avoided. The first is the expectation that newcomers to the West will wholeheartedly embrace "Western values": values that are, furthermore—need it be mentioned?—not unanimously agreed upon even among natives of the West. Indeed, the most virulent critiques—from the Right to the Left of the political spectrum—come from within the democratic societies themselves. There have been Marxist and Trotskyist critiques of Western society, and critiques from the Far Right on the illusion of the principles of equality and justice or on the myth of universal democratic participation. In the United States, as we have discussed in chapter 2, the position of African Americans continues to demonstrate the limits of American democracy and its pretensions of universality. Even without having recourse to extremist positions, one can still point out the vast distance that separates the citizen/individual and the workings of democratic institutions. The second, opposite mistake (noted in chapter 2) is to consider all Muslims to be resistant *a priori* to any and all Western political values.

But why such warnings here? Because one should not assume, based on the information presented in this chapter, that Muslims will automatically adapt to Western democracies—as if they arrived in the West with no reservations about Western culture or criticisms of Western democratic values. In chapter 5 especially, we set out existing forms of resistance to Western norms and values, which can go as far as outright rejection, or even (rare though it may be) the will to destroy. Such extreme forms of resistance are rare. But among the Muslims of Europe and the United States, there are other ways of distancing oneself, many of which we have described in this chapter.

These alternate forms are by far the most common: without requiring the embrace of radical causes, they nonetheless express a certain reserve and critique of the cultural bases of democratic norms. These critiques are largely unspoken and implicit in the interviews that we conducted, surfacing only in the discussion of certain topics, such as women or the family, in sermons, conferences, and debates on both sides of the Atlantic.

The moral and cultural code of the Muslim woman is constantly seen as the antithesis of that of the Western woman, an opposition also claimed by Western-born female converts to Islam. A feminist Islamic discourse can be seen in the headscarf controversy in France between 2003 and 2004, and emerges in the taking-on of leadership roles by women such as Ingrid Mattson (vice president of the ISNA, mentioned above) and Amina Wadud (discussed in chapter 9).[39] Islamic orthopraxis, especially in terms of the dress code, constitutes a critique of the universal application of the principle of gender equality. These Islamic practices imply that, on the contrary, the principles of equality and individualism are not as universal as we Westerners would like to believe.

In this sense, Islamic orthopraxis in Europe and America must be differentiated from political Islam in the Muslim world. A reactionary moral position espoused in the suburbs of Lyon or New York does not necessarily imply a reactionary political stance, even if many Westerners still automatically associate the suburbs of Vénissieux with FIS in Algeria or Jamaat-Islamiyya in Cairo. Islamic demands in the West are mostly made within the context of the democratic system; whereas in the Muslim world, political demands are formulated within the context of authoritarian regimes, in which often no option is left open other than that of violence.

Muslim leadership in the West has therefore placed its emphasis primarily on issues of morality and the maintaining of differences, and even a kind of hierarchy of generations and genders. This situation clearly illustrates the divide between democratization and liberalism. In essence, the democratization of religious practice is *not* always followed by an acceptance of individual prerogative in matters of the family or personal morality. What many Muslim clerics describe as the Muslim point of view in regard to family or moral issues is largely a means of keeping their distance from the cultural underpinnings of the West, and thus functions as an implicit critique of Western democracy. In short, the internalization of democratic values by some Muslims, and Muslim leaders in particular, is colored by a good deal of skepticism for the universality of certain principles. Cultural education programs—such as the one announced on May 11, 2004 for the training of imams in French culture—may be helpful in quelling this skepticism.[40]

At the same time, however, current conditions—particularly since September 11—hinder the free expression of Muslim critiques of the West. The emergence of an "Islamically correct" language in mosques, described above, is a good example of the current impossibility of expressing one's skepticism. Even if this skepticism is expressed indirectly, for example, on issues of family or personal morality, it risks censorship and rebuke. Thus the Algerian imam of Vénissieux, who had spoken in support of polygamy and the stoning of adulterous women, was expelled from the country on April 21, 2004 by the French Ministry of the Interior. (The administrative court of Lyon, however, eventually stayed the expulsion, on the grounds that it had no basis in fact but rather on "general statements resting on subjective opinions." [41]). The Imam's opinions are no doubt objectionable, and Can be subject to both civil disciplinary measures and criminal prosecution; what remains an open question, however, is the way in which his comments were politicized by the Minister of the Interior, who made the decision to deport the Imam on grounds of public security.

We are thus dealing with classic dilemma of the new immigrant, obliged to display a wholehearted embrace of the values of the new political community of which he or she wants to be a part. In other words, the new immigrant must be more enthusiastic about his or her host society than its native inhabitants—all the more so in the unfriendly environment of post–September 11. The result among Muslims in the West is an ambivalence that is neither hypocrisy nor dishonesty, but a means of survival. This ambivalence demonstrates the extent to which Islam remains a alien phenomenon in Western societies. Islam will only cease to be alien once Muslims living in the West are able to express their criticisms of the democratic process, without being accused of disloyalty or being seen as a danger to society.

In this respect, it is interesting to point out that the only criticisms which are accepted, and even expected, from Muslims in the West are those that take issue with Islamic tradition itself. As chapter 9 shows, reformist trends, ranging the spectrum from moderate to radical, are currently beginning to develop within the Islam of the diaspora.

CHAPTER 9

The Reformation of Islamic Thought

In the West, a reformist trend is beginning to emerge in Islamic thought. It is, of course, still very much a fringe movement, and western Muslims remain, by and large, more conservative and more conformist than one might suspect. But it is nevertheless a first effort to break the vicious circle of the apologist mindset. The trend is particularly visible in the United States, largely due to the concentration there of Muslim elites from a variety of countries and cultures.

There are also efforts to reform Islamic thought, of course, within the Muslim world. Indeed, most of the chief reformist thinkers come from countries of the Muslim world: it was there that they began their studies, and they continue to maintain friendships and associations in their countries of origin. But it is easier for these thinkers to express certain ideas and methodologies in the West than in the Muslim world, for the obvious reason that the West makes specific provisions for the free expression of thought.

Some of the ideas these thinkers present are particular to Islam's status as a minority culture in the West; others, such as the status of women, human rights, or democracy, have a more universal import and have been subjects of debate and controversy in the Muslim world for decades. We discuss how residence in the West often gives a new dimension to these debates.

The international relevance of any one thinker's ideas can be measured by such criteria as the number of his works that have been translated into Arabic or other languages, the number of works taught in the universities of the Muslim world, and the thinker's ties to the Muslim world by professional affiliations or visits to various institutions in that part of the world. All of the thinkers presented below meet these criteria.[1] But relevance must be measured in two ways: the preeminent thinkers and controversies of the Muslim world must be judged not only in terms of their influence in the Muslim world itself, but also according to their place in the intellectual life of Western Islam. A truly international intellectual community—one that claims members as diverse as Rached Ghannouchi and Abdolkarim Souroush, Fatima Mernissi and Hassan Hanafi—is beginning to take shape. In this chapter, we only discuss thinkers who write and publish in the West.

Reforms in Legal Thought: Minority Rights

Since the 1980s, Muslim settlement in Europe and the United States has given rise to intense debate over the legal conditions connected to minority status. Islamic law initially developed in a context in which Islam was the dominant political culture; reflection on the legal status of minorities was for the Jewish or Christian "Other," not for the Muslim living in non-Muslim lands. Some interpretations, certainly, came out of the situation of the Christian reconquest of Spain in the fifteenth century. But there was nothing that would truly place in question the *summa divisio* between the *Dar al-Harb* and the *Dar al-Islam*, the Abode of War versus the Abode of Islam, which for centuries has shaped the relationship between Muslims and non-Muslims.

There are at least six different definitions of the *Dar al-Islam* in Islamic law: Does it refer to the territories in which Islamic law is applied? Is it where Muslims hold political power? Where the governors behave as good Muslims? Complicating the situation, the various schools of Islamic jurisprudence differ in their opinions on the status of the *Dar al-Harb*. The Malekites reject the idea that Muslims can live in the *Dar al-Harb*. The Hanbalis and Shiites tolerate it, on the condition that expatriate Muslims can still observe the Five Pillars of Islam. The Hanafis solve the problem by making a distinction between what is required, what is recommended, what is permitted, and what is forbidden. It is required, for example, for a Muslim to leave the *Dar al-Harb* if his life is in danger or it becomes impossible to practice Islam. On the other hand, a Muslim may remain in the *Dar al-Harb* if he can continue to observe the Five Pillars without difficulty. Hanafis also stipulate that some laws—including those with an ethical character, such as the prohibition against earning interest—can be suspended if one lives outside the *Dar al-Islam*.

Today some Muslims—primarily Wahabis—continue to use the dichotomy *Dar al-Islam/Dar al-Harb* to explain the condition of European and American Muslims. But there are also those who feel that this dichotomy has become obsolete or inadequate, and seek to replace it—especially the idea of the *Dar al-Harb*—with a different concept. In 1987, Sheikh Faisal Mawlawi, of Beiruit, was the first to propose a different way of thinking on this topic. At the UOIF's request, he published a brochure in which he described how the opposition between *Dar al-Islam* and *Dar al-Harb* could be fruitfully replaced by an opposition between *Dar al-Islam* and *Dar al-Ahd*—the Abode of Accord—or *Dar al-Dawa*—the Abode of Mission or of Invitation to Islam.[2] (This latter term is a reference to the Mekka period, in which Muslims made up the minority in a society that rejected the Revelation; thus Muslims took upon themselves the responsibility for transmitting Islam's message.) In his writings, Mawlawi begins by questioning the definition of an Islamic State, on the grounds that nowhere today in the *Dar al-Islam* are the Islamic laws respected in their totality. On the status of Muslims in a non-Muslim State, Mawlawi makes it clear that the countries in which Muslims live are not part of the *Dar al-Harb* (the Abode of War), but rather of the Abode of Accord, since the Muslims who live there came on the basis of agreements with their countries of origin. Consequentially, the relations between Muslims and non-Muslims are based on a mutual respect for the law of the State—as long as this law does not contradict the dictates of Islamic faith. "Our rights in these countries," he states, "are the rights that their laws give to us." Interpersonal relationships in these countries are based on two additional principles: piety (the Muslim must be pious and follow the "straight path") and justice (injustice is prohibited, even in a conflict with a non-Muslim).

These countries are seen as the "Lands of Mission" (*Dar al-Dawa*): "We are living in the Dar al-Dawa, as the Prophet and the Muslims did in Mecca before the Hejira. Mecca was not the *Dar al-Harb*, nor was it the *Dar al-Islam*, but the *Dar al-Dawa*." Such a view makes it necessary for the Muslim to be - welcoming and conciliatory. The idea of the West as a land of Islamic proselytizing is demonstrated in the actions and words of many of the Islamic leaders who hold positions of authority. For the time being, at least, most of the Islamic authorities have shifted their focus away from the enforcing of Islamic law in family or personal life. The emphasis is instead on keeping the Muslim community—particularly the younger generations—to the "straight path," in light of the dangers posed by an religious, or even an antireligious environment. The concept of "the Abode of Accord" is the expression of Muslims' decision, of their own free will, to settle outside the *Dar al-Islam*, with all the consequences of civil participation and good conduct that this entails.

Rached Ghannouchi is a dissident Tunisian Islamist living in exile in London since the beginning of the 1990s. In his writings, he elaborates upon the idea of democracy in the context of Islamic philosophy. He holds the position that there is no existing Islamic government worthy of the name, and that Muslims should therefore be pragmatists in their political approach. Citing the list of necessities drawn up by the fourteenth century Andalusian jurist Al-Shatibi—Protection of Faith, Protection of Life, Protection of Posterity, Protection of Property, and Protection of Reason—Ghannouchi considers that all of these conditions are sufficiently fulfilled in the West. There is therefore no reason why a Muslim should not live there. Ghannouchi is also in favor of the sharing of power, and thus of Muslim participation in the democratic process.[3]

Still others, such as the U.S. resident Taha Al-Alwani, completely reject the traditional opposition of *Dar al-Islam* and *Dar al-Harb*. Their claim largely rests on the Hanafi argument that a Muslim majority does not necessarily entail an Islamic character for a country or a society. They conclude that Islamic principles can still apply outside those lands that have historically been Muslim.

Taha Al-Alwani describes the legal condition of Western Muslims as follows: "The different schools of jurisprudence in Islam have not yet dealt with the situation of the Muslim minority. The only instances that have been discussed have to do with exceptional periods, such as the time in Andalusia, which necessitated an exceptional jurisprudence based on the principle of necessity. Today, the situation is completely different: to be a minority is the norm, not the exception. We must thus settle the question of the relationship between Islamic law and societies that are not governed by Islam. For example, jurists have long regarded it as a problem for a Muslim to acquire citizenship and national status in a non-Muslim country. They believed that it was not possible to be both a citizen of a non-Muslim country and a faithful Muslim. But today, all our efforts are intended to prove the contrary: to understand that citizenship of a non-Muslim country is, in fact, *not* incompatible with Islamic religious observance. The contributions of all the schools of law have proven helpful in legitimating the idea of citizenship, as they have with all the different social and political consequence of the minority condition. My own primary goal is to engage in interpretation that reflects the requirements of life in the United States."[4] Al-Alwani is currently working on an epistemology of minority rights based on the following three concepts: *tawhid* (unity), *tazkiyya* (purification), and *al-umran* (civilization).

Tariq Ramadan, for his part, rejects the necessity of minority rights law. Instead, he believes that Europe and the United States now constitute part of the Muslim world, and that it is indeed possible to live there according to Islamic principles. He proposes the term "World of Witness (*Shahada*)" to define this situation, seeing it as one in which the Muslim gives witness—through his behavior and his participation in the institutions of democracy—to his faith and identity as a Muslim. Non-Muslim governments in which Muslims are able to participate democratically, he argues, are more Islamic than authoritarian governments run by Muslims. The electoral structures and the freedom of thought that form the basis of the democratic process are Islamic principles as well, principles that make any theocracy or autocracy unjustifiable.[5]

Deconstructing the Revealed Text

Historical interpretation of the Qu'ran—in which it is treated as a text shaped by its cultural and political circumstances—is still very much an innovation and a taboo within Islam. Fazlur Rahman wrote the pioneering work on this subject, bibliography of which remains fairly limited. Rahman was born in 1919, in the British colony that would later become Pakistan. His academic career brought him to India, England, and eventually, the United States. After teaching in England and Canada, he returned to Pakistan in 1966 to direct the Institute for Islamic Research in Karachi, where his modernist views quickly earned him the opposition of the religious establishment. He subsequently returned to the Western academic world, accepting a chair at the University of Chicago in 1968, where he worked on his reinterpretation of Islam until his death in 1988.

Rahman rejected the middle way of "excusing" or defending certain practices described in the Qu'ran by arguing that they could only be possible in a fully realized Islamic society. Many Islamists—including, for example, the Muslim Brothers—hold this view in regard to certain practices such as corporal punishment. For Fazlur Rahman, however, this kind of practice should be rejected entirely, as it is a product of the societal standards in place at the time of the Prophet, and is thus no longer relevant. He believes that Islam began to decline as soon as the Qu'ranic text was considered as something absolute, independent, and divorced from any historical context. This bias is reinforced by the selective use of verses and *suras*, taken individually and without regard for the meaning of the text as a whole.

In order to counteract this kind of atomistic and anachronistic approach to the revealed Text, Rahman argues for a method of interpretation that would move from the historically particular to the general and from the general back to the particular. This method entails studying the specific historical situations in which the verses of the Qu'ran were revealed, revealing the transcendent and universal aspects of Qu'ranic laws, and reapplying those laws to present-day situations. Nasr Hamid Abu Zayd,[6] for one example, uses this method in his discussion of dowry practices. He demonstrates that, while providing a dowry for women was a form of progress according to the prevailing social standards of the time of the Prophet, today it is equality between man and woman that is the progressive position.

Mohammed Arkoun, born in Kabylia in 1928 and currently professor of Islamology at the Sorbonne, attempts in his work to construct an Islamic humanism based on a historical analysis of the Qu'ran. A historicist approach would provide a way to think about the Qu'ran beyond the antimonies of secular/Westernized and traditionalist that currently dominate contemporary interpretations. Arkoun joins Abu Zayd in maintaining that it is possible to engage in a historical analysis of the Qu'ran without renouncing its divine source. To support his claims, Arkoun introduces the idea of the difference between the unthought and the unthinkable. Islamic tradition and orthodoxy fall into the former category. Tradition here refers to the series of texts recognized as authentic by the Muslim community, including the *Hadith*, the methodology for interpreting *Shari'a*, and the body of legal texts. Arkoun argues for a historical analysis of these works, as well as of the foundations of Islamic law and religion. He criticizes the idea of a "return to the source," which has become a sort of leitmotif in contemporary Islam and operates as at once a methodology, an epistemology, and a theory of history.[7]

In contrast to Arkoun, the goal of Khaled Abou El Fadl is not to bring the unthinkable or the unthought in Islam to light, but to deconstruct the modes and methods of religious authoritarianism in contemporary Islam. El Fadl, born in 1961 and currently a professor of Law at UCLA, is one of the most prominent figures of the reformist movement in Islam. A Kuwaiti American, he has been an important participant in the ongoing debate within the American Muslim community, particularly after September 11. His strong criticism of conservative and puritanical strains of Islam have earned him several death threats. But it has also allowed him to gain a name for himself in Washington political circles, where he currently sits on a variety of commissions and committees on Islam and human rights. In his book, *And God Knows the Soldiers* (2001), El Fadl attempts to deconstruct the fatwa issued by The Society for Adherence to the Sunna in support of basketball player Mahmoud Abdul Rauf, who refused to stand for the singing of the American national anthem. El Fadl describes how Wahabi thought simply obscures the multiplicity of sources and discussions that make up the richness of Islamic tradition. There is nothing new, of course, in the phenomenon of competing interpretations on the same theme. But the originality of El Fadl's argument is his critique of the abuse of the *usul al fiqh*, the foundations of

Islamic law. In Wahabi thought, the *usul al fiqh* cannot be contested because they come out of the sacred Text. The wearing of *hijab*, for example is—in most contemporary cases, without discussion—placed in the category of fundamental precepts, and is therefore nonnegotiable. El Fadl, in contrast, shows that *hijab* was actually an active subject of debate for the jurists of the classical period: What should one cover? The chest, the hair? Who should cover herself? For example, among other exceptions to the rule, female slaves were not required to cover themselves. El Fadl writes, "The historical setting and the complexity of the early context do suggest that the inquiries into the juristic base of the *hijab* cannot be considered heretical. In this sense, labeling the *hijab* as part of the *usul* and using that label as an excuse to end the discussion on this matter, is obscenely despotic."[8] El Fadl applies the same kind of deconstruction to the term *maslaha*, or public good, currently often used to justify the authoritarian application of Islamic laws and precepts.

Muslim progressives, with Omid Safi[9] foremost among them, have the even more ambitious agenda of following up on changes in Islam's ideology with changes in leadership and religious practices.

The Acknowledgment of Secularism

Islam's approach to the concept of democracy was turned upside-down once Muslims began to establish communities in the West. The changes that are currently taking place are even more remarkable in that for the majority of Muslims, the concepts of democracy and secularization are associated with Western domination, both colonial and postcolonial.

This is how Egyptian Islamist Abdulwahab al-Massari describes his view of Western civilization and its problems:

The price of progress, quantification, mechanization, standardization, instrumental value-free rationalization, alienation, the crisis of meaning, the domination of utilitarian values, the spread of moral and epistemo-logical relativism, anomie, disintegration of society, increasing contractu-alization, the problem of the *Gemeinschaft* versus the *Gesellschaft*, the tightening of the grip of the state over the individual through its various apparati, the hegemony of companies and bureaucracies, the decline of the family, the atrophy of identity, the minimal self, the decentering of man, the rise of anti-humanist philosophies, philosophical nihilism, interna-tionalization or globalization, the subversion of individuality and privacy, the Americanization of the world, Cocacolization, commodification, reification, fetishism, the cult of progress, the cult of change and fashion, consumerism, the culture of the disposable-instantaneous gratification, the culture of narcissism, post-ideology, the modern world as an iron cage, the death of God and the death of man, disenchantment of the world, the rise of ethnicity, racism, pornography, deconstruction (and a number of verbs with the prefix "de": dehumanize, debunk, demystify, deconstruct).[10]

Today, such a vision of Western culture and political philosophy has been completely destabilized by Muslim intellectuals living in the West. We should first mention that the question of who should rule, over which so much ink has been spilled since the first *salafiyya* is not experienced by European or American Muslims as a major political problem, but rather as an advantage. Second, on the theoretical level of what constitutes "good" government, the old debate about the compatibility between Islamic values and political principles and those of the West has been largely replaced by the ideas of pluralism and tolerance.

In his work, El Fadl distinguishes between God's will and human efforts to articulate this will within the structures of the Law. In his opinion, the idea that God is a kind of legislator of human affairs is, from the standpoint of theology, an indefensible fiction. Justice and mercy are the two Islamic principles that should guide all human efforts in political and collective matters. He further demonstrates how these principles are completely in harmony with the idea of civic responsibility within the democratic system.

El Fadl's research on the compatibility of Islam and democracy follows in the footsteps of Abdolkarim Soroush's thought. Both men emphasize secularization and human rights in their discussion of a new attitude toward democracy. Soroush, an Iranian exile living in the United States, has been at the forefront of the reformist movement in Iranian Islamic thought, and remains part of the Irani religious intelligentsia. He was born in 1945 and studied pharmacology and philosophy in both England and Iran. In Iran, he was a preeminent figure in the first phase of the Islamic regime, sitting on the High Council of Cultural Revolution, from which he later resigned. His critical stances on Islam and politics gradually caused him to be shunned by both the Iranian political and intellectual worlds. In 1999, he came to the United States, teaching at Harvard and Princeton. He currently divides his time between Iran and the United States. His tenure in the United States has enabled him to attract a wider audience, and has given an international dimension to his thinking.

Soroush belongs to that class of reformists who attempt to reconcile Islamic values and Western culture, in contrast to those who adopt one or the other system exclusively. He bases his ideas on a distinction between religion and knowledge about religion. The latter is the work of human beings, and is thus subject to change and criticism. He wholly rejects the ideological use of Islam, which in his view destroys the complexity of the religion and reduces it to a political tool. The ideological use of religion, according to him, plays into the identity-politics version of Islam, which has come to supplant the true Islam, that is, the Islam of faith and values. Soroush is in favor of democratic rule, which, he says, is the only form of government and the only ethical system compatible with the principles of Islam. Faith and religion can never be the basis of citizenship or political rights; thus the status of religion within society should be independent of both politics and law.

At the same time, however, a Western-style separation of religion and politics is not a realistic option. Soroush's vision of democracy is essentially a plea for equality between Muslims and non-Muslims. His critics have noted the absence of theory and historical perspective in his thought, pointing out that there is no historical example of a society both democratic and religious. It is true that Soroush does not spell out what "a religious democracy" would mean, in terms of either methodology or institutional organization.[11]

The Question of Human Rights

In its current usage, the term "human rights" has two meanings. The first refers to the various struggles for freedom and social justice that have taken place throughout history. The second is the specific conception of freedom and justice set out in the Universal Declaration of Human Rights (created in 1948) and other international treaties. According to these treaties, these rights are an essential characteristic of every human being, without distinction for religion, culture, race, or sex. The paradigm of the universality of human rights is set down in various national and international treaties, and alludes to the universal character of constitutional rights as they appear in Western democracies. The 1948 Universal Declaration of Human Rights and the 1966 International Convention of Economic, Social and Cultural Rights are two examples of international documents that have put this vision into concrete form.

Within the Muslim community, two political and intellectual attitudes have emerged in opposition to this vision. The first is a defensive stance, which consists in the rejection of the very concept of human rights as a foreign product hostile to Islamic tradition. This has been the attitude taken by the first phase of the Islamic regime in Iran, as well as by the Sudanese Nimeiri regime[12] and, most recently, the Taliban. One surprising fact is that this rejectionist attitude has been strengthened by many Western academic analyses, particularly those coming from so-called postmodern schools of thought.[13]

The second attitude can be called the inclusive attitude;[14] it attempts to claim the concept of human rights as an achievement of Islamic culture. The Islamicization of human rights is particularly noticeable at the international level, where it is transformed into Islamic versions of various treaties, including the Universal Islamic Declaration of Human Rights (1981), a draft of an Islamic Constitution (Al Azhar, 1979), and the Cairo Declaration of Human Rights in Islam (1993). In each case, Islamic law is the gold standard for the evaluation and inclusion of human rights provisions. As Article 25 of the Cairo Declaration states, "The Islamic *Shari'a* is the only source of reference for the explanation or clarification of any of the articles of the Declaration." Despite the statement in Article 1 that all human beings are equal, the Declaration largely maintains the idea that there exist fundamental differences between people. Article 6 presupposes that men have the dominant role in the home: "Woman is equal to man in human dignity and has rights to enjoy as well as duties to perform; she has her own civil entity and financial independence, and the right to retain her name and lineage. The husband is responsible for the support and welfare of the family." Article 10 violates the principle of equality entirely by stipulating, "Islam is the religion of unspoiled nature. It is prohibited to exercise any form of compulsion on man or to exploit his poverty or ignorance in order to convert him to another religion or atheism." Such a statement is in direct contradiction of the principle of equality among religions as it exists in the human rights model.

In the intellectual sphere, the inclusive or Islamicizing attitude avails itself of two types of arguments. First, it plays on the confusion between the two meanings of the term human rights, demonstrating that the different formulations of *Shari'a* have always respected the fundamental character of human rights.[15] Second, it perpetually repeats the following assertions: Divine law comes before human law, Collective rights take precedence over individual rights, and Equality between individuals is conditioned by sex and religious affiliation.

In contrast to this inclusive or apologist ideology, there is another, attitude, more critical and realistic, which is articulated primarily by Muslim intellectuals living in the West. Abdullah An-Na'im is one of the chief figures in the critical discourse on human rights in an Islamic context. Originally from Sudan, he studied at Cambridge University in England and later at the University of Edinburgh in Scotland, from which he received his law degree. A disciple of Mahmoud Mohamed Taha,[16] the reformist leader executed by the Sudanese government in 1985, An-Na'im has taught in the Sudan, Canada, and the United States. He has been active in the struggle for human rights as the long-standing director of Africa Watch, a human rights advocacy group in Washington, and is currently a professor of Law at Emory University.

One of An-Na'im's primary contributions has been to recognize the inherent tension between the human rights model as it has emerged as a result of Western history, and the principles of *Shari'a*. Even if the moral or philosophical bases of human rights, as defined in the Universal Declaration of Human Rights, are found in many religious traditions, it is still the case that theology often conflicts with this particular model. Thus many of the principles of *Shari'a* have to be reinterpreted before reconciliation and real intercultural dialogue are possible.[17] Certain underlying assumptions of *Shari'a*, such as the inequality of men and women, the unequal status of different religions, and the status of the apostate in Islamic tradition, must all be reexamined in light of the Western conception of human rights.

"Gender Jihad"

It is the discourse on women, above all, that serves as a yardstick for the various interpretations of Islam, from the most reactionary or the most apologist to the most modern. The overwhelming majority of Islamic literature available in the West on the subject of women either defends Islam against attacks by westerners, or acknowledges the problems of certain practices but simply deems them non-Islamic. The use of the term "Islam" without specifying what sources the author is referring to—Qu'ran, *Hadith, Madhab*[18]— exploits people's confusion and ignorance and reinforces the kind of authoritarianism described by Abou El Fadl.

In these works, the prevailing point of view seems to be that while men are naturally superior, women should be treated with lenience and kindness.[19] The conservative slant of this interpretation, favoring the social separation of the two genders, is meant to respond to the anxieties of Muslims living in the modern world, who fear that they will lose their standards of morality. The division of gender roles—between the "public" man and the "private" woman—is a solution that speaks to many believers, especially since the number of converts to Islam, and female converts in particular, is constantly on the rise in both Europe and the United States. The irony of this model, however, is that it is quite a bit dissimilar to the idea of woman as it exists in classical Islamic texts.[20] The image of woman as mother and homemaker described by today's conservative literature is a shift in emphasis from the vision of woman in classical legal tradition. The jurists of the classical period, for their part, focused on a woman's wifely duties toward her husband, particularly her sexual duties.[21]

Increasingly, however, women Muslims are offering interpretations to counter this dominant model. Adopting the feminist approach of the social sciences and cultural studies fields, Azizah al-Hibri and others show how Islamic law has up to now been interpreted in a patriarchal manner. Still others, such as Asma Barlas, maintain that the Qu'ran itself is solidly egalitarian in its positions.[22]

Amina Wadud offers one of the most original approaches to the question of gender in the Qu'ran. An African American convert to Islam and professor of Islamic Studies at the University of Virginia, her career is a kind of case study of Western influence on Islamic thought. While many analyses of women's status in Islam, including that of Fatima Mernissi, deal with interpretations of sacred text, taking issue with the patriarchal aspects of religions tradition, Wadud chooses to interpret the Qu'ran directly. Using the technique elaborated by Fazlur Rahman, she has developed a hermaneutics of the Qu'ran by studying the historical context of the revealed Text, the grammatical structure of the Text (How does it express concepts? What words/phrases does it use?), and the vision of the world it presents.[23]

In contrast to other feminist approaches to Islam,[24] Wadud recognizes that the Qu'ran does indeed make distinctions between men and women, but these distinctions are not, she maintains, essentialized. In other words, they do not presuppose the fixed social and religious gender roles that have been canonized by Islamic tradition. Wadud reopens the debates on the supposed superiority of men over women or the definition of modesty. To accomplish this, she identifies two levels of text in the Qu'ran—the historical and the universal or mega-text—and claims the right to disagree with the text, even as a practicing and believing Muslim, particularly in her discussion of the Qu'ranic verse that allows a husband to beat his wife.[25] She also claims the right to wear *hijab* only from time to time, and advocates "gender jihad": that is, the struggle for equality between the sexes, in the name of God.

Wadud's intellectual stance resonates with the daily aspirations of many Muslim women, especially in the United States, who are demanding to be allowed to hold positions of religious authority. The role of the imam, for one, has become a hotly debated issue among educated Muslim women, who refuse to be led in prayer by a man often less competent than themselves in matters of Islam.

The woman's magazine *Azizah*[26]—whose motto proclaims, "For the woman who doesn't apologize for being a woman, and doesn't apologize for being a Muslim"—is the reflection of these discussions. Its French equivalent, *Hawa*, created in 2000, fell far behind in terms of both its longevity and its audience, and went out of circulation completely in 2003. In the same way, the fledgling women's studies groups that have sprung up in several communities, most notably among German converts to Islam, still cannot compare in either depth or intensity to the feminist discourse of the American Muslim community. The proof can be found, for example, in the worldwide popularity of Amina Wadud's book among women Muslims. Her book has been translated into numerous languages, including Arabic, Urdu, and Malay, and she herself is regularly invited to speak at universities and women's associations throughout the Muslim world.

Interfaith Dialogue

Today, the theory of Islam's inherent superiority to other religions is being challenged by the advocates of interfaith dialogue. The trajectory of Ismael Faruqi is typical of this process of understanding. Assassinated along with his wife in 1986 in unclear circumstances, his American career typifies the evolution from militant nationalism to Islamic philosophy. Born in Jaffa in 1921, he served as governor of Galilee until the creation of the State of Israel. He went into exile in the United States and began a career as an academic. Faruqi eventually came to believe in Islam's superiority over other, national and political, ideologies. He graduated with a degree from Al Azhar and received his doctorate in Philosophy from the University of Indiana, taking a post as professor at Temple University in 1968. Inspired by the *salafiyya* of the eighteenth and nineteenth centuries, Faruqi went on to dedicate his life to the reform of Islam through its integration with Western philosophical and sociological concepts. He was also actively involved in the creation of a number of Islamic organizations: the MSA in 1963, AMSS, American Islamic College, and the IIIT.[27] In 1967, his pioneering thesis, *Christian Ethics*, became the first work by a Muslim educated in an American university to analyze the ethical system of Christianity.

Faruqi argues for the necessity of an interfaith dialogue that would preserve each religion's right to internal coherence. No interfaith communication is allowed to violate this internal coherence: in other words, a Christian cannot exhort a Muslim to accept the idea of the Trinity, nor could a Muslim require a Christian to renounce it. Faruqi insists upon the primacy of reason in the analysis of religious belief. In light of this, he considers all those debates in which reason and faith are set up as opposites—such as that between the Mutazilites and the Asharites,[28] or between the theologians and the philosophers—to be overrated. In their place, he argues for an analysis of ethical systems: "Let us drop our old questions regarding the nature of God, which have brought nothing but deadlocks, and let us turn to man, to his duties and responsibilities which are in fact, none other than God's will. Let God be whom He may, it is not possible, nay necessary, that all men agree to establish divine will first?"[29]

But this belief in reason as a means to arrive at an interfaith dialogue that would transcend differences in religious doctrine, however, itself contains a number of biases. It assumes, first of all, that the participants in the dialogue will be able to agree on transcendental ethical principles and leave aside their differences of legal and religious practice. Faruqi cannot quite rid himself, furthermore, of the notion of Islam's superiority *vis-à-vis* other religions, and his argument often seems to be an attempt to convince Christians to adopt the Islamic version of religious history. This is particularly apparent in the distinction he draws between "Christianism" and true Christianity: that is, the ethical principles of Christianity divorced from historical and religious contexts.[30] Nonetheless, Faruqi can take credit for having opened up the possibility of de-absolutizing the Islamic message.

This possibility has also been explored by the scholar Fathi Osman. Like Faruqi, he subscribes to movements of progressive *Salafiyya* and the Muslim Brothers. Born in Cairo, he received his Ph.D. from Princeton University in 1976, and served as the editor-in-chief of the London-based magazine *Arabia* from 1981 to 1987. He is currently scholar-in-residence of the Ibn al Khattab Foundation and director of the Institute for the Study of Islam in the Contemporary World at Los Angeles, after a term as scholar-in-residence at the Los Angeles Islamic Center until 1996. He advocates a dialogical structure for interfaith communication in which the point of view of the other is taken into account, and all different systems of belief are given the opportunity to express themselves.[31] We should also note here the example of Rifat Hassan, who since 1979 has been an active participant in dialogue between Christians, Jews, and Muslims.[32]

The Status of the Apostate

Apostasy is another one of those subjects for which the traditional approach of Islam has been transformed by the phenomenon of Western Islam. Abduallah An-Naim's position is representative of the majority of critics in Islam today: "Although I know this to be the position under *Shari'a*, I am unable as a Muslim to accept the law of apostasy as part of the law of Islam today. ... The *Shari'a* law of apostasy can easily be abused and has been abused in the past to suppress political opposition and inhibit spiritual and intellectual growth. This aspect of *Shari'a* is fundamentally inconsistent with the numerous provisions of the Qu'ran and Sunna which enjoin freedom of religion and expression."[33]

The relation to the Other becomes central in this new approach to Islamic tradition. The work and activism of Farid Esack exemplify this new focus. Born in 1959, Esack was an important figure in the Muslim contingent of the anti-Apartheid movement in South Africa. He helped to break down the Islamic religious establishment's resistance to cooperation with non-Muslims in the struggle for liberation, arguing that the struggle for social justice takes priority over religious differences—and is, furthermore, in itself eminently Islamic, even if it means cooperating with non-Muslims. His work is not only political, but also theological. To live the Qu'ran with integrity, he holds, means having to question the division between Muslim and *kafir*. Esack urges Muslims to take personal responsibility in their readings and interpretations of the Qu'ran: "Affirming the dynamic nature of the terms islam, *iman*, and *kafir* comes back to affirming the fundamental spirit of the Qu'ran for justice."[34] His attitude to the religious Other took on an even more universal dimension after 2000, when he came to live in the United States. Today he is professor of Islamic Studies at the University of Cincinnati.

Finally, we should note the work of Sherman Jackson, mentioned above, at the University of Michigan. Jackson's work revisits the texts of twelfth century philosopher Abu Hamid Al Ghazali, in regards to tolerance of the apostate.[35]

All these approaches to Islamic tradition which have emerged in Europe and the United States demonstrate a critical evaluation of religious texts not seen since at least the colonial period. They signal a definite concern to escape from the defensive and apologist attitude in which many figures of Muslim political and intellectual life find themselves trapped, largely due to the international political conditions discussed above. As a result, the manifestations of Muslim reform in the United States are more conspicuous than those in Europe. This is due in part to the high concentration of Muslim elites in the United States, particularly in the university system: a situation which has no parallel as yet in European countries. The other difference between American and European figures of Islamic reform has to do with the emergence, in the United States, of women's voices, which in Europe remain weak. What is particular to the American situation is that these women— Asma Barlas, Amina Wadud, Kecia Ali—are at once believing, practicing (in varying degrees) Muslims who are nonetheless casting a critical eye on their own tradition. This combination is almost unthinkable on the other side of the Atlantic, where critics of Islam are most often Muslim women and men who reject identification as Muslims, even to the point of declaring themselves Islamophobic.

Lastly, this reformist trend forms a integral part of religious and intellectual dialogue within the Muslim world. Its influence is felt in two ways: in the many intellectuals of the Muslim world (such as Abdolkarim Souroush and Abdullahi An-na'im) who have sought refuge in the United States and from there developed their thought; or on the other hand, in those born or educated in the United States (such as Amina Wadud and Omid Safi, mentioned above) who acquire a transnational notoriety through the reaction to their work in both the United States and the Muslim world. The reformation of Islamic thought is thus a product at once of western freedoms of thought and of cultural globalization.

CONCLUSION

Toward a Reconciliation of Islam and the West?

I n order to understand the situation of Muslims in the democratic and
secular societies of the West, it has been necessary to examine those
dimensions of Muslim life that are crucial to the formation of both
identities and religious practices. These dimensions are the meta-narrative
currently circulating on Islam, the influence of the cultural and political
structures of the host countries, the complex interaction between religion
and ethnicity, and the influence of global Islam.

The Meta-Narrative on Islam

The September 11 attacks only exacerbated the view of Islam as Enemy,
already present in centuries of orientalist imagery. This persistence of the
orientalist tradition has made it all but impossible, in popular opinion, to
dissociate Western Muslims from the external political enemy.

In such a situation, in which the relationship between dominator and
dominated has had such vast consequences, three modes of integration are
possible for Muslims: acceptance, avoidance, or resistance.[1] These three
modes underlie all the possible types of Islamic discourse and activity, both
within the Muslim community and in relation to the non-Muslim world.
Acceptance here means that the dominant discourse of the host culture is
adopted, accompanied by a cultural amnesia and the definite will to assimi-
late. This tendency is of only marginal import among immigrant Muslims.
Avoidance refers to types of behavior or language that attempt to separate

Muslims from the non-Muslim environment as much as possible: for example, by developing a sectarian form of Islamic religious belief. Resistance means actively refusing the status given to Islam within the dominant discourses and policies. Resistance need not be violent: it can take the form of an oppositional stance to dominant narratives, including the production of a body of literature that functions as an apology for Islam. The preferred themes of this literature are democracy and women: that is, the writers strive to convince both Muslims and non-Muslims that Islam is intrinsically democratic or favorable to emancipation of women. Resistance may also involve what Irving Goffman calls "contact terrorism": using Islamic symbols, clothing, or behavior to play on the Other's fear of and repulsion for Islam. Resistance does, on occasion, take more radical forms, such as an attraction to violent Islamist movements. This latter form of resistance—which, however, remains marginal—is incarnated by individuals such as Khaled Kelkal, a French citizen born in France to Algerian parents who participated in the GIA battle, or John Reid and John Walker Lindh, both of whom joined the ranks of Al Qaeda. But there are also more constructive forms of resistance, more and more common, in which Muslims reappropriate elements of Islamic practice, creating a religious life based on personal commitment and faith even while "keeping up with the times." As far as the discourse on Islam is concerned, what is new in all these modes of integration is a critique of Muslim governments' monopoly on Islamic tradition, as well as the emergence of new themes relating to European or American contexts.

How Political and Cultural Differences within the West Influence Islam's Evolution

The ethnic diversity of Muslims is constantly, and correctly, emphasized in studies of Islam. For a complete picture, however, one must also take into account the differences that exist among the host countries of Muslim immigration. The status given to religion, methods of acquiring citizenship, the degree of multicultural tolerance: these and other aspects, different for each country, equally affect the development and identity-formation of Muslim minorities in the West. One of the greatest differences between Europe and the United States, for example, is the higher degree of secularization in European public life. This secularization means that in European countries, forms of social and cultural activity that are based on religious principles are frequently seen as illegitimate, and certain types of interaction between Muslims and non-Muslims, such as interfaith dialogue, are frowned upon or dismissed. Thus if European Muslims fail to develop certain kinds of activities, the reason must be looked for not among the Muslim community, but in the various opportunities and limitations presented by the host societies. The examples of identity-formation being shaped by the characteristics of mainstream culture and politics are innumerable. Britain's multicultural policies, for example, long hindered the full religious expression of its Muslim minority, at least until the Rushdie Affair. By the same token, the authorization of religious teaching in German and Austrian public schools spurred Muslims to create textbooks that reflected Islamic religious tradition, particularly in terms of Islam's minority status.[2]

In the United States, racial tension and multiculturalist ideologies both contribute to Muslims' continued tendency to identify with their particular ethnic groups. At the same time, however, the combination of two factors— societal recognition of religious organizations' activities, and the cultural capital of many Muslim-Americans—facilitates the emergence of Muslim voices at a more rapid pace than in Europe, through organizations such as ISNA, ICNA, and CAIR. The major question with regard to the United States is what the consequences of September 11 have been and will be for this level of acceptance. Indeed, America's erstwhile tolerance has been irrevocably altered less by the growing hostility of civil society than by the institutional discrimination of the War on Terror.

Something both European and American Muslims share in common is the importance of the local community in Muslim identity-formation. This is so much the case that, even though national representation for Muslims exists in many countries, such as Belgium, dialogue between government authorities and Muslims is still almost always carried out on the municipal level. Moreover, the visibility and legitimacy of the new generation of Islamic leadership now coming into its own is nearly always grounded in local and community-based activities.[3] The disputes that occur on the local level feed into the national debate on Islam and vice versa, according to a subtle dialectic between the two areas of Islamic mobilization and visibility; this, in turn, influences the international debate on Islam and its political role. This process is seen, for example, in the various "headscarf affairs" in France: after the expulsion of two young sisters, Alma et Lila Lévy, from their Aubervilliers high school in September 2003, media attention on the issue helped to hasten the adoption of a law banning Islamic headscarves from the public schools. Similarly, in Italy, the 2002 rejection of a proposal to build a mosque in Lodi became a factor in nationwide discourse, serving to justify hostility to the construction of mosques throughout Italy. What is more, this hostility was given additional support by the international situation after September 11.[4]

Ethnicity Versus Religion

In both Europe and the United States, the identification with Islam most often comes out of the development of ethnic communities. For the Turks of Germany, the Indo-Pakistani of Great Britain and even to a certain extent the Maghrebi of France, Islam is inseparable from ethno-national identity as it operates in European society. This is especially the case for first-generation immigrants. Muslim Americans, for whom racial and ethnic divisions are even more marked, are undergoing a similar process of identification.

At the same time, however, more and more "transethnic" forms of Islam have emerged, particularly since the 1990s. In Great Britain, a new generation of Muslim leaders is in the process of shaking off the ethnically based and often isolationist version Islam dominated by first-generation immigrants from the Indian subcontinent, mostly from Barelvi or Deobandi groups. After the trauma of the Rushdie Affair, these new leaders entered into dialogue with national authorities. Throughout Europe, a new generation of organizational and religious leaders is emerging as part of the larger phenomenon of Islam's acculturation to secular society. This acculturation takes place by two, apparently contradictory, methods: the individualization of Islamic religious practice and a greater social role for Islam.

A similar process is taking place in the United States, with the emergence of a pan-Islamic discourse based on the rejection of "old-world" Muslim culture and the search for a "true Islam," whose values would better correspond to those of American society. There is nonetheless a tangible difference between European and American Muslims, stemming from the opportunities and constraints presented by the respective host societies. In the United States, the pan-Islamic approach is often promoted by an immigrant elite, individuals practiced in political lobbying and who use their position as religious leaders to gain a foothold in public discourse. Karen Leonard has called these leaders "Professional Muslims."[5] This strategy, however, does not mean that these "professional Muslims" necessarily identify as pan-Islamist in their personal Muslim practice. In other words, while their public discourse may take a universalist stance, the social reality of these leaders is such that they still often choose to marry and socialize, for example, within ethnically determined circles. In Europe, on the other hand, the existence of third- or even fourth-generation immigrants results in a more developed French-, British-, or Belgian-Muslim identity (with regard to points of cultural reference, language, customs, interaction with non-Muslims, etc.), as opposed to the ethno-national culture of the first immigrant generations.

In both cases, the European as in the American, one must keep in mind the real gulf between the reality of daily practices and the theological/intellectual discourse. The day-to-day, concrete practice of Muslims demonstrates an acculturation to their secular environment, a makeshift or adaptive character, and the internalization of cultural relativism, which is not always reflected in intellectual discourse, particularly in Europe.

Global Islam

Cultural globalization is a complex process involving the deterritorialization of cultures and communities, religious, ethnic, sexual, or otherwise. In this context, Islam becomes a powerful source of collective identity, recreating connections between groups otherwise separated by widely diverging geographies, languages, and cultures.

In the past few decades, two forms of global Islam in particular have attracted an increasing number of followers. The first, which too often goes unnoticed, are those diaspora communities that create networks of solidarity across national and cultural borders. Sometimes termed "transnational networks," these communities comprise a variety of nongovernmental figures—imams, immigrants, entrepreneurs—who establish ties between different political and cultural spaces. Three main factors give these communities their transnational character: (a) the idea of a common cultural or religious identity; (b) the existence of certain international associations; and (c) the development of financial, political, or even imaginary relations between people living in different countries.[6]

The second, and much more visible, form of global Islam concerns those theological or political movements that emphasize the universal ties of the Community of Believers (the *Ummah*). This form of global Islam includes movements such as the Muslim Brothers, Wahabism, and Tabligh. The rapid growth of communication and transportation technology have made the concept of the Ummah more real than ever before. Unlike, for example, Protestantism—in which theological and interpretive schisms led to the creation of distinct communities and the proliferation of sects—the unity of the Ummah as an imagined community with a common and constantly renewed destiny remains alive and well.

A distinction must be made between radicalism and fundamentalism. Many of those who subscribe to the movements mentioned above do so on the basis of a tradition of Islamic scholarship, inspired by the first *salafiyya*, that attempts to enter into a direct relation with the revealed Text.

These are the fundamentalists; that is, those who base their religious observance on the direct reading of Islam's source texts, the Qu'ran and the Hadith. Such a return to the original texts often does go hand in hand with a conservative or puritanical interpretation, as demonstrated by the growing popularity of Jamaat-Islamiyya in England and the United States, or the inspiration many young Muslims are finding inspiration in the Tabligh and (in the European suburbs) the teaching of leaders such as Sheikh Albani. Nonetheless, this return to the revealed Text can be the source of more open interpretations which explicitly takes into account the social and political concerns of their various European contexts.

Global Islam also includes the various forms of "virtual Islam." The development of electronically based forms of religiosity—through cassette production, satellite television, and the Internet—has exerted an immense influence on the globalization of Islamic identity. This explosion of available techniques for the spreading of Islam's message has resulted in the multiplication of (sometimes contradictory) interpretations of Islamic tradition. It thus weakens the interpretive monopoly of the traditional guardians of Islamic orthodoxy and its various nationalized versions within the Muslim world.[7]

Thorough study of the interactions between local, national, and international forms of Islamic mobilization demonstrates the limits of most current research on Islam in Europe and the United States. Because transnational networks are so crucial to the development and activity of Muslim communities, any analysis that limits itself to Muslims' adaptation in their different national societies runs the risk of providing only a partial view of the religious and cultural reality of these groups. In fact, Islam's adaptation to a democratic context is a multifaceted process in which both transnational and national forms of identification come into play.

Global Islam is thus at crossroads: one characterized by a crisis in religious authority and the rise of both the theology of intolerance and the language of hate. Muslims in Europe and the United States serve as a sort of lightning rod for this crisis. Their position at the very heart of the West crystallizes the debates and controversies that are currently shaking the entire Muslim world: the question of democracy, Muslim relationship to the Other, the status of women, the lure of fundamentalism.

At the same time, however, there are hints of a *renaissance* in Islam. Islamic practices are being revamped and secularized, and Islamic thought is at a peak of activity. In this study, we have tried to emphasize the emergence of a kind of intellectual freedom not seen in Islam since at least the first *salafiyya*. The only real drawback to this critique of current Wahabi dominance is the fact that it comes from only a handful of young intellectuals including Khaled Abou El Fadl, Farid Esack, and Abdullahi An-Naim.

"Resisters" are also to be found in the Muslim world, of course, but Western working conditions allow them a particular visibility and opportunity for development. American Muslims play an especially crucial role in this regard. They function as a sort of microcosm of the Muslim elite, and do not share the inferiority complex of their European coreligionists. In the words of Dr. Hassan Hathout, president of the Southern California Islamic Center: "We have no more lessons to learn from the Muslim world; from now on it is up to us to give them lessons in democracy."[8]

The ideas of Islamic reformers may hardly touch the life of the ordinary Muslim in Cairo or Kuala Lampur; but neither any longer can they be considered a marginal group. Their position is confirmed by their roles as producers and consumers of virtual Islam, and especially, by their contributions to transnational Islamic thought. They are thus introducing a new narrative: one of reconciliation between Islam and Western society, which deconstructs the stereotypes underlying the "clash of civilizations" between East and West.

The paradox, however, is that despite this reformist ferment, many European and even American Muslims are still trapped in the vicious cycle of reaction and defensiveness in the face of Western anti-Islamic sentiment— a cycle which shows no signs of weakening, but rather grows stronger with every terrorist act committed throughout the world "in the name of Islam." It is this cycle, above all else, which engenders political violence and unrest.

The real challenge for the coming decades lies in the ongoing development of the tension between the two poles of western Muslim communities: the one, reformist and open to influence; the other, radical and closed in on itself. The evolution of this tension will be determined not only by Muslims themselve, but also by the various policies of western governments for the integration and institutionalization of Islam. The worst case scenario is one in which the changes now taking place within Muslim communities are paralyzed or even reversed by the current foreign and domestic policies of western governments, policies which are frequently seen by Muslims as being hostile to Islam. This perception increases Muslims' feeling of being humiliated, which in turn provides fertile ground for the theology of intolerance or of hatred.

Appendix I

Table AI.1 Estimates of population identified as Muslims, European Union member States (end of 1990s)

Country	Estimated Muslim population (×1000)	Origin or citizenship	% of total population (estimate)
Austria	200	Turkey : 120 Bosnia : 50	2.6
Belgium	370	Morocco : 165 Turkey : 100	3.8
Denmark	150	Turkey : 36 Iran : 6 Pakistan : 7	2.8
Finland	20	Tartars & Turks	0.4
France	4,000–4,500	Algeria : 1,500 Morocco : 1,000 Tunisia : 350 Turkey : 350 Sub-Saharan Africa: 250	7
Germany	3,040	Turkey : 2,300 Former Yugoslavia Maghreb	3
Greece	370	Albania : 250 Western Thrace: 120	3.7
Ireland	7		0.2
Italy	600	Morocco : 150 Albania : 92 Tunisia : 50 Senegal : 35 Egypt : 26	1
Luxembourg	5	Bosnia	0.8

Table AI.1 Continued

Country	Estimated Muslim population (×1000)	Origin or citizenship	% of total population (estimate)
Netherlands	696	Turkey : 284 Morocco : 247 Surinam : 36	4.6
Portugal	30–36	Former colonies	0.3
Spain	300	Morocco : 170	0.7
Sweden	300	Iran, Turkey, Bosnia	1.2
United Kingdom	1,590	Indian subcontinent: 918	2.7
Total European Union	11 à 12.000	Maghreb & other Arabs : 3,700 Turkey : 3,100 Indian subcontinent : 950	3%

Sources: Census figures and national experts.

Table AI.2 Estimates of population identified as Muslim, other European countries (end of 1990s)

Country	Estimated Muslim population (×1000)	Origin or citizenship	% of total population (estimate)
Bulgaria	1,100	Turks a majority Gypsies, Pomaks	13
Hungary	2–20		
Norway	23	Iran : 7 Turkey : 6	0.5
Poland	15	Tartars : 5	0.04
Romania	50	Turks : 40% Tartars : 60%	0.3
Switzerland	250	Turkey Ex-Yougoslavia	3

Source: Maréchal, Brigitte, Dassetto, Felice, Nielsen, Jorgen, Allievi, Stefano (eds.), *Muslims in the Enlarged Europe, Religion and Society*, Leiden, Brill, 2003.

APPENDIX II

American Muslim Organizations

Islamic Society of North America (ISNA), *www.isna.net*

Address:
Islamic Society of North America
P.O. Box 38
Plainfield, IN 46168, USA

The Islamic Society of North America (ISNA) is a product of the resolve of the Muslims in North America to live an Islamic way of life. In keeping with its charter, ISNA works for the pleasure of Allah to advance the cause of Islam and Muslims in North America. ISNA activities include support for better schools, stronger outreach programs, organized community centers, and other Islamic programs. ISNA serves to help foster unity among Muslims, which is vital to an Islamic way of life.

ISNA's Mission

ISNA is an association of Muslim organizations and individuals that provides a common platform for presenting Islam, supporting Muslim communities, developing educational, social, and outreach programs and fostering good relations with other religious communities, and civic and service organizations.

Goals/Strategic Priorities

- Imam Training and Leadership
- Involvement of Youth

- Sound Financial
- Public Image
- Interfaith and Coalition Building
- Community Development (Goal Committee Chair: Zia Mahmood)

Fiqh Council of North America, http://www.fiqhcouncil.org (nonfunctional), http://www.isna.net/Library/fiqhqa/fiqh.asp

Leader is Taha Jabir Alalwani.
Associated closely with ISNA. Claims to represent all legal schools within Islam.

Dr. Taha Jabir Al Alwani is the president of The Graduate School of Islamic and Social Sciences and occupies the Imam Al-Shafi'i Chair in Islamic Legal Theory as a professor in his specialty field. Particularly interested in the social implications of Islamic law, he is a major participant in the activities of Muslim social scientists, publishing works such as his *Ethics of Disagreement, The Rights of the Accused in Islam,* and *Linking Ethics and Economics: The Role of Ijtihad,* in the Regulation and Correction of Capital Market (a co-authored occasional paper). Since coming to the United States in 1984, Dr. Alalwani has been a regular contributor to the American Journal of Islamic Social Sciences and a keen observer of intellectual trends throughout the Muslim world. Following his early education in the classical Islamic disciplines, Professor Alalwani left his native Iraq and received the degrees of M.A. and Ph.D. at Al Azhar University in Cairo. Included among his works are the monumental edition of Razi's al-Mahsul fi 'ilm Usul al-Fiqh, *Contemporary Islamic Cultural Undertaking, the Horizons of Change and its Approaches, Crisis in Fiqh and the Methodology of Ijtihad,* and *Source Methodology in Islamic Jurisprudence.* Recent publications include: *An Epistemological Perspective on the Political Dimensions to the Concept of Sovereignty, Taqlid and the Stagnation of the Muslim Mind, The Testimony of Women in the Law of Islam,* and *The Islamization of Knowledge: Yesterday and Today.*

Islamic Circle of North America (ICNA), www.icna.com

President: Dr. Talat Sultan
Islamic Circle of North America (ICNA) is a nonethnic, non-sectarian, open to all, independent, North America wide, grassroot organization.

ICNA's Goal

The goal of ICNA is to seek the pleasure of Allah (SWT) through the struggle of Iqamat-ud-Deen (establishment of the Islamic system of life) as spelled out in the Qur'an and the Sunnah of Prophet Muhammad (peace be upon him).

ICNA's Program

- To invite mankind to submit to the Creator by using all means of communications.
- To motivate Muslims to perform their duty of being witnesses unto mankind by their words and deeds.
- To organize those who agree to work for this cause in the discipline of ICNA.
- To offer educational and training opportunities to increase Islamic knowledge, to enhance character, and to develop skills for all those who are associated with ICNA.
- To oppose immorality and oppression in all forms, and support efforts for civil liberties and socioeconomic justice in the society.
- To strengthen the bond of humanity by serving all those in need anywhere in the world, with special focus on our neighborhood across North America.
- To cooperate with other organizations for the implementation of this program and unity in the ummah.

The Muslim Student's Association of the United States and Canada (MSA), www.msa-national.org

Address:
MSA of the US and Canada
P.O. Box 18612
Washington, DC 20036
Tel. 703-820-7900

President, MSA of the US & Canada: Tarek Elgawhary
The aims and purposes of MSA are to serve the best interest of Islam and Muslims in the United States and Canada so as to enable them to practice Islam as a complete way of life. Toward this end, it works in cooperation with the Islamic Society of North America to:

- help Muslim student organizations carry out Islamic programs and projects;
- assist Muslim students organizing themselves for Islamic activities;
- mobilize and coordinate the human and material resources of Muslim student organizations.

History

In January 1963 some of the most respected personalities in the Islamic movement came together at the University of Illinois Urbana-Champaign and formed the MSA of the United States and Canada. Over 70 people from across the country, including Brs. Ahmad Sakr, Mahdi Bhadori, Ahmad Totonji, Ilyas Ba-Yunus, and others, then all students, met in what would be the first of a number of historic gatherings to discuss the state of Muslims in North America.

Muslim student organizations were popping up all over the country, mainly in the mid-west, and comprised largely of foreign graduate students bent on returning home after their studies. Many of them did. But a significant portion realized that they would still have the responsibility of spreading Islam as students in North America. The main goal was always Da'wah. When the chapters realized that working on a national level, in a coordinated and concerted effort may be advantageous, they decided to put their heads together. MSA of the US & Canada was the result.

The very same year—1963—the first MSA of the US & Canada National Convention was held in Urbana-Champaign. Every year since then, MSA has held some form of national convention without failure. It was not until at least 1982 that the Islamic Society of North America (ISNA)—an off-shoot of MSA—held their first major convention in place of the MSA National Convention.

MSA was originally funded by Saudi monies to establish the interpretation of Islam in the United States according to their sectarian vision. As such, many members of MSA retain a strong Sunni identity, and while many do not openly follow Wahabbism, or hire Wahabbi Imams, there are still strong and open Salafi tendencies in the national leadership and at local centers. MSA organizations are seen as the voice of Islam on many university campuses.

Executive Committee

Tarek Elgawhary
President, MSA of the US & Canada
Altaf Husain
Ex-officio
Lina Hashem
Vice President US
Mohamed Sheibani
Vice President Canada
Eman Hasaballah
Treasurer

Muslim American Society (MAS), www.masnet.org

Address:
P.O. Box 1896
Falls Church, VA 22041
Tel. (703) 998-6525

The Muslim American Society (MAS) is a charitable, religious, social, cultural, and educational, not-for-profit organization. It is a pioneering Islamic organization, an Islamic revival, and reform movement that uplifts the individual, family, and society.

Muslim American Society (MAS) traces its historical roots back to the call of the Prophet Muhammad (Peace be upon him). Its more recent roots, however, could be traced to the Islamic revival movement that started evolving at the turn of the twentieth century. This movement brought the call of Islam to Muslim masses all over the reestablish Islam as a total way of life. The call and the spirit of the movement reached the shores of North America with arrival of the Muslim student and immigrants in the late 50ls and early 60ls. These early pioneers and Islamic Movement followers established in 1963. Muslim Student Association (MSA) of U.S and Canada as the rallying point in their endeavor to serve Islam and Muslims in the North America scene. Other services and outreach organization soon followed, such as North America Islamic Trust (NAIT), Islamic Medical Association (IMA), Muslim Arab Youth Association (MAYA) and Muslim Youth of North America (MYNA), to name a few. Twenty years later, Islamic Movement followers and sympathizers in North America launched the Islamic Society of North America (ISNA) as an outgrowth of the Muslim Students Association (MSA) to serve the needs of the ever-growing number of indigenous Muslims and immigrants who had opted to reside permanently in North America. Since its inception, ISNA and other organizations affiliated with it have been working diligently under the leadership of many future MAS founding members toward the advancement of the cause of Islam and Muslims in North America. Mindful of the dynamic changes that are taking place within the Muslim community and its surroundings and keeping an eye on the future, a number of Islamic workers and Islamic movement followers decided in 1992, after a painstaking slow and tedious process of soul searching and consultation to launch the Muslim American Society (MAS) to complement the work that has been accomplished in the last three decades and to lay the ground for the Islamic work needed to face the challenges of the next century.

Objectives

- To present the message of Islam to Muslims and non-Muslims and promote understanding between them.
- To encourage the participation of Muslims in building a virtuous and moral society.
- To offer a viable Islamic alternative to many of our society's prevailing problems.
- To promote family values in accordance with Islamic teaching
- To promote the human values that Islam come to emphasize: brotherhood, equality, justice, mercy, compassion, and peace.
- To foster unity among Muslims and Muslim organizations and encourage cooperation and coordination.

MAS appears to be heavily involved with ICNA, a Jamaati Islami influenced group. They are involved in moral/ethical education and propagating a particular understanding of Islam. Most involvement seems to occur through their website. The political wing, Freedom Foundation, does not have a real impact in the American context. They are also attempting to establish a university for da'wah. The group is also involved in supporting Islamic secondary schools and offers an on-line fatwa service.

American Muslim Council (AMC), www.amconline.org (does not work)

1212 New York Ave. NW, Suite 400
Washington, DC 20005
Phone: 202-789-2262
Fax: 202-789-2550

The American Muslim Council is a national organization that was established in 1990 to increase the effective participation of American Muslims in the U.S. political and public policy arenas. One of his founder, Abuduraham Alamoudi from Erythrea, was recently under investigation for supposed links with Libyan government. AMC aims to promote ethical values that enhance the quality of life for all Americans and to catalyze the greater presence of American Muslims in mainstream public life.

The aim of the AMC is to empower Muslims through education, both social and political. AMC believes that the way to political success is through social work and through cultivating both your own community as well as others. The AMC intends to help Muslims take advantage of the political system through participation. They believe that soon there will be Muslim elected officials from the local level to the Senate and maybe more. The organization believes that the challenge is to get Muslims out, active and involved in the social, political and civic arenas.

Muslim Public Affairs Council (MPAC), www.mpac.org

MPAC Los Angeles
Executive Director: Salam Al-Marayati
Address:
3010 Wilshire Boulevard, # 217
Los Angeles, California 90010
Tel. (213) 383-3443

MPAC's Vision Statement

MPAC was established in 1988 in order to establish a vibrant American Muslim community that will enrich American society through promoting the Islamic values of Mercy (21:107), Justice (4:135), Peace (8:61), Human Dignity (17:70), Freedom (2:256), and Equality for all (49:13).

MPAC's Mission Statement

To effect positive change in public opinion and in policy with the purpose of realizing the vision. The scope of the mission includes, but is not limited to, the following:

- Promoting an American Muslim identity.
- Fostering an effective grassroots organization.
- Training a future generation of men and women who share our vision.
- Promoting an accurate portrayal of Islam and Muslims in mass media and popular culture;
- Educating the American public, both Muslim and non-Muslim about Islam;
- Building alliances with Muslim and non-Muslim groups;
- Cultivating relationships with opinion and decision makers

As the American Muslim community continues to deal with the after-effects of September 11, 2001, MPAC is seeking to take a leap forward in its role of serving the American Muslim community. In addition to responding to current events around the nation and the world, MPAC is seeking to be pro-active in its efforts by establishing a set of issues to focus its resources on.

Platform Issues as a Basis for Work

Platform issues are those issues that MPAC deems important enough to dedicate its resources to becoming national leaders. Through these issues MPAC will work on behalf of our community to create meaningful, positive, and constructive change in our country.

Domestic Platform Issues Include

- Patriot Act Repeal
- Protecting American Muslim Zakat Monies & Charities
- Protecting Civil Liberties
- Assisting Victims of Hate Crimes
- Combating Anti-Muslim Bias
- Pursuing Political Efforts to Eradicate Homelessness
- Community Development
- Promoting Progressive Islamic Philosophy

Electoral Involvement Include

- Foreign Platform Issues
- Palestine and U.S. Policy in the Middle East
- Kashmir and U.S. South Asia Policy
- Promoting a Foreign Policy Based on Human Rights
- Reigning In the Excesses of the War on Terror

The group has a multiethnic leadership core, but its current activities focus predominantly on the Arab world. Domestically, it suffered a setback in 1999 when the head of the organization, Salman al-Marayati was suggested to have condoned terrorist activities. They are heavily involved in interfaith coalition building and attempting to establish a clear domestic agenda for American Muslims. While having strong name recognition, active membership does not seem to represent the diversity of the nation.

American Islamic Congress (AIC), _www.aicongress.org_

Address:
1770 Massachusetts Avenue, #623
Cambridge, MA 02140
Tel. 1-617-621-1511

The American Islamic Congress (AIC) is a social organization that is dedicated to building interfaith and interethnic understanding. AIC grew out of the ashes of September 11. The vicious terrorist attacks made many American Muslims realize that they had been silent for too long in the face of Muslim extremism. AIC believes that American Muslims must take the lead in building tolerance and fostering a respect for human rights and social justice. AIC feels a responsibility toward helping the United States rebuild from the attacks of September 11 and toward Islam in order to reassert that Muslims are moderate and peace-loving people.

The American Islamic Congress is dedicated to representing the diversity of Muslim American life. AIC founders and members represent an array of ethnic, racial, religious, and professional backgrounds. Members and activists come from the across the United States (Arizona, Tennessee, Nebraska, Oklahoma, Vermont, and beyond) and around the world (Egypt, Malaysia, Nigeria, Kuwait, Morocco, and beyond). Many non-Muslims are also enthusiastic about AIC efforts, and have joined in solidarity.

Founded shortly after September 11, 2001, the group is composed of a mixed Arab and South Asian leadership, and ideologically has both Sunni and Shi'ah on the board of directors. Primary focus seems to be on inter-faith understandings and media input.

American Muslim Alliance (AMA), _www.amaweb.org_

Address:
39675 Cedar Blvd. Suite 220 E
Newark, CA 94560
Tel. 510-252-9858

AMA Mission Statement

AMA believes that political power is not a function of numbers alone but is a combined product of initiative, innovation, and determination. Therefore there is a need to unlock our creativity energies and transform our present pent-up frustration, anger and pain into creative and meaningful steps toward political empowerment of the American Muslim community. One way of doing that is to methodically gain influence in the American political system commensurate with the sum total of our skills and creativity, resourcefulness, imagination, moral and ethical concerns, our intellectual contributions, and our strength of numbers.

AMA's main goal is to organize the American Muslim community in the mainstream public affairs, civic discourse, and party politics all across the United States. As a nationwide community we must organize ourselves nationwide: in every state and every congressional district. It is the AMA's mission to organize Muslims in all 50 states and have an AMA chapter in each of the 435 Congressional Districts. Currently, AMA has 98 chapters in 31 states.

AMA Goals

- To get a qualified American Muslims elected to the US Congress.
- To identify and train American Muslims to run for public offices at all levels in the American Political System.
- To get qualified Muslim Americans elected as delegates to the Democratic and Republican state and national conventions.
- To develop long-term Muslim political strategies.
- The AMA is in the business of producing American Muslim leaders for the American mainstream and our ultimate goal is to earn the right to coauthor America's vision of itself and its destiny.

AMA Activities

- Political education and leadership training.
- Candidate, campaign and issue research and analysis.
- Maintenance of a comprehensive database of American Muslim candidates and campaigns.
- Developing political strategies and articulating policy positions.
- Issuance of election advisories.
- Voter registration, education and mobilization.
- Organized participation (including hospitality suites) at the national and state conventions of Democratic and Republican Parties.
- Formation of political clubs.
- Workshops, seminars and conferences on 'Political Access / Action Though The Internet' and 'Public Debate and Public Policy'.

Group no longer appears to be active. May have joined with MPAC.

Council on American Islamic Relations (CAIR), www.cairnet.org

Address:
453 New Jersey Avenue, S.E.
Washington, DC 20003
Tel. 202-488-8787

Council on American Islamic Relations (CAIR) is a non-profit, grassroots membership organization. CAIR headquarters is in Washington, D.C., and there are CAIR chapters across America. CAIR was established to promote a positive image of Islam and Muslims in America. CAIR believes that misrepresentations of Islam are most often the result of ignorance on the part of non-Muslims and reluctance on the part of Muslims to articulate their case.

CAIR's Mission
CAIR is dedicated to presenting an Islamic perspective on issues of importance to the American public. In offering that perspective, CAIR seeks to empower the Muslim community in America through political and social activism.

CAIR, started in 1994, has a strong Arab element in its founding membership, and continues to exist in its executive leadership. Ostensibly open to all Muslims, CAIR has taken cases that serve a particular constituency and cultural interpretation of Islam. While not Wahabhi, there are Salafi elements in their understanding of Islam, particularly as interpreted in a Sunni Arab cultural context.

CAIR attempts to define Islam by claiming to represent Muslims in civil rights issues. Court cases are used as a platform to define Islam as five pillars, in dress and in mannerisms. The recent mosque report done by CAIR excluded large numbers of Shi'ah mosques.

Recently CAIR has come under attack for its ties to terrorist organizations and indirect support of the 1993 World Trade Center attack.

Chapters are loosely defined and are often more represented than the national organization. However, almost all "action alerts" are driven by the national group defining the agenda.

AMPCC: American Muslim Political Coordinating Council (Federation of Islamic Associations), (no website available)

The Federation of Islamic Associations (FIA) was formed by Lebanese Immigrants in1953. The FIA included Muslim associations in Canada as well as in the United States, and this broader North American base was adopted by the Muslim Student Association (est.1963) as its student leaders graduated and formed the Islamic Society of North America (ISNA). The FIA, MSA, and ISNA were initially led by Muslims from Arabic-speaking backgrounds. Certain Arab American leaders were organizing members of a specifically Muslim community by the 1980s, when Muslims had become the majority among Arab immigrants and many more Muslims had immigrated to the United States from around the world. During the same year in which the FIA was established the federal government first allowed Muslim servicemen to identify their religion as Muslim, and the 1953 McCarran-Walter Act, officially named the Immigration and Nationality Act, removed racial boundaries and allowed more immigration from non-European countries.

Today the Federation of Islamic Associations is known as The American Muslim Political Coordination Council (AMPCC). AMPCC is composed of the American Muslim Council (AMC), the American Muslim Alliance (AMA), the Council on American Islamic Relations (CAIR), the American Muslim Political Action Committee (AMPAC), and cooperating organizations such as ISNA, ICNA, the United Muslim American Association (UMAA), and the Islamic Community of America led by Imam Warith Deen Muhammad.

These organizations have decided that it was in the best interests of Muslims in America and Muslims worldwide to participate in politics without creating a political party. This became the decision of a large number of well-educated and mature professionals who are involved in the future of Muslims in America.

Project Islamic H.O.P.E. (helping oppressed people everywhere), www.projectislamichope.org

Address:
P.O. Box 43 A 122
Los Angeles, Ca 90043
Tel. 323 769 5267

Project Islamic H.O.P.E , Is a 501 C3 Non-profit national civil rights organization, that works collectively with other ethnic and religious groups to stand on the frontlines in the war against poverty, hunger, and social injustice.

Mission Statement

To Develop and Improve the spiritual, social, mental, and physical life of youth and adults in the community in accordance with the Holy Quran and the example of Prophet Muhammad (pbuh) and to provide services that will establish better economic social and moral conditions for youth and adults in the community.

Founded and run by Najee Ali, the group caters predominantly to African Americans and African-American concerns. Clearly identifying with the Sunni interpretation of Islam, Ali is focused on issues of social justice at the local level, prison reform issues and he encourages boycotts of socially damaging products. There does not appear to be a regular membership but rather a regular pool of people that help in grassroots organizing. Najee Ali was involved in boybotting the White House Iftar Dinners of 2003.

Progressive Muslims Network,
www.geocities.com/pmndc/index.htm

Progressive Muslims Network-DC, or PMN-DC was formed by some members of the international group, Progressive Muslims Network (PMN), as a regional offshoot. The organization has been active in organizing forums, activities, and marches on issues such as war, social justice, solidarity with Palestine, Kashmir, and progressive Islam. The progressive movement focuses on God and the divine message of the Quran, in their theology and struggle for social justice. Progressive, as defined by those who align themselves with the movement, is not progress within the context of a linear model of progress or reform, but is a political ideology that seeks social progress in the spheres of community, kinship, economics, and polity, and struggles against all forms of oppression.

Progressive Muslims stand in solidarity with the oppressed and disadvantaged of the world and maintain that Islam's emphasis on social justice and challenge to the status quo is an answer to the intersection of all forms of oppression.

Progressive Muslims distinguish progressivism from liberalism by maintaining that liberals seek to reform present structures of society in order to create social change, or as a means of preventing meaningful social change; however, progressives realize that the structures in themselves perpetuate injustice and, therefore, go beyond just reforming existing societal structures to creating new and more just ones.

American Muslim Society of Warith Deen Mohammed, (no website available)

Warith Deen Mohammed (1933-) Successor to Elijah Muhammad as head of the Nation of Islam is the founder of Muslim American Society (Calumet City, Ill.).

W.D. Muhammad resigned as spiritual leader of the American Muslim Mission in 1978 but still remained head of the organization. In 1985 he dismantled the leadership council he had set up. While each mosque then became an independent entity with its own name and leadership, most remained affiliated to the organization, the Muslim American Society (also known as the Ministry of W. Deen Mohammed), based in Calumet City, Ill. (Note: this Muslim American Society is not the same group as the Muslim American Society based in Falls Church, Virginia. MAS changed its name to American Society of Muslims (ASM) in 2002 because another Muslim organization was using the same name). W.D Muhammad officially resigned as head of the Muslim American Society in September 2003.

Integration of the MAS, still overwhelmingly African American, with mainstream Sunni Islam in the United States is by no means complete 25 years after it began. Mosques, schools, businesses and organizations (including the International League of Muslim Women) affiliated with W.D. Muhammad's MAS (or ASM) retain their distinctiveness through separate conferences and networks. Also, they cooperate in distribution of the organization's weekly newspaper. Headquartered in Hazel Crest, Ill.,

"Muslim Journal" was known as "Muhammad Speaks" when it was the official publication of the Nation of Islam.

Recently reports have placed the number of MAS followers at near 2.5 million persons with a percentage of immigrant and naturalized American citizens from various Muslim ethnic peoples, European Americans, and a majority of African Americans representing five generations since the earliest history of Elijah Mohammed's leadership (1933) and in some cases before.

Nation of Islam, www.noi.org
7351 South Stoney Island Avenue
Chicago, Illinois 60649
Tel. (773) 324-6000

The Nation of Islam began in 1930 with the arrival of Wallace Dodd Fard to the black ghetto of Detroit, Michigan. To the black underclass, Fard presented himself as a merchant allegedly from "the holy city of Mecca." Before his disappearance in 1934, W.D. Fard passed all his knowledge to Elijah Muhammad initially named Robert Poole.

The Nation of Islam believes that first people of the world were the original members of the Tribe of Shabazz from the Lost Nation of Asia. The lost people of the original nation of African descent, were captured, exploited, and dehumanized to serve as servitude slaves of America for over three centuries. W.D. Fard's mission was to teach the downtrodden and defenseless Black people a thorough Knowledge of God and of themselves, and to put them on the road to Self-Independence with a superior culture and higher civilization than they had previously experienced.

Today, Mosque Maryam serves as the headquarters and National Center for the Nation of Islam in Chicago, Illinois and its current leader is Louis Farrakhan. After Louis Farrakhan accused the son and eventual predecessor of Elijah Muhammad, Warith D. Muhammad from straying from the true path of The Nation of Islam, Farrakhan, severed his relationship with Warith D. Muhammad in 1977 and established what became known as the "revival" of the Nation of Islam.

Today, Farrakhan is known as an outspoken and charismatic leader and spokesperson for the Nation of Islam. His message is clear and urges black followers to become educated and independent American citizens. The Nation of Islam offers positive social programs to the Black community. Its members are active in jails and prisons, recruiting men behind bars and dissuading them from a life of crime. They have a strong emphasis against drugs, against prostitution and pimping, and against violence and gang involvement. They urge blacks to set up black-owned and black-operated businesses, thus working to raise the standard of living in poor neighborhoods. They also look with disfavor on black reliance on the government welfare system, which they perceive as often perpetuating the cycle of poverty. The Nation of Islam look to restaurants and food service industry as one focus for economic growth.

The Nation of Islam owns thousands of acres of Georgia farmland, and has operated countless restaurants, bakeries, clothing stores, bookstores, hair care shops, and other enterprises.

Ahmadiyya, www.alislam.org
Address:
Centers throughout North America: regional addresses can be found on their website.

The Ahmadiyya Movement in Islam is a religious organization, international in its scope, with branches in over 176 countries in Africa, North America, South America, Asia, Australasia, and Europe. At present, its total membership exceeds 200 million worldwide, and the numbers are increasing. The Ahmadiyya Movement was established in 1889 by Hadhrat Mirza Ghulam Ahmad (1835–1908) in a small and remote village, Qadian, in the Punjab, India. He claimed to be the expected reformer of the latter days, the Awaited One of the world community of religions (The Mahdi and Messiah).

Although the Mirza began as a polemicist within the Islamic fold his extreme claims soon ensured that his followers were alienated from the mainstream of Muslim life and it was inevitable that they should form a separate group. They are known by the title they gave themselves—*Ahmadiyya*—which they say refers to Muhammad's other name and not, to their founder. Their own general antagonism toward traditional Islam finally led to the point where leading Pakistani theologians sought to have them denounced as non-Muslims.

Within a century, the Ahmadiyya Movement, has spread across the globe. Despite being bitterly persecuted in some countries the Movement endeavors to exert their perspective of Islam through social projects, educational institutes, health services, Islamic publications, and construction of mosques.

The Ahmadiyya Movement encourages interfaith dialogue, and diligently defends Islam and tries to correct misunderstandings about Islam in the West. It advocates peace, tolerance, love, and understanding among followers of different faiths. It firmly believes in and acts upon the Qur'anic teaching.

After the demise of its founder, the Ahmadiyya Movement has been headed by his elected successors—Khalifas. The present Head of the Movement, Hadhrat Mirza Masroor Ahmad, was elected in 2003. His official title is Khalifatul Massih V.

The second Khalif, known as Hudoor, established the central consultative body (*Majlis Mashawarat*) of the Jamaat in 1922. Elected representative of various chapters of the Community gather at the Center once a year on the express orders of the Caliph and offer their consul and opinion on matters presented before them. The Khalifat al-Masih agrees with the counsel, if he deems appropriate. In this way all the members of the Jamaat have a chance to get involved in the affairs of the Community by offering their opinion.

APPENDIX III

Muslim Umbrella Organizations in Europe

United Kingdom

The Muslim Council of Britain (MCB), www.salaam.co.uk
Address:
Boardman House, 64 Broadway, Stratford, London E15 INT, G.B.
Tel. 0208 432 0585/6

The Muslim Council of Britain is the main representative body of British Muslims with a membership based of over 380 grassroots community organizations, mosques, professional bodies, and cultural associations. It was inaugurated—after several years of wide-ranging consultation and careful planning—on November 23, 1997 at the Brent Town Hall in Wembley by representatives of more than 250 Muslim organizations from all parts of Britain including Northern Ireland. The MCB's status as a coalition of organizations and institutions was officially confirmed during its fifth annual general meeting on April 28, 2002.

The MCB network provides an outreach to 70 percent of the 1.6 million Muslims in England, Wales, and Scotland. The MCB is a broad-based organization and its affiliated members represent the social and ethnic diversity of the community.

Membership of the MCB
Membership is open to any organization based in the United Kingdom whose activities are primarily for the benefit of Muslims of Britain, or which operates from Britain with staff drawn from Britain for the benefit of the Muslim *ummah*. No

organization is eligible for membership unless its own membership is open only to those who profess the Muslim faith. The MCB has three types of affiliated bodies—national, regional, and local. A "national" body is one that has branches across the United Kingdom; a "regional" body is one with branches in one or more counties, or an association or council of mosques operating with a town or city. "Local" or specialist bodies are typically mosques, Islamic centres, charities, schools, and similar institutions at one location. Each affiliate is assigned to a geographical zone within the United Kingdom. The MCB has defined 12 zones, largely based on postcode boundaries and to ensure an even distribution of members within each zone.

The Forum Against Islamophobia & Racism
(FAIR), www.fairuk.org

Address:
Suite 11, Grove House
320 Kensal Road
London W10 5BZ
Tel. 020 8969 7373

The Forum Against Islamophobia & Racism (FAIR) was founded in the wake of September 11, 2001. As an independent charitable organization, FAIR aims to establish a Safe, Just and Tolerant Britain in which Islamophobia and racism have no place.

FAIR emphasises partnership and works with organizations across numerous disciplines and with communities towards common purposes.

Programs
As part of its organization FAIR has set-up "The Media & Popular Culture Watch" to monitor and identify specific incidences of Islamophobia and issues of concern to the Muslim community, and to respond appropriately.

The project aims to be comprehensive, including coverage of print, radio, television, Internet, novels, cinema, theatre, museums, art galleries, fashion, music, sports, and local events. As well as monitoring the media one of the longer term aims of the Project is to develop proactive initiatives to facilitate a more balanced and fair reporting of Muslims in the media. To this end FAIR is working to implement the training of young Muslim professionals to represent the Muslim community on a range of issues, encourage Muslims to take a greater part in shaping and creating media and enter the media profession.

As part of its organization FAIR is also involved in issues of Policy Research and Lobbying. Through analysis of its project work FAIR formulates policies and advises relevant agencies on tackling Islamophobic and Muslim alienating trends in society.

The Islamic Cultural Centre, http://www.islamicculturalcentre.co.uk/ iccnew/History/BriefHistory.asp

The Islamic Cultural Centre which includes the London Central Mosque was established since 1944. It was officially opened by His Majesty King George VI in November 1944. The 2.3 acres of site adjacent to Hanover Gate in Regent's Park, was presented as an unconditional gift from the British Government to the U.K. Muslim Community. A Mosque Committee comprising of various prominent Muslim diplomats and Muslim residents in the United Kingdom gratefully accepted the gift which was intended mainly as a tribute to the thousands of Indian Muslim soldiers who had died defending the then British Empire.

The Mosque Committee registered the London Central Mosque Trust Limited as a Trust Corporation in September 1947. The delay from 1944 to 1947 was caused by disruptions to civil life due to war. Seven representatives from six Muslim countries acted as Trustees. In 1995, the Council counted its members from 29 different countries. The Board of Trustees of the Islamic Cultural Centre is the Diplomatic Representatives of Muslim countries accredited to the Court of St. James.

The Centre has, since its establishment, has acted on behalf of all British Muslims vis-à-vis the British Government, and Local Authorities and other official bodies, in matters such as health, education and welfare.

The Muslim Public Affairs Committee (MPAC), http://www.mpacuk.org/mpac/data/newhome/index.jsp

The Muslim Public Affairs Committee is a non-profit organization working to strengthen the Muslim community. Its aim is to defend Muslim interests and Islam throughout Britain and the world. Originally set up as a web-based media monitoring e-group, MPACs first mission was to fight the bias in the media and to re-address the balance. MPAC has since flourished. Rather than being a concentrated group of activists funded by the community, MPAC aims to give the power to the Muslim community.

UK Islamic Mission, www.ukim.org

The U.K. Islamic Mission is a nationwide organization with over 40 branches and Islamic Centres working all over British Isles. It has nationwide membership and a three-tier program consists of Da'wah that is, Invitation toward Islam, Educating Community and Relief & Welfare for the needy. The basic purpose and priority of all programs affiliated with the U.K. Islamic Mission is to convey the message of Islam in the United Kingdom. Thus the U.K. Islamic Mission has established mosques and Islamic centers as well as madaris and libraries in major cities. These activities carried on by all their branches are centerd on disseminating Islamic teachings and thought.

U.K. Islamic Mission is a registered charity, which offers a range of services including welfare and relief to individuals and communities. Donations and contributions are received and spent to help the less fortunate in society. U.K. Islamic Mission workers are engaged in providing funds to relieve the miseries of those caught up in wars and natural disasters like, famine, floods, and earthquakes all over the world.

The Federation of Students Islamic Societies In the UK & Eire, http://www.fosis.demon.co.uk/index.htm

FOSIS, the Federation of Student Islamic Societies in United Kingdom and Ireland, is the premier Muslim Student representative body in the United Kingdom and Ireland. It was established in 1962 after a meeting held in Birmingham by students from the cities of Birmingham, Dublin, Leeds, Liverpool, London, and Wolverhampton who realized the need to coordinate the work of Islamic societies across the country.

FOSISs main aim is to unify Muslim Students under one banner that can represent their voice and their interests. To do this, FOSIS encourages as many Islamic Societies in the United Kingdom and Ireland to affiliate to FOSIS so that they can say that FOSIS truly represents Muslim Students.

Italy

UCOII (Union of Islamic Communities in Italy), www.islam-ucoii.it

Address:
Via Quattro Fontane 109, 00184 Roma
Tel. 39 0183 764735

The largest Muslim organization in Italy is UCOII (Union of Islamic Communities in Italy). UCOII is the Italian section of the Muslim World League that was formed in 1990 by the grouping of a number of local associations. Its foundation was promoted by the Islamic Centre of Milan and Lombardy, which initially claimed to be the only representitive of Islam in Italy. According to some observers, UCOII vehicles a political version of Islam, influenced by the ideology of the Muslim Brotherhood. Its roots are widespread throughout the entire Italian territory.

As one of the more structured Islamic organizations in Italy, UCOII was the first to to propose a draft (1992) for a possible agreement with the Italian State under Article 8 of the constitution which declares: "All religious denominations are equally free under the law. Denominations that are different from Catholicism have the right to establish organisations according to their regulations, unless the denomination concerned conflicts with Italian law and order. Their relationship with the state is determined by law and based on an agreement with the organisations that represent their corresponding denominations."

Centro Islamico Culturale d'Italia (CICI): Islamic Cultural Centre of Italy, www.alhuda.it

The Centro Culturale Islamico (Islamic Cultural Centre) is based in Rome. The Centre has played a leading role in the construction of the most important mosque in Italy. Its Board is largely composed of the ambassadors of Islamic States. Besides serving as a spiritual and social focal point, organizing celebrations of religious holidays and observance of other religious rites, the Centre plays an important educational role. It provides Arabic language classes and religious instruction and has an extensive library on Islamic history, culture, and contemporary affairs.

CICI is the only Islamic organization that is not considered as an association by the state of Italy. Instead CICI is recognised as a religious legal entity (*ente morale di culto*) by a decree passed by the President of the Republic. Recognized religious legal entities are regulated by the norms defined by l.n. 1159/1929 and r.d. n. 289/1930. These norms concern the recognition itself and the control to be exercised over the entities. The recognition is granted by the president of the Republic, on proposal by the Interior Minister, who exercises the control on the religious entities. However, doubts are put forward about the constitutional legitimacy of some of those provisions. Some rights and privileges are granted to recognised religious legal entities. The nature of recognized religious entities as public law entities or private is regarded irrelevant by authorities.

The CICI, which promotes the official Islam of the States, has its seat at the Great Mosque in Rome. Its board of directors is formed mainly by ambassadors of Muslim sunni States accredited to the Holy See or to the Italian State. The influence of Saudi Arabia in the CICI is balanced by that of other States, above all Morocco. Saudi Arabia is the prominent member of the World Muslim League, which politically and financially supports the Centro.

The Association of Italian Muslims (AMI), http://village.flashnet.it/users/fn034463/history.html

Address:
Via Giovanni Barracco 12/6
Rome, Italie

Founded in 1982, the Association of Italian Muslims (AMI) is one of Italy's smaller Islamic organizations, composed predominantly of Italian citizens who have converted to Islam. Its original legal seat was in Naples, but was moved to Rome in 1985. The founders unanimously decided to elect Shaykh 'Ali Mo'allim Hussen as President. Shaykh 'Ali Mo'allim Hussen is an Italian citizen coming from Somalia, a Qadi and Qari descending from Ahmad al-Badawi as-Siddiqi and retired officer of the Italian Army.

AMI held its first General Assembly in Naples in 1984. During this Assembly, Shaykh 'Ali presented a wide plan of activities, and clarified that the AMI will inspire its programs to moderateness and tolerance, and oppose fanaticism and chauvinism, thus not affiliating itself with any other Muslim organizations.

AMI wants its members to strictly abide by the Italian civil and penal law, and promotes interfaith dialogue with Christians and Jews. It claims to have always been in good relations with the Catholic Church, the Federation of the Italian Evangelical Churches and the Italian Jewish Community.

In 1991, some AMI members founded in Rome the Cultural Institute of the Italian Islamic Community (ICCII) whose goal was to increase knowledge of Islamic sciences in Italy. On April 3, 1993 the AMI Board and the ICCII Direction assembled and decided to unify the two organizations under a single set of articles. This decision of unification was nevertheless accepted out of a request coming from the Italian Government after the proposal of an agreement between the State and the Islamic Community. A single representation in front of the State was regarded as a necessary step toward the preparation of bill on rights of Islam in Italy.

COREIS (Italian Islamic Religious Community), www.coreis.it

Via Meda 9, 20136 Milan, Italie
Tel: 02 8393340

COREIS was founded in 1997 as a part of the International Association for the Information of Islam (which was founded in 1993). Abdel-Wâhid Pallavicini is the president of COREIS. Inspired by the French sufi, Rene Guenon, the goal of COREIS is to participate in interfaith dialogue and to teach both Muslims and non-Muslims that Islam is compatible with Italian society and Law.

COREIS has also established some smaller organizations of its own. It has established the Institute of Islamic Studies (IHEI) and the Center for Metaphysics Studies. CORIES is currently managing a proposal for a future mosque of Via Meda in Milan.

France

National Federation of the Muslims of France (FNMF), (no website available)

Address:
33, rue Polonceau, 75018 Paris
Tel. 01 46 06 26 65

President: Mohammed Bechari

The FNMF was established in 1985, and aims to meet the religious, cultural, educational, social, and humanitarian needs of Muslims in France. The National Federation of French Muslims (FNMF) was founded in December of 1985 by a French Muslim convert. It has established itself as the main rival of the Mosquee de Paris, promoting a French Islam freed from the influence of countries of origin. Daniel Youssouf Leclerc, who served as director of the organization during the first "headscarf affair" of 1989, espoused this view charismatically. According to the federation's directors, it has more than 500 local associations; this claim is difficult to verify. During 1995, Moroccans came to dominate its leadership when Mohammed Bachari became president.

The Paris Mosque, www.mosquee-de-paris.com
Address:
2, bis place du puits de l'ermite
75005 Paris
Tel. 33 1 45 35 97 33

Leadership: Dalil Boubakeur

The Paris Mosque (established in 1926) is France's main mosque and numbers more than 500 local associations among its members. The mosque was a gift of the French government to honor the Muslims who died for France during the World War I. Although the the French governement did provide the grounds and initial funding for the mosque, a significant portion of funding was also made by Muslims in Algeria.
Educated in Algeria, Dalil Boubakeur is the Rector of the Paris Mosque.

The Union of the Islamic Organizations of France (UOIF), www.uoif-online.com
Address:
20, rue de la Prévôté
93120 LA COURNEUVE – FRANCE
Tél : +33.1.43.11.10.60

President: L.T. Breze
Secretary Genereal: Fouad Alaoui

The UOIF is the French branch of the Union of Islamic Organisations in Europe. The UOIF was founded by immigrant Muslim Tunisians in 1983. They had close ties with islamist Tunisian Party known as Ennahda, founded by Rached Ghanouchi (exiled in London). Some of them came from North Africa for university studies, and then remained in France to work and start families. They began to make connections with the immigrant world, which had until then been unfamiliar to them, during the first "headscarf affair" of 1989. Since then, they have undertaken a series of efforts to organize a French Muslim minority. Professors, students, and businessmen, the leaders of the movement are part of the emerging Muslim French elite. They promote the strict observance of Islam, as well as openness toward other cultural and religious sectors of French society. Since the organization's founding, most of the original leaders have retired. When the administrative council was modified in December of 1995, a new group of leaders surfaced, most of Moroccan origin and living in Bordeaux. Today, the UOIF claims 200 local organizations of different statuses: active (50), friends (50), and sympathizers (100).

UOIF functions on both the national and regional levels. On the national level, the General Assembly elects an executive bureau, which then elects a president. On the regional level, member organizations elect 12 city delegates, who choose a regional representative. Since 1994, regional conferences have occurred in Acquitaine and the South East region of France. The organization's most significant accomplishment is its annual congress in Le Bourget in the outskirts of Paris, which features different lectures and roundtables.

This event attracts several thousand young people from all over France, who gather for three days for both festivities and studying. Its other important achievement has been the founding of an Islamic university institute. UOIF leaders were among the first to understand the critical importance of training imams in France. They founded the European Institute of Human Sciences, including an institute for imams and Islamic educators. With about 80 students—the majority of them French—it has not yet shown itself capable of producing religious leaders in France, chiefly because public authorities often view it with mistrust. In 1997, the institute's first graduating class of imams included only four people, of which one was a woman. In addition, the institute conducts yearly summer seminars for those unable to pursue the complete program of study.

Outside the training of Islamic leadership, educating Muslim youths is UOIF's chief priority. For this purpose, the organization created French Muslim Youth (JMF) in 1992. This group's members are men and women between the ages of 18 and 30. Its leaders are young men, students or upwardly mobile professionals. Their operation is decentralized. Today there are six federations grouping together sections in Paris (Dreux, Evreux, Montfermeil), as well as Lille, Nantes, St. Nazaire, Cholet and Marseille. They see themselves more as a consciousness-raising movement than as providers of services. They do, however, organize conferences (at the local level) and forums (at the regional level), where guest lecturers speak on assorted subjects. In 1996, one of this forum addressed the theme, "Young People and Belief." Several UOIF members lectured. More than 300 young people, with an average age of twenty, gathered at this forum.

Association des Etudiants Islamiques en France (AEIF), (no website available)

Address:
23, rue Boyer-Barret, 75014
Tel. 01 45 42 04 82

Association of Islamic Students (AEIF), founded in 1963 by Professor Hamidullah, drew its original membership from foreigners studying in France. Since then, some young people of immigrant origin have joined the organization.

The AEIF was prides itself as being one of the first organizations to establish "official" prayer spaces throughout France. The AEIF library was also considered to be one of the only places where Muslims could go to conduct research on issues concerning Islam. The AEIF was one of the first organizations to bring books on French Islam to Grance. Professor Hamidullah translated the Qu'ran, the biography of the Prophet and other books regarding Islam. As a student organization, headed by Professor Hamidullah, AEIF was and still is an environment of intellecual debate, student meetings and conferences.

The organization looks to help students coming from abroad to find a place of Islamic practice and belief within the University setting. they left in their country of origin.

Étudiants Musulmans de France (EMF), www.emf.asso.fr, http://membres.lycos.fr/emfrouen/
Leaders: Fethi Belabdelli, président ; Abdelkrim Amine, vice président

EMF is associated with UOIF. The president of EMF is Fethi Belabdelli and the vice president is Agdelkrim Amine. Upon its creation, EMF recieved 10,000 euros from the Saudi government and its aim is to create an environment for all Muslim students in France. Presently, EMF is affiliated with 12 academies in three regions of France.

Union des Jeunes Musulmans (UJM) et Collectif National des Jeunes Musulmans de France (CJMF): Union of Young Muslims in France, (no website available)

The Union of Young Muslims in France is an activist group based in Lyon that started in 1987. UJM works nationally with other young Muslim organizations in order to be active in their community. UJM not only concerns itself with issues pertaining to young Muslims in France but also plays an active role helping Muslim immigrants from North Africa and students from Arabic countries.

UJM organizes different cultural and interreligious conferences and events. UJM has created a bilingual libarary (Arabic and French) and have created a publishing house called Tawhid in 1990. Tawhid was created in order to fill a need for Islamic literature written in French. Tawhid concerns itself with issues related to Muslims in France such as interreligious issues and laïcité.

Mouvement des musulmans laïques de France (MMLF): Movement of Secular Muslims in France

Address:
Espace B, 16, rue Barbanègre, 75019 Paris
MMLF@free.fr

MMLF was created in 2003 by different Muslim activists, intellectuals, and journalists such as Djida Tazdait, ex-deputy of Europe Rachid Kaci, president of the Democratia movement, and member of the right-wing French political party UMP, Betoule Gekkar-Lambiotte, inspector of national education, (who resigned from CFCM), Nadia Amira, ex-vicepresident of France Plus, Soeib Bencheikh, the grand mufti of Marseille, the writer Malek Chabel, Anthropologist Mezri Haddad, philosopher and journalist Michel Renard, director of the review *Islam de France*. The intention of the MMLF is to participate in the national understanding of laïcité through national congresses, conferences, and reports. It also intends to diffuse information on religious topics such as imams, hallal slaughtering, and so on.

Conseil Français des musulmans laïques (CFML): French Council of Secular Muslims

CFML was created in May 2003 by Amo Ferhati and Tokia Saifi, Secretary of State. The CFML claims the support of 500 Muslim organizations and its aim is to create a representive council that would be the secular counterpart of CFCM.

Conseil des Démocrates Musulmans de France (CDMF): Democratic Council of Muslims in France.

The CDMF was created in October of 2003 by Abderrahmane Dahmane, a politician from the UMP party. One hundred persons were present at the founding meeting. Their ambition is also to be the secular counterpart of CFCM.

Convention Laïque pour l'Egalité des droits (CLE): Secular Convention for the Equality of Rights

CLE was started in June 2003 by Yazid Sabeg a businessman who is concerned with Muslim equal rights and discrimination in the workplace and within French society with a special emphasis on social and economic integration.

Germany

ISLAMRAT für die Bundesrepublik Deutschland, www.islamrat.de

Address:
Adenauerallee 13
D-53111 Bonn
Tel. 0228 53961 0

The Islamic Council with more than 30 member organizations is dominated by Milli Görüs, an Islamic community considered extremist, the 19 members making up the Central Council represent a wide range of nations and attitudes, though it scarcely embraces 200 mosques.

ZENTRALRAT für die Muslime in Deutschland (ZMD): Central Council of the Muslims in Germany, www.zentralrat.de

Address:
Indestr. 93, 52249 Eschweiler
Franz Liszt Str. 35, 52249 Eschweiler

The "Central Council of Muslims in Germany" (ZMD) emerged from the "Islamic Working Group Germany" (Islamischer Arbeitskreis Deutschland) in 1994. Today, the ZMD represents only 10,000 members, a small minority of the about 3.3 million Muslims in Germany (the other two Muslim parent organisations, the "Islam Council" (Islamrat) and "Turkish-Islamic Union" (Türkisch-Islamische Union), count 185,000 and about 125,000 members, respectively).

Turkisch-Islamische Union (DITIB): The Turkish Islamic Union, (no website available)

DITIB is the largest Muslim non-profit organization in Germany consisting of many member associations. According to its own figures, in mid 1999 DITIB had 776 member associations throughout the country.

Föderation der Aleviten Gemeinden in Deutschland (AABF), www.alevi.com

Address:
Stolberger Str. 317
50933 Köln
Tel.: 0049/(0)221/ 94 98 56 – 0

The AABF is a Sufi group of the Alevi-Bektashis. Originally a minority group from Turkey and the Anatolian region, Kurdes make up a large portion of the Bektashi membership. The Alevis-Bektashis have develped a humanistic and modern ideology that was agreeable with the Kemal presidency of Turkey. Their modern ideology have made them a minority among the more extreme Muslim groups in Turkey. The president of the European Federation of the AABF is Turgut Oker.

Council for Christian and Muslim Dialogue

The Council for Christian and Muslim Dialogue was founded in 2003 by the German government. The Council is composed of many local Muslim and Christian associations and deals with issues that concern the coexistance of both religions.

Spain

Federación Espalola de Diocesis Islamicas (FEERI): Spanish Federation of Islamic Religious Entities, (no website available)

President: Abdelkarim Carrasco

FEERI was established in 1989 by a number of small Islamic organizations that were existing in Spain. This movement led by converts is the main political Muslim group in Spain. It is well organized and has engaged in negotiations with the Spanish government over the status of Muslims in Spain. This group was behind the building of the Granada mosque.

Union de Comunidades Islamicas de Espana (UCIDE),
The Union of Islamic Communities of Spain,
(no website available)
President: Riay Tatari, imam of Syrian origin of the Estrecho mosque in Madrid.

UCIDE was established in 1990, a year after the creation of FEERI. By Muslim immigrant groups who did not want to merge with FEERI.

Sweden

Förenade Islamiska Församlingar i Sverige
(FIFS, United Islamic Communities in Sweden),
(no website available)
Address:
Kapellgrand 10
116 25 Stockholm
Tel. 08 509 109 24

Förenade Islamiska Församlingar i Sverige (FIFS, United Islamic Communities in Sweden) was formed in 1974 to fill the need among the Muslim communities for an umbrella organization. This need was created by the structure for state support which presupposed a national organization that would distribute economic support to the different local communities. This was done by SST that in the middle of the 1970's reformulated its task from supporting the different national free churches, to give support to every kind of religious community including what was called the immigrant churches (which among others included Islamic communities). Thus FIFS organized different Muslim communities including Shias, Sunni, communities of different ethnic background and so on, the only exception being the Ahmadiyyas who have a separate organisation.

Sveriges Förenade Muslimska Församlingar (SMuF, United Muslim Communities of Sweden), (no website available)
Address:
Kapellgrand 10
116 25 Stockholm
Tel. 08 509 109 23

Sveriges Förenade Muslimska Församlingar (SMuF, United Muslim Communities of Sweden): due to the sensitive issues of economy, there were quarrels and some choose to leave FIFS and form SMuF in 1982. These were mainly Sunnis of Arabic language background, but do contain Shi'a communities. In 1990, a new split occurred and IKUS was formed.

Islamiska Kulturcenterunionen (IKUS, Union of Islamic Centres of Culture), (no website available)
Address:
Box 3053
145 03 Norsborg
Tel. 08 531 707 95

IKUS has a leaning toward the Suleymanli, but they also coordinate quite a few Somali communities (which is obvious in their charter that bans female circumcision and the chewing of Kat). In IKUS there are no Shi'a communities.

Sveriges Muslimska Råd (SMR – The Muslim Council of Sweden), (no website available)
Sveriges Muslimska Råd (SMR – The Muslim Council of Sweden) was formed in 1990 by FIFS and SMuF to be their active part in their relations with the Swedish majority society. The most active person in SMR is Mahmoud Aldebe who also has held the chairmanship of SMuF for quite a while; SMR can be seen as his project. The specific mission of the SMR is to:

• Create mosques and Islamic schools.
• Create information material about Islam directed towards the non-Muslims in Sweden.
• Take active part in the public debate in society.

Switzerland
League of Muslims in Switzerland (LMS), (no website available)
Address:
Rue Temple 23
2400 Le Locle
Tel. +41 (0) 32 931 45 95

The League of Muslims in Switzerland was created in 1994 to combine the efforts of Muslims of all origins. It was created with the goal to serve the development of religious activities and to encourage Muslims to strive for a responsible and positive integration within Swiss society. The League considers the recognition of the Islamic religion as the second largest official religious community in the country as beneficial for the entire Muslim community, since it will enable them to feel respected and taken into account and to better assume their responsibilities as citizens.

The Netherlands
There are approximately 700,000 Muslims in the Netherlands with a majority of them immigrants from Turkey and Morocco. The different Muslim organizations are

a representation of the different ethnicities and nationalities that make up the Muslim population in the Netherlands.

Islamic Foundation of the Netherlands

The Islamic Foundation of the Netherlands is predominately comprised of Diyanet Turkish Muslims. The Foundation controls 140 mosques over the 400 currently present in the Netherlands.

Milli Görüs

Milli Görüs is a Turkish association that used to be an an Islamic Party called Refah. Milli Görüs controls 30 mosques in the Netherlands.

Foundation Islamic Center

The Foundation Islamic Center is associated with the Turkish Suleyman organization of Turkey. The Centre controls 30 Islamic centers in the Netherlands.

HAK-DER, www.hakder.nl

Hak-Der is an Alevie Group that controls 30 Islamic centers in the Netherlands.

Union of Moroccan Muslims Organization

As the name indicates, the Union of Moroccan Muslims is an organization for Muslims from Morocco. The organization claims 100 mosques and organizations in the Netherlands.

World Islamic Mission (WIM)

The World Islamic Mission (30 mosques) is primarily composed of Muslims from Surinam and Pakistan.

NB: A Muslim Council of Mosques (close to the Islamic Foundation of the Netherlands) as well as a Muslim Council of the Netherlands have been created. However none of them have been recognized by the State.

Islamitische Scholen Besturen Organisatie (ISBO): Organization of Islamic Schools

In 1983, the formal ties between the State and Religious organizations were severed. However, the State can still fund primary and secondary high schools: 32 Muslim primary schools are thus funded by the State and members of the Organization of Islamic Schools.

Austria

Islamic Center of Austria

The foundation stone for the building of the first Islamic Center in Austria was laid in 1968, and its Trustee Council was formed under the chairmanship of

Hassan Al-Tuhamiy, Egypt's ambassador to Austria at the time, who later became secretary-general of the Organization of Islamic Conference (OIC). In November 1977 the Center was inaugurated and has since been playing an important role in teaching the Muslims in Austria matters related to their religion.

Norway
World Islamic Mission (WIM), www.wim.no
President: Mr. Talib Hussain Minhas
Address:
Akeberg Veien 28B
0650 Oslo (Norway)
Tel: 02 -268 2708

World Islamic Mission (WIM) is an international organization founded in the Holy city of Mecca in 1972 by the Muslim scholar and missionary, Maulana Shah Ahmad Noorani Siddiqui. WIM is active in several countries in Europe, North America and Asia organizing conferences and seminars to bring people together to work for peace and understanding. In Norway, the WIM is in charge of 60 mosques.

Denmark
Muslimernes Landsorganisation (MLO) Organisation Nationale Musulmane, www.mlo.nu
Address:
Blågårdsgade 30, 2200 København N
Tel : 45/ 70 20 66 25
Leader: Fatih Alev

Islamic Union in Denmark
The Islamic Union in Demark is directed by Mohammed Fouad Baraze. The association affiliates itself with the Wahabi Islam of Saudi Arabia. The Islamic Union has worked in creating a mosque and Muslim cemetery in Copenhagen.

Center of Islamic Information
The Muslim population in Denmark is estemated to be approximately 170,000 (making up 3 percent of the population). A majority of the Muslim population immigrated from countries such as Turkey, Pakistan, Morocco, and Yougoslavia. Representing the different Islamic associations in Denmark, the Center of Islamic Information is an organization that represents Muslims from different countries. In July 2003 the main Muslim organizations appealed to the government in order to create a council that would represent all Muslims in Denmark.

Glossary

'Abd: Servant, the believer in relation to God.

Adhan: Call to prayer given five times daily; *Mu'adhdhin*: the one who gives the call.

Ahl Al Kitab: "People of the Book," the Qur'anic reference to Christian, Jews, and others who possess Scripture.

Ashura: The tenth of the first month of the Islamic calendar (*Muharram*). A Shi'a sacred anniversary commemorating the martyrdom of the third imam Husayn in 680.

Bid'a: Innovation in Islamic doctrine and practice. *Bid'a* is considered by Traditionalists to be a punishable deviation from the straight path of faith and practice.

Caliph: The "successor" or "vice regent" of the Prophet who was elected to head the Muslim State. The office of caliph or Caliphate was subsumed in 3 periods: the *Rashidun* (632–661), the *Ummayads* (661–750), the *Abassids* (750–1258).

Dar al-Harb: "Abode of war" referring to lands outside of Islam (sometimes called *Dar al-Kufr* ("abode of apostasy").

Dar al-Islam: "Abode of peace," referring to lands where Islamic Law is enforced.

Da'awa: "Call or invitation," summoning others to heed the call of God to Islam; propagation of the faith.

Dhimmi: A tolerated religious people of the Book living within lands under Islamic rule. According to the *Shari'a*, *Dhimmis* are granted the right of retaining their non Muslim religious status in exchange for payment of a poll tax (*jizya*) and meeting certain obligations to the Muslim body politics.

Dhikr: "Remembrance," the congregational Sufi ritual of remembering God.

Dîn: "Judgement" but also Religion oppposed to Dunya.

Dunya: Everyday world, earthly existence.

Fatiha: First chapter of the Qu'ran.

Fatwa: Legal decision of a religious authority.

Fiqh: The Science of Islamic jurisprudence.

Fitna: Sectarian strife that disrupts the social order. The first of several fitna in Islam was occasioned by the assassination of Caliph 'Uthman (644–656).

Hadith: Tradition that reports the words and deeds of Prophet Muhammad through a chain of trusted human transmitters.

Haj: Pilgrimage to Mecca, prescribed for every Muslim, if possible, once in a lifetime.

Halal: Legally permissible in opposition to *haram*.

Haram: Unlawful, prohibited.

Hijab: Head covering worn by women as a sign of piety and Muslim identity.

'Ibadat: The ordinances of Muslim worship and rituals explained and interpreted in the Shari'a by the Ulama. The *ibadat* generally includes rules governing ritual purity, prayer, alms, fasting, and pilgrimage.

Ijma: Consensus of the community, one of the four accepted sources of Islamic law.

Imam: For Sunnis, the one who leads the prayer, for *Shi'a* a direct descendant of the Prophet who is the divinely mandated leader of the Community.

Iman: Faith, submission to God through the heart.

Ijtihad: Interpretation of the Islamic law.

Jahiliyya: "The time of ignorance," said to apply to the Arabian society before the revelation of the Qu'ran.

Jihad: Struggle against the lower forces of one's nature or against the enemies of God.

Ka'ba: The Holy House or Shrine of Islam, in the grand mosque at Mecca.

Kufr: Rejection of the reality and being of God, unbelief.

Mahdi: The divinely guided leader who will return to establish justice on earth before the Resurrection.

Masjid: Literally, the place of prostration for Muslim prayers. A larger central *masjid* in a Muslim city is know as a "*jami*" because it is a place of gathering or assembly for the Friday prayer (*jumu'a*).

Mihrab: A "niche" within the *masjid* wall that is closest to Mecca. The *mihrab* serves to orient Muslim worshippers toward Mecca during the prayer (*salat*).

Niyya: Declaration of intention to carry out a religious responsibility, as in *salat*, or prayer, in the right spirit of mind and heart.

Qadi: Judge, one who decides civil and criminal cases according to the *Shari'a*.

Qibla: The direction of prayer facing the *Ka'ba* in Mecca.

Qiyas: Reasoning by analogy. One of the four accepted sources of Islamic Law.

Salam: peace.

Riba: Usury or interest in excess of the legal rate.

Salat: The formal or ritual prayer to be performed five times a day.

Salat Al Fajr: at dawn and before sunrise

Salat Al Dohr: after the sun passes its highest point

Salat Al 'Asr: afternoon

Salat Al Maghreb: sunset

Salat Al 'Isha: before midnight.

Sawm: Fast.

Shahada: Bearing witness that there is no God but Go and that Muhammad is his Prophet.

Shari'a: Sacred law which is derived from revelation (Qur'an) and the example of the Prophet (Hadith) through the interpretation of the *Ulama*.

Shi'a: The identifying name for those who are the part of Ali, as distinguished from the majority Sunni.

Shirk: The sin of associating anything or anyone with God.

Shura: The principle of consultation by which decisions are made in the Islamic community.

Sufi: One who follows one of the schools of mystical thought in Islam.

Sunna: The customary practice of the Prophet Muhammad as reported by his companions, concerning Muhammad's deeds, utterances and unspoken approval.

Sunni: The vast majority of orthodox Muslims who acknowledge the authority of the Qur'ran and the *Sunna as* intepreted by the Ulama, but not the authority of the 'Alid imams.

Tariqa: Way or path under the leadership of a shaykh or pir; a Sufi order or brotherhood.

Tawhid: The essential unity of God, affirmation of God's oneness and consequent human responsibility to live ethically.

'Ulama: The learned religious and legal scholars of Islam.

'Umma: The Community of all those who affirm Islam.

'Umra: The lesser *haj*, or pilgrimage to Mecca performed at any time of the year.

Wudu': Ritual washing before performance of the *salat* or prayer.

Zakat: almsgiving.

Sources

Cesari, Jocelyne. *Etre musulman en France aujourd'hui* (To Be a Muslim in France Today). Paris: Hachette, 1997.

Martin, Richard C. *Islamic Studies, A History of Religious Approach.* Upper Saddle River, New Jersey: Prentice Hall, 1996, 2nd edition.

Smith, Jane. *Islam in America.* New York: Columbia University Press, 1999.

Notes

Introduction

1. See John E. Reilly, ed., *American Public Opinion and U.S Foreign Policy 1995* (Chicago Council on Foreign Relations, 1995), 21. Also *Le Monde,* September 20, 1991, 12, quoted by Samuel Huntington, *The Clash of Civilizations and the Remaking of World Order* (New York: Simon & Schuster, 1996), 215.
2. See Frank J. Buijs and Jan Rath, *Muslims in Europe, The State of Research* (report for the Russel Sage Foundation, New York, 2003).
3. Runymede Trust, *Islamophobia: A Challenge for Us All* (London: Runnymede Trust, 1997).
4. See Bobby Said, *A Fundamental Fear: Eurocentrism and the Emergence of Islamism* (London: Zed Books, 1997).
5. Yvonne Yazbeck Haddad and Adair T. Lummis, *Islamic Values in the United States: A Comparative Study* (New York: Oxford University Press, 1987).
6. See Vincent Geisser islamophobie, *La Nouvelle islamophobie* (Paris: Editions La Découverte, 2003).
7. Oriana Fallaci, *La rage et l'orgueil* (Paris: Plon, 2002).
8. Debate on LCI, October 24, 2003.
9. See chapter 2 for a more extensive discussion of this topic.
10. T. Gerholm and Y. G. Lithman, eds., *The New Islamic Presence in Western Europe* (London: Mansell, 1988).

    Jack Goody, *Islam in Europe* (London, Cambridge: Blackwell, 2004).

    Shireen Hunter, ed., *Islam, Europe's Second Religion: The New Social, Cultural and Political Landscape* (Westport, London: Praeger, 2002).

    Bernard Lewis and Dominique Schnapper, eds., *Muslims in Europe* (London: Pinter, 1994).

    Felice Dassetto, Brigitte Maréchal and Jorgen Nielsen, eds., *Convergences musulmanes, Aspects contemporains de l'islam dans l'Europe élargie* (Louvain la Neuve: Bruylant, 2001).

    Gerd Nonneman, Tim Niblock and B. Szajkowski, eds., *Muslim Communities in the New Europe* (Reading, Berkshire: Ithaca Press, 1996).

    W.A.R. Shadid and P.S. Van Koningsveld, eds., *The Integration of Islam and Hinduism in Western Europe* (Netherlands: Kampen, 1991); *Religious Freedom and the Position of Islam in Western Europe* (Netherlands: Kampen, 1995); *Muslims in the Margin: Political Responses to the Presence of Islam in Western Europe* (Netherlands: Kampen, 1996).

Steven Vertovec and C. Peach, eds. *Islam in Europe: The Politics of Religion and Community* (St. Martin's Press, 1997); Steven Vertovec and Alisdair Rogers, eds, *Muslim European Youth, Reproducing Ethnicity, Religion, Culture* (London: Ashgate, 1998).

11. Iftikar Haider Malik, *Islam and Modernity: Muslims in Europe and in the United States* (London: Pluto Press, 2004).

12. Hofert Alamut and Armando Salvatore (eds.), *Between Europe and Islam* (Brussels: P.I.E. Peter Lang, 2000).

13. These discursive practices can include the practices themselves. Talal Asad, *Genealogies of Religion: Discipline and Reasons of Power in Christianity and Islam* (Baltimore: John Hopkins University, 1993).

14. Appadurai, Arjun, *Modernity at Large: Cultural Dimensions of Globalization* (Minneapolis: University of Minnesota Press, 1996), chs. 2–3, 27–65.

Chapter 1

1. Obtaining precise statistics is difficult, if not impossible, since in most European countries, questions on religion are not included in population censuses. At most, an estimate can be made based on the number of immigrants coming from countries in which Islam is the main religion; however, one must also take into account naturalized Muslims or Muslims with citizen status according to law. For details by country, see the statistical appendix.

2. According to French law, the term "immigrant" includes foreign-born individuals with foreign citizenship as well as foreign-born individuals who have acquired French citizenship. In this way, the law distinguishes immigrants from foreigners, who numbered 3.26 million in 1999. The numbers of both immigrants and foreigners have declined since the 1900 census (3.6 million and 4.16 million, respectively). Immigrants from the Maghreb increased by 6 percent since the 1990 census, three quarters of which represented by immigrants of Moroccan origin. INSEE et Ministère des Affaires Sociales, <http://www.social.gouv. fr.htm/actu/rapleb99.htm>. It should be noted that this estimation is lower than that given by the statistical appendix, reflecting the fact that the appendix also counts second-generation immigrants in its figures. See appendix 1.

3. Since the end of the 1990s, a figure of 5 million Muslims has been in circulation, but this "amplification" has little basis in sociological fact.

4. See <www.statistics.gov.uk/census2001>.

5. Stefano Allievi, *Les convertis à l'islam* (Paris: l'Harmattan, 1998).

6. It is almost impossible to keep track of the number of conversions, since Islamic conversion is generally an individual act that requires no institutional mediation, and only stipulates that there be two Muslim witnesses present. Moreover, in cases where conversion is exclusively a matter of individual conscience, can the conversion be deemed any less valid? See Allievi, *Les convertis à l'islam*, 69.

7. Chaplains for International Students in the Netherlands, *Religion in the Netherlands*, <http://www.geocities.com/Athens/Olympus/8858>. There are more than 700,000 Muslims in the Netherlands, or almost 4 percent of the total population, half of these coming from Turkey and a third from Morocco, with a significant portion also from Surinam. U.S. Department of State, *Annual Report on International Religious Freedom for 1999: The Netherlands*. Released by the

Bureau for Democracy, Human Rights, and Labor, (Washington, D.C., September 9, 1999).

8. The number of Muslims in Spain is estimated at 300,000, or less than 1 percent of the total population, mostly from Morocco.

9. Tom W. Smith, *Estimating The Muslim Population in the United States* (New York: The American Jewish Committee, October 2001). A study conducted by the American Religious Identification Survey, published in 2001, similarly estimated the number of American Muslims at 1.8 million.

10. The figure of 6 or 7 million is based on a number of additional considerations, including statistics on immigration from countries considered Muslim by definition, as well as statistics on the membership of existent Islamic centers. The problem with this reasoning is that many immigrants from Muslim countries are actually Christians, particularly those from the Arab world. In fact, the majority of the Arab-American community is Christian. Moreover, statistics acquired from Islamic centers are highly imprecise, since they count not only members, but all those "associated" with the center. See Isan Bagby, P.M., Perl and B.T. Frohle, *The Mosque in America: A National Portrait* (Washington, D.C.: Council on American Islamic Relations [CAIR], 2001). One other statistical approach is to ask questions about ancestry. This method puts the number of Muslims in the United States at 4 million.

11. R. Felicia Lee, "A Sketch of Arab-Americans: Survey Touches Off Disputes Over Who Should Study Whom." *New York Times*, November 15, 2003.

12. Nick Galifianikis, "U.S. Muslim Population Grows," *Rockland Journal News*, February 10, 1994.

13. Ibid.

14. M.M. Ally, *History of Muslims in Britain 1850–1980* (M.A. Thesis, University of Birmingham, 1981).

15. Jorgen Nielsen, *Towards a European Islam* (London: Macmillan Press, 1992).

16. A. Sinno, *Deutsche Interessen in Palestina 1841–1898* (Berlin: Baalbeek, 1982).

17. Felice Dassetto, Brigitte Maréchal and Jorgen Nielsen, eds., *Convergences musulmanes, Aspects contemporains de l'islam dans l'Europe élargie* (Louvain la Neuve: Bruylant, 2001).

18. See Patrick Weil, *La France et ses immigrés* (Paris: Calmann-Lévy, 1991).

19. See Chantal Saint Blancat and Ottavia Schmidt di Friedberg, "Why are Mosques a problem? Local Politics and Fear of Islam in Northern Italy", in *Mosques conflicts in Western Europe*, (special issue of the *Journal of Ethnic and Migrations Studies*, Sussex, (forthcoming). One must also take into account the number of converts and illegal immigrants, at a combined estimate of about 500,000. See Allievi, *Les convertis à l'islam*. One-third of these Muslims come from Morocco, the rest from various countries including Tunisia, ex-Yugoslavia, Senegal, Albania, Iran, Somalia, Egypt, and Pakistan.

Chapter 2

1. What we profess to know about Islam is to a large extent the product of a vision constructed upon centuries of conflict, political as much as religious. The fluid and often paradoxical reality of Muslims—from their most private behavior to their most public—is frequently obscured by the mass of stereotypes that have built up

over the centuries. These stereotypes emerge out of specific historical events and encounters, and permanently crystallize different, even contradictory, sets of images, such as violence, heresy and debauchery, or sensuality, brutality, and cruelty. Many such stereotypes descend from the orientalist tradition of orientalism. While the most conspicuous forms of orientalism have been profoundly modified by sociology, anthropology, and political science, its more latent forms (the result of these amassed stereotypes) continue to exert an influence on culture. Edward Said is thus correct in asserting that the Orient and Islam exist only as *topoi*, a collection of meanings or a sum of imaginary characteristics. In the orientalist interpretation, which is often supported by actual quotes from religious texts, Islam is always presented as a closed system, a prototype for the traditional closed society. Muslims and Islamic society are thus permanent denied any capacity for change. Such interpretations are, of course, clearly motivated in part by the same ideology that has sought to justify, since the nineteenth century, the attempts to dominate these parts of the world.

2. Edward Said, *Orientalism* (New York: Pantheon Books, 1978).
3. See *Le Monde*, June 3, 2002.
4. See Dassetto, Maréchal and Nielsen, 126.
5. Yunas Samad and John Eade, eds., *Community Perception of Forced Marriages*, (Bradford: Community Liaison Unit, 2002), 18.
6. Community Cohesion, *A Report of the Independent Review Team* (Home Office, December 2001).
7. M. Krishnan, "Anti-Muslim Feelings Plague Bradford," *The Rediff Special* <http://www.rediff.com/news/dec/20brad.htm>.
8. In Portes and Zhou's theory of segmented assimilation, "negative assimilation" is a result of physical proximity to dominant disadvantaged classes. "Classic" or "positive assimilation" consists of adopting middle-class values. Maintaining a solidarity based on the values and culture of the immigrant group helps, in certain cases, to ease the transition into the dominant society. Alejandro Portes and Min Zhou, "The New Second Generation: Segmented Assimilation and its Variants," *The Annals* 530 (November 1993), 74–96
9. See Williams Julius Wilson, *The Truly Disadvantaged, The Inner City, the Underclass, and Public Policy*, (Chicago: The University of Chicago Press, 1987). See also Chapour Haghighat, *L'Amérique urbaine et l'exclusion sociale* (Paris: PUF, 1994), 208.
10. Wendy Murray Zoba, "Islam USA," *Christianity Today*, vol. 44, no. 4, 3 (April 2000), 40–50.
11. Islam was obviously present in the black community before the Nation of Islam, through such movements as the Moorish Science Temple of Noble Drew Ali. See Richard B. Turner, *Islam in the African-American Experience* (Indiana University Press, Indianapolis, 1997), 115 onward.
12. The first change Elijah Muhammed effected was to move the organization's headquarters from Detroit to Chicago. More important, he elevated Fard to almost divine status and himself to the rank of prophet. The movement is for this reason considered heretical in the eyes of both Sunni and Shiite Muslims, who do not recognize the Nation of Islam as a Muslim group. Elijah Muhammed also developed a theory of world history in which truth and primacy belonged to the black race, who were then subjugated by the white or "Caucasian" and deprived of their

central role in the development of the world. He considered himself to be the new messenger of Islam in charge of fighting against the "whitening of history."

13. Elijah Mohammed's most talented disciple was Malcolm Little, later known as Malcolm X, who preached Islam in Philadelphia and New York, and became an major figure among young blacks "rotting" in the ghettos of the American North. He was the first to attempt to use Islam in the political mobilization of African Americans.

14. Warith means "Inheritor of the Faith" in Arabic.

15. Sunni Islam is also represented by other movements, such as Darul Islam of Brooklyn, New York (founded in 1962). Based on the strict observance of the Qu'ran and the Sunna, the group was long regarded as a fundamentalist and exclusively African-American movement. It was only toward the end of the 1970s that immigrant Muslims were accepted into the mosques of this organization.

16. The members of Warith Deen Muhammad's organization are called Bilalians, in reference to the choice of Prophet Muhammad in favor of the Ethiopian Bilal to give the first call to prayer.

17. Followers of the Nation of Islam fast on fixed dates during the month of December.

18. *Chicago Tribune,* September 2, 2003.

19. See Don Terry, "A Leap of Faith," *Chicago Tribune Magazine,* October 20, 2002, 14.

20. Malcolm X, "Black Man History," ed. Imam Benjamin Karim, *The End of White World Supremacy: Four Discourses by Malcolm X* (New York: Merlin House/Seaver Books, 1971).

21. Quoted by Jane Smith, *Islam in America* (New York: Columbia University Press, 1999), 83.

22. Robert Dannin, *Black Pilgrimage to Islam* (New York: Oxford University Press, 2002), 237–260.

23. *Shahada*: The first Pillar of Islam, consisting of testifying that "There is no God but God and Mohammed is his Prophet." This sentence must be recited by the convert to Islam, preferably before two Muslim witnesses.

24. Interview with the author, December 12, 1999.

25. "Antisemitism and Xenophobia Today," ≤http://www.axt.org.uk/antisem/archive1/uk/uk.html≥ (1996).

26. Interview with the author, April 16, 1999.

27. It should be noted that some Muslim groups in Europe have contributed to this critique (see, e.g., the Ramadan controversy, ch. 6). As a corollary, we should note that attacks on European Jews and acts of vandalism against synagogues and Jewish schools have been on the rise in the past three years, especially in France. Although the annual report of the National Consultative Commission on Human Rights, published on April 1, 2004, counted 817 racist attacks, in contrast to 1,313 in 2002 (a decline seen also in instances of threat and intimidation), anti-Semitism remained the primary form of racism according to the report, and largely as a response to the Israeli–Palestinian conflict. Quoted in *Le Monde,* April 1, 2004. For a criticism of anti-Semitic attitudes among certain French-Muslim communities, see also Emmanuel Brenner, *Les Territoires perdus de la République. Antisémitisme, racisme et sexisme en milieu scolaire.* (Paris: Mille et une nuits, 2002).

28. *Le Monde,* June 16, 2004.

29. Institute for Jewish Policy Research, *Antisemitism World Report 1997: Germany.*

30. "Normality," in this case would mean that Haider signed a declaration, entitled "Responsibility for Austria," which declared that the Austrian government would make efforts to combat xenophobia, anti-Semitism, and racism.
31. *Le Monde*, June 13, 2004.
32. In an interview given to *De Volkskrant*, Fortuyn made the following statement on immigration: "I think that sixteen million Dutch people have had enough." He also announced his intention to close the border and reduce the number of immigrants from 40,000 to 10,000 per year.
33. Hanz G. Betz, *Radical Right-Wing Populism in Western Europe*. (New York: St.Martin's Press, 1994), 94.
34. Ibid. 96
35. Cf. EMNID-Spiegel poll, November-December 1991.
36. *The New York Times*, March 20, 2001.
37. Quoted in Peter Schwartz, "The Debate over a 'Defining German Culture': The Christian Democrats March to the Right," *World Socialist Website*, <www.wsws.org./ articles/2000/nov2000/cult-n25.shtml> (November 25, 2000).
38. *Financial Times*, March 8, 2001.
39. *El Pais*, March 12, 2001.
40. *Sedes sapientiae*, no. 75, September 30, 2000.
41. *Libération*, September 28, 2001.
42. *Le Monde*, May 22, 2004.
43. IFOP survey (October 5, 2001) carried out with a sample of 940 non-Muslims and 548 recorded as belonging to a Muslim family. Survey New Reuters/ Zogby poll, September 17, 2001, carried out with a sample of 1,018 people.
44. Beginning with... the Qu'ran. The rise in sales of the Qu'ran has been a surprising sign of how much the public has bought into the essentializing tendencies of popular discourse: as if the keys to understanding contemporary Islamic terrorism, essentially a classic political question, could be found in the sacred texts of Islam.
45. See "Islam Attracts Converts by the Thousands, Drawn Before and After the Attacks," *New York Times*, October 22, 2001.
46. European Monitoring Center on Racism and Xenophobia, *Anti-Islamic Reactions in the EU after the Terrorist Acts against the USA* (Vienna, November 29, 2001).
47. See petition published in *Le Monde*, December 12, 2001.
48. See the September 17 survey carried out by Reuters/Zogby, cited above. After the Oklahoma City bombing in 1995, Americans are also aware that the enemy can come from the very heart of American society, particularly from the Extreme Right.
49. Council on American Islamic Relations, *American Muslims: One Year AFter* (Washington D.C., 2002).
50. Council on American Islamic Relations, *Unpatriotic Acts* (Washington D.C., 2004).
51. The enhanced procedures for receiving foreigners into the country, announced on June 5, 2002, consist of the following: taking photographs and digital fingerprints at passport control, regular surveillance of any foreigner in the country for a stay of less than 30 days, and greater authority for the INS to deport foreigners whose visa has expired. These measures apply to visitors from any country designated a supporter of terrorism by the United States, including Iran, Iraq, Sudan, Libya, and Syria. See *Le Monde*, June 6, 2002.

It should be noted that antiterrorist measures had already been in place since 1996, through a procedure used in proceedings against illegal immigration and known as "secret evidence" (as specified by the Illegal Immigration Reform Law). According to this procedure, the government had the power to create ad hoc tribunals to investigate any illegal immigrant considered a potential threat to the country. In these tribunals, certain key elements in the government's case may be kept secret from defense attorneys for reasons of national security. Muslim immigrants were particularly targeted in this procedure, and many Muslim organizations mobilized against it. Ironically, during his campaign for the presidency, George W. Bush had promised to put an end to the practice.

52. See Reuters, September 8, 2002.

53. According to the Fourth Amendment, "The right of the people to be secure in their persons, houses, papers, and effects, against unreasonable searches and seizures, shall not be violated; and no Warrants shall issue, but upon probable cause."

54. Survey conducted by the website Beliefnet and the Ethics and Public Policy Center, "Evangelical Views of Islam." <www.beliefnet.com/story/124/story_12447.html>

55. M. Ergun and Emir Caner, *Unveiling Islam. An Insider Look at Muslim Life and Beliefs.* (Grand Rapids: Kregel Publications, 2002). See also Richard Cimino, "Evangelical Discourse on Islam after 9/11" (American Sociology of Religion Congress, Atlanta, August 15–17, 2003).

56. Dan Eggen, "Alleged Remarks on Islam Prompt an Ashcroft Reply," *Washington Post,* February 14, 2002.

57. *Los Angeles Times,* October 16, 2003.

58 "U.S. General Violated Rules with 'Satan' Speeches." <http://www.reuters.com/newsArticle.jhtml?type=topNews&storyID=6013543>, August 19, 2004.

59 See Andrea Shalal-Esa, "General who Made Anti-Islam remark tied to Pow case" Reuters, May 11, 2004. <http://www.reuters.com/newsArticle.jhtml?type=topNews&storyID=5109973>. See also: "Anti Islam Gen Under Fire", New York Post, May 12, 2004. <http://www.nypost.com/news/worldnews/20687.htm>.

60. Comment made at the "Islam in America" conference, held at Harvard University, March 8–9, 2003. Comment recorded by the author on March 9, 2003.

61. *Newsday,* <www.newsday.com> (September 2, 2003).

62. Jesse Bradford, "Muslim Immigrants In the Wake of 9/11: A Case Study in Reactive Identity Formation" (HLE-513 Harvard University, September 2003).

63. *Newsday* <www.newsday.com> (September 2, 2003).

Chapter 3

1. Adam Seligman, "Toleration and Religious Tradition," *Society* 36, no. 5 (1999): 47–53.

2. Khaled Abou El Fadl, "Islam and the Theology of Power," *Middle East Report* 22 (Winter 2001), 6.

3. Danièle Hervieu-Leger, "The Transmission and Formation of Socio-Religious Identities in Modernity," *International Sociology* 13, no. 2 (June 1998): 213–228.

4. Yves Lambert and Guy Michelat, eds., *Crépuscule des religions chez les jeunes? Jeunes et Religions en France* (Paris: L'Harmattan, 1992).

5. A recent poll by SOFRES-*Le Nouvel Observateur* shows a definite trend: 49 percent of those surveyed consider Islam to be a private issue, 87percent declare Islam compatible with the French Republic, and 57percent disapprove of the creation of a Muslim party. See *Le Nouvel Observateur*, January 15–21, 1998.
6. They make the profession of their faith (*Shahada*) every day: "There is no God but God (Allah) and Muhammad is his prophet."
7. With the exception of public figures, all names have been changed to respect the anonymity of the speakers.
8. Interview with the author, July 20, 1998.
9. Interview with the author, June 13, 1998.
10. Interview with the author, New York, February 26, 1999.
11. Interview with the author, New York, February 15, 1999.
12. For a description of these movements see part II, chapter 4.
13. Interview with the author, Boston, January 11, 2003.
14. Interview with the author, Los Angeles, March 17, 2000.
15. Interview with the author, New York, May 17, 2000.
16. Interview with the author, Los Angeles, March 17, 2000.
17. Marcia K. Hermansen, "In the Garden of American Sufi Movements: Hybrids and Perennials," in *New Trends and Developments in the World of Islam,* ed. Peter B. Clarke (London: Luzac Oriental Press, 1997), 155–178.
18. *Dhikr*: the technique, widespread in Sufi orders, of reciting God's names to achieve knowedge of God (*marifa*) through contemplation or extasis.
19. Laleh Bakhtiar, *Sufi Women of America, Angels in the Making* (Chicago: The Institute of Traditional Psychoethics and Guidance, 1996), 40.
20. Ibid., 42.
21. Interview on http://spahirnet.information/article_649.html, June 4, 2003.
22. Interview with the author, February 26, 1999.
23. Interview with the author, November 23, 2003.
24. *Toronto Star*, June 11, 2004.
25. This document was ratified on September 19, 1981, by representatives from countries throughout the Muslim world, including Egypt, Pakistan, and Saudi Arabia, on the initiative of the Islamic Council, a private organization, based in London, affiliated with the World Islamic League. The Declaration was first presented to UNESCO in Paris.
26. This is not without certain dangers, given that in many cases the judge does not know Islamic law: Halima Boumidienne cites the example of a judge who did not understand that ordinary or definitive repudiation can lead, in Islamic law, to an abrogation of the wife's rights. "African Muslim Women in France," in *God's Law versus State Law*, ed. Michael King (London: Grey Seal, 1995), 49–61.
27. "Angrezi Shari'a" is an Urdu translation of "British Muslim Law," or Islamic law as redefined by British law. David Pearl and Werner Menski, *Muslim Family Law* (London: Sweet and Maxwell, 1998), 74.
28. Ibid., 7.
29. Marie-Christine Meyzeaud-Garaud, "La femme face à la répudiation musulmane: analyse de la jurisprudence française" ("Women and Muslim Repudiation: An Analysis of French Law"). Presentation at the Addawa Mosque, rue de Tanger, Paris, March 6, 2004.

30. See Rik Torfs, "The Legal Status of Islam in Belgium," in *Islam and European Legal Systems,* ed. Silvio Ferrari and Anthony Bradney (Ashgate: Aldershot, 2000), 73–95.
31. Zaki Badawi is one of the most prominent figures of British Islam. A graduate of Al Azhar University, he immigrated to Great Britain in 1951. In 1986, along with his wife, a convert to Islam, Badawi founded the Muslim College, which provides a two-year university-level program of study in the Qu'ran , Shari'a, and Islamic history.
32. Zaki Badawi, "Muslim Justice in a Secular State," in King, *God's Law Versus State Law,* 73–80.
33. Javier Martinez-Torron, "The Legal Status of Islam in Spain," in Ferrari and Bradney, *Islam and European Legal Systems,* 47–61.
34. Marie-Christine Foblets, "Famille, Droit Familial et tribunaux en Europe," in *Convergences musulmanes, Aspects contemporains de l'islam dans l'Europe élargie,* ed. Felice Dassetto and Brigitte Marechal and Jorgan Nielsen (Louvain la Neuve: Bruylant-Academia, 2001), 77–96. This principle allows for the recognition of marriage on the grounds of the existence of a married lifestyle.
35. The Marriage Act of 1949 recognizes not only municipal buildings but also the religious spaces of the main registered religions—temples, churches, and synagogues—as authorized spaces for the civil marriage ceremony. According to this law, however, the building designated for cultural activities must be distinct and separate from the buildings dedicated to other activities—which is not always the case with mosques and Islamic centres. The 1990 and 1994 amendments to this law (Marriage Registration of Building) repealed this stipulation , thus making it possible for Islamic centers to be recognized as authorized spaces for civil marriage.
36. These so-called common-law marriages had previously existed in medieval England, but were abolished in 1842. Cf. Richard Freeland, "Islamic Personal Law in American Courts," (Islamic Legal Studies Program, Harvard University, Autumn 2000); also, Asifa Quraishi and Najeeba Syeed-Miller, "No Altars: A Survey of Islamic Family Law in the United States" <http://els4.law.emory.edu/ifl/cases/USA.html>.
37. The issue of dowry does not appear to be incompatible with most existing legal systems. The dowry, another element of Islamic marriage, tends to be viewed by Western courts as a form of prenuptial agreement. Islamic rules on inheritance can be an issue in countries whose legal system is influenced by Roman law (as in the case of most Romance-language countries), but is less frequently problematic in countries with legal systems based on common law, such as the United States or Great Britain.
38. The council is made up of theologians and jurists representing the four juridical schools of Sunni Islam. Between the years of 1982 and 2002, the council handled more than 4,500 cases. See <www.islamic-sharia.co.uk/whoitrepresent.html>.
39. This council, headed by Dr. Taha Al Alwani, is made up of theologians and sholars from all the schools of Sunni Islam. Privately run, the Council issues fatwas (legal decisions) on all aspects of Muslim American life, partticularly regarding the adaption of shari'a to secular American law. For a more comprehensive examination of he Council, see chapter 7.
40. Amina Wadud, *Qur'an and Women, Rereading the Sacred Text from a Woman's Perspective* (New York: Oxford University Press, 1999); Azizah Al-Hibri, "Islamic

Law and Muslim Women in America," in *One Nation Under God, Religion and American Culture*, ed. Marjorie Garber and Rebecca L. Walkowitz (New York, London: Routledge, 1999), 128–142.

41. In Islam, a divorced or widowed woman may not remarry until eight months after her separation or her husband's death, respectively. The goal of such a rule is to avoid any uncertainty regarding the paternity of children born to a new marriage. In traditional Muslim law, several conditions are in place to make sure that this time period is respected, including locking up the divorced/widowed woman or carefully restricting her freedom. These conditions are not always followed to the letter in Europe or the United States.

42. In these situations, the division of inheritance according to Islamic law is either abandoned or somehow circumvented.

43. In the United States, circumcision is widely practiced for nonreligious reasons, as it is considered hygienic.

44. In England, female circumcision was banned by special legislation, the 1985 Prohibition of Female Circumcision Act.

45. Quoted in Gerhard Robbers, "The Legal Status of Islam in Germany," Ferrari and Bradney, *Islam and European Legal Systems*, 147–154.

46. In Spain, this right was included in a 1992 agreement between the state and the Islamic Commission. In Great Britain, *halal* meat is made available as a matter of course in schools and prisons. In France, *halal* food packages are made available in the army but not (for the most part) in public schools. Also in the United States public schools do not provide *halal* meat for Muslim students, in this case because of the strict separation of Church and State.

47. Cf. Sebastien Poulter, "Multiculturalism and Human Rights for Muslim Families in English Law," in King, *God's Law Versus State Law*, 83.

Chapter 4

1. Article 8 of the Italian constitution states that "religions are equally free under the law. Non-Catholic religions may seek an agreement with the State." What this indicate is that according to the Italian system, there is a fundamental difference between religions that benefit from such an agreement and those that do not. Other than Catholicism, the only religions who currently claim this agreement are Protestantism and Judaism. Religions without an agreement are governed by a law that dates from the Fascist era, guaranteeing only "the public or private practice of their rites, on the condition that they do not interfere with either moral standards or the public order." An agreement, on the other hand, provides the signatory religious organization with such benefits as the ability to take advantage of State assistance from tax revenues and the control of the nomination of imams. Since its creation in 1990, the UCOII (Union of Islamic Communities and Organizations in Italy), has been in a process of negotiation with the Italian government to sign an agreement (*intesa*) recognizing it as the official representative body for Italian Muslims. (The two other organizations competing for this honor are CoRels and the AMI: see appendix.) At the time of this writing, the *intesa* process appears to be at a standstill. The government of Italy cannot afford to draw up an agreement with an organization whose legitimacy is not accepted by the vast majority of Muslim associations, particularly

since once the agreement is signed, it can be neither abolished nor amended without the agreement of both parties.

2. Muslim Bosnia was a constituent State of the Austro-Hungarian Empire in 1912. This law regulated Islam's status that time.

3. To be eligible to vote in this process, one had tobe at least 18 years old, to be a declared Muslim, and to have lived in Belgium for at least a year. On the day of elections 74,000 Muslims registered to vote; 45,000 voted on mosques or community centers. To be a candidate for the General Assembly, one had to be at least 25 years old, to have lived in Belgium for at least five years, and to speak at least one of the national languages. it was also required to have finished high school. It was forbidden, however, to act on behalf of a political agenda or to possess a diplomatic passport: both stipulations being designed to prevent the influence of foreign governments over the Assembly. To provide for a genuinely representative assembly, quotas were fixed for Muslims of Moroccan, Turkish, and other origins, as well as European converts. For more details see Lionel Panafit. *Quand le Droit écrit l'islam, l'intégration juridique de l'islam en Europe* (Brussels: Bruylant, 1999).

4. <http://fr.groups.yahoo.com/group/suffrage-universel/message/2240>.

5. The number of school-age Muslim children in Spain has been estimated at 50,000, with the majority concentrated in Melilla, Ceuta, Madrid, and Andalusia. In Madrid, more than 5,000 children were listed as being eligible for Islamic instruction. The most delicate issue has been the more than 500 new professors this instruction necessitated (*El Pais*, October 4, 1999). The first classes were scheduled to begin in Melilla for the 2001–2002 school year (*Spanish Newswire Services*, June 7, 2001). The selection of teachers had already begun under the auspices of the Islamic Commission, in cooperation with the regional headquarters of the Minister of Education. The events of September 11, however, delayed the start of the program.

6. According to the existing legislation—similar to that of Austria—religious groups in Germany can have one of three kinds of legal status:

(1) The most basic kind of status is the common law provision for the freedom to assemble for the purpose of religious activity. A 1964 law extends provisions for freedom of assembly to foreigners—with a few exceptions, such as that of assembling for the purpose of endangering domestic security. It is as a result of this law that immigrant-based organizations have increased tenfold in the past 20 years.

(2) The second degree of recognition is the status of religious community, which groups "persons of the same denomination for the carrying-out of duties determined by a common faith" under the status of an associative body. This law grants the right to both constitutional protection of the free practice of religion and religious education in schools. Nothing in this law states that individuals must be of a particular nationality to form such a community; however, Muslims have found themselves denied this status on the grounds that religious activities are already part of nationality-based organizations such as the Dyanet, an official body connected with the Turkish State.

(3) The third kind of status, that of public organization, grants religious groups freedom in the conducting of religious activities; financial privileges such as full independence in matters of employment; recognition of the community's religious oath in a court of law; freedom to organize councils and chains of

command; the automatic membership of the religion's followers with the community; fiscal protection and exemption from real-estate taxes on property designated as belonging to the public domain; and the right to receive a percentage of the national revenue based on tax-payers' declarations of membership. See Renaud Detalle, "L'islam en Allemegne," *L'islam et les musulmans dans le monde,* ed. Mohammed Arkoun, Rémy Leveau et Bassem EI Jisr (Beiruit: Centre Culturel Hariri, 1993), 291–306, 297.

7. Only in the states of Brandenburg and Bremen, where religious education is not required and where the churches provide their own teachers and curricula without government intervention.

8. Valérie Amiraux, "Expérience de l'altérité religieuse en Allemagne: Islam et Espace public," *Cahiers d'Etudes sur la Méditerranée orientale et le monde turco-iranien,* no.33, (January–June2002): 128–146; and Irka-Christin Mohr, "Islamic Instruction in Germany and Austria, a comparison of Principles Derived from Religious Thought," *Cahiers d'Etudes sur la Méditerranée orientale et le monde turco-iranien,* no. 33, (January–June 2002): 149–172.

9. "Founded in 1971 in Braunschweig by Neemettin Erbakan under the name Turkish German Union, it adopted its current name in 1994" (Pascal Beucker, "Milli Görüs, l'islamisme loin du Bosphore," *Courrier International,* no. 586, (January 24, 2002).

10. Reports from the Bureau of Protection of the Constitution noted that members of the Federation professed, in all knowledge, Islamic extremist aims. "Islamic Teachings to be Allowed in German Schools," *IPS,* February 29, 2000.

11. <http://www.arabia.com/Life/article/english/html>.

12. Sonia Phainikar, "When Faith is More Important than School," *Deutsche Welle,* April 23, 2004, <http://www.dw-world.de/dwelle/cda/detail>.

13. Ibid.

14. "Learning about Mohammed and the Koran in Germany," *Deutsche Welle,* August 19, 2003, <http://www.dw-world.de/dwelle/cda/detail>.

15. It should be recalled that France had retained control of Algeria for approximately 130 years.

16. The text of the law reads as follows: "[C]ompromising, in the application of the principlr of secularism, the wearing of symbols or clothing in public elementary, middle, and high schools which display a religious affiliation." See <http://www.legifrance.gouv.fr/WAspad/UnTexteDeJorf?numjo=MENX0400001L>.

17. At the time of this writing, Islam still has no official institutional status in Denmark, although there are certain Islamic associations that receive funding from the state. Another particularity of Denmark is the preponderance of *halal* slaughterhouses, administered by the World Islamic League, which supply the rest of Europe.

18. Due to the fact that Greece was a part of the Ottoman Empire until the mid-nineteenth century, Islam has a long-standing presence in the country. The "historical" Turkish Muslims, mostly concentrated in the region of Thrace, enjoy a somewhat different status from the Muslim immigrants from Albania, Bangaladesh, Pakistan, Iran, and other countries who have settled in Greece during the past two decades. The primary issue is whether the institutions representing Greece's "historical" Muslims, such as the Grand Mufti, can also be extended to immigrant Muslim

communities. The Mufti is responsible for the application of civil Islamic law, which controls issues of family life(marriage, divorce, circumcision, etc.) and religion (mosque) for Thracian Muslims. See Thanos P. Dokos and Dimitri Antoniou "Islam in Greece." in *Islam, Europe's Second Religion: The New Social, Cultural and Political landscape*, ed. Shireen T. Hunter (Westport: Praeger et Center for Strategic and International Studies, 2002), 175–189. See also Konstantinos Tsitselikis, "Personal Status of Greece's Muslims: A Legal Anachronism or an Example of Applied Multiculturalism?" Presentation at the colloquium, "The Legal Treatment of Islamic Minorities in Europe and in the United States," Turin, 19–21 June 2003.

19. <www.familiesonline.co.uk/article/static/163>.
20. Some of the arguments cited include the idea that state-aided schools must provide for the development of critical and analytical thinking (which Islamic schools, according to this argument, fail to do); and the idea that just because other religions can claim this privilege does not mean that the Muslim minority is equally entitled—particularly as State policy has leaned toward the phasing out of such schools.
21. *The Guardian*, October 7, 2000.
22. <www.familiesonline.co.uk/article/static/163>.
23. *The Guardian*, February 10, 2001.
24. "Islamic School Ruled Out," *Oxfordshire*, May 22, 2004.
25. "New scrutiny for Islamic Schools Plan," *Lancashire News*, December 12, 2001. Also London Schools, www.familiesonline.co.uk/article/static/163.
26. Tariq Modood, ed., *Church, State and Religious Minorities* (London: Policy Studies Institute, 1996).
27. That is, each community—whether Protestant, Catholic, or other denominations—had representation at all levels of public administration. This representation was eventually also extended to non-theistic groups (such as Humanists and Freethinkers) and political parties. After the 1960s, this system began to break down, with a number of groups and organizations asserting their independence from institutionalized and publicly recognized communities. See Jan Rath, R. Penninx, K. Groenendijk, and A. Meyer (eds.), *Western Europe and Its Islam: The Social Reaction to the Institutionalization of a "New" Religion in the Netherlands, Belgium and the United Kingdom.* (Leiden, Boston, Tokyo: Brill, 2001).
28. Woelmet Bœnder, "Teaching Dutch Ways to Foreign Imams, Between Government Policy and Muslim Initiative." Presentation at the conference, "European Muslims and the Secular State," Paris, La Sorbonne, June 30–July 1, 2003. See <http://www.euroislam-info>.
29. See Rath et al., eds., *Western Europe and Its Islam*.
30. The government granted their request, at the same time granting the Islamic association concerned, World Islamic Mission, authorization to conduct their call to prayer. See *BBC News*, March 30, 2002.
31. Note that the term "laïcité" implies more than the legal separation of Church and State; it is also a philosophy of public life in general and a fundamental principle of French culture.
32. The highest court of France as well as a consultative body for proposed legislation. [Trans.].
33. The Fauroux report on Islam in France, submitted to the Ministery of the interior on December 14, 2000, largely agreed with the recommendations of

the Conseil d'État. Their conclusion led to the resignation of certain members of the Commission who held a stricter conception of secularism.

34. Mathias Malhmann, "Religious Tolerance, Pluralist Society and the Neutrality of the State: The Federal Constitutional Court's Decision in the Headscarf Case." *German Law Journal*, vol. 4, no. 11, (2003): 999–1107, 1103.

35. U.S. Department of State, *Germany Country Report on Human Rights Practices*, 1998. Mathias Malhmann, "Religious Tolerance, Pluralist Society and the Neutrality of the State: The Federal Constitutional Court's Decision in the Headscarf Case," *German Law Journal*, vol. 4, no. 11 (2003): 999–1107, 1103.

36. Not to mention the fact that many of the first American colonists were escaping persecution by State religions in Europe. It should also be noted that a large percentage of the writers of the U.S. Constitution were professed Freemasons.

37. Settlers later also included English Catholics, especially in Maryland.

38. David Martin, *A General Theory of Secularization* (Oxford: Basil Blackwell, 1978).

39. In 2003, the organization changed its name to the American Muslim Society (AMS) (see appendix).

40. Interview with the author, May 14, 2000.

41. Islamist party founded it 1941 by Mawdudi. It controled Pakistan during the period of General Zia's rule in 1977.

42. Interview with the author, February 12, 2004.

43. "Consulate backs down on Passport Photo," *Chicago Tribune*, December 4, 2000.

44. The reasons behind this support are primarily tied to the American position on the Israeli-Palestinian conflict. Ironically, they are also tied to the 1996 anti-terrorist law and the "secret evidence" procedure, which, as a candidate for the presidency, Bush had initially promised to abolish.

45. See Abdus Sattar Ghazali, "There may not be a Muslim bloc vote this time but," *American Muslim Perspective*, ≤http://www.amperspective.com/html/there may not be.html≥, August 12, 2004. And also: "Poll: Muslims voters favors Kerry, Nader", ≤http://www.cair-net.org≥, June 29, 2004.

46. For a description of thisc sect, see chapter 3.

47. For details on this Sufi order see chapter 3.

48. Moqtedar Khan (1998) quoted in Karen Leonard, *Muslims in the United States* (New York: Russel Sage Foundation, 2003), 23. A typical member of the new generation of Muslim activists, Muqtedar Khan is professor of International Relations at Adrian College in the Washington D.C. area, as well as the creator of the website www.ijtihad.org. He is also president of American Muslim Social Scientists and a member of several Muslim organizations, including the Center for the Study of Islam and Democracy.

49. See Daniel Pipes, "What Bush got right- and wrong," *Jerusalem Post*, September 26, 2001,
    • "We're going to conquer America:, New York Post, November 12, 2001.
    Paula R. Kaufman, "Pipes helps U.S. identifies the Enemy," *Insight on the News*, April 15, 2002.

50. Murray Dubin, "Islam expert suddenly in the spotlight," *Philadelphia Inquirer*, November 29, 2001.

51. Interview in the *San Jose Mercury News* (September 16), quoted in Leonard, *Muslims in the United States*, 25.

Chapter 5

1. Anthony Giddens, *Modernity and Self-Identity: Self and Society in the Late Modern Age* (Cambridge: Polity Press), 64.
2. Ulrich Beck, *What is Globalization?* (Cambridge: Polity Press, 2000), 105.
3. On the concept of the "imagined community" as it applies to nationalism, see Benedict Anderson's classic work, *Imagined Communities. Reflections on the Origins and Spread of Nationalism* (New York: Verso, 1983).
4. Arjun Appadurai, *Modernity at Large: Cultural Dimensions of Globalization* (Minneapolis: University of Minnesota Press, 1996).
5. Barrie Axford, *The Global System: Economics, Politics and Culture* (Cambridge: Polity Press, 1995). Also Timothy W. Luke, "New World Order or Neo World Orders: Power, Politics and Ideologies in Informationalizing Glocalities," in *Global Modernities* Michael ed. Featherstone et al. (London: Sage, 1995), 91–107.
6. Susanne Hoeber Rudolph and James P. Piscatori, eds., *Transnational Religion and Fading States* (Boulder: Westview Press, 1997). See also Dale F. Eickelman et James Pescatori, *Muslim Politics* (Princeton: Princeton University Press, 1996).
7. For a description of these movements, see below.
8. See S. Abdul Hassan Ali Nadwi, *Hazrat Maulana Muhammad Ilyas Aur Un Ki Dini Dawa't* (Lucknow: Tanwir, 1964).
9. The six principles of Tabligh are: (1) *Kalima* (attestation of faith i.e there is no deity but God, Mohamed is the Apostle of God, (2) *Namaz* (Prayer), (3) *Ilm* and *Dhikr* (Knowledge and remembrance of God), (4) *Ikram-e-Muslim* (Respect for Muslims), (5) *Iklas-e-Niyat* (purity of intention and sincerity), (6) *Tafri-e-waqt* (sparing time for Tablighi tour, self-reformation, and proselytizing).

    About the missionary work itself: (1) *dawah* (missionary work) is not just for Islamic scholars or specialists, but for all Muslims; (2) the Muslim must seek contact with others; (3) missionary work and preaching is conducted by itinerant and self-funded groups; (4) these groups must be made up of Muslims from all class backgrounds; (5) the most important goal of these groups is to deepen the faith of those who are already Muslims; and (6) unity is the most important virtue and has priority over any theological and political controversies. See Jan Ali, , "Islamic Revivalism: The Case of Tablighi Jamaat," *Journal of Muslim Minority Affairs* 23, no.1 (April 2003): 173–181.
10. Zygmunt Bauman, *Globalization: The Human Consequences* (Cambridge: Polity Press, 1998), Ch. 1, 6–26; Ch. 4, 77–102.
11. See e.g., the position taken by Mohamed Abduh, Grand Mufti of Egypt, who toward the end of the nineteenth century came out against polygamy and for equality between the husband and the wife in divorce proceedings.
12. Conservative jurist of the Hanbalite school during the Middle Ages (1263–1368). His ideas are considered the inspiration for Wahhabi doctrine.
13. See <www.saudinf.com>.
14. *New York Times*, October 20, 2001.
15. Cloth covering the face according to Wahhabi law. In the Tabligh movement, women don't cover their face.
16. Sheikh Abdul Azeez Ibn Baaz, born in 1909 in Riyadh, began his religious education in the family of Ibn Abdul Wahab, the founder of the Saudi dynasty. He held

numerous posts at the university and within the kingdom's religious hierarchy, and was Grand Mufti of the Saudi kingdom from 1992 until his death in 1999.

17. Fatwa delivered in 1997. For the complete text of this fatwa in English, see http://www.allaahuakbar.net/tableegi_jamat/.

18. French-language site: <http://assabyle.com/index.php?id=510>.

19. <www.allaahuakbar.net/womens/choice_between_burqa_and_bikini.htm>.

20. <www.assabyle.com>.

21. Khaled M.Abou El Fadl, *Conference of the Books, The Search for Beauty in Islam* (New York: University Press of America, 2002), 125. For more details on Abou Fadl's work, see chapter 8.

22. Mikhail Bakhtin, *The Dialogic Imagination: Four Essays* (Austin: University Press of Texas, 1981).

23. Ibid., 15.

24. Ibn Baaz, <www.fatwa-online.com/fataawa/innovation/celebrations/cel003/9991018_11.htm>.

25. Qu'ran 4 : 34.

26. <www.islamqa.com>.

27. A dissonance is thus created between the theoretical vision of the ideal woman and the reality of women within Tabligh. In other words, one consequence of women's participation in Tabligh is to modernize, in a certain fashion, the condition of women and to make women more autonomous—in spite of the extremely conservative discourse on the role of the Muslim woman which dominates Tabligh. See Yoginder Sikand, "Women and the Tablighi Jama'at," *Islam and Christian-Muslim Relations* 10, no. 1 (1999): 41–52.

28. Khaled Abou El Fadl, *And God Knows The Soldiers: The Authoritative and Authoritarian in Islamic Discourses* (Lanham: University Press of America, 2001). Here again, some differences need to be introduced between Tablighi and salafi. It is possible to find some Tablighi, individuals or groups involved in civic actions or interfaith dialogue. For example, a member of this movement is member of the CFCM (Conseil Francais du Culte Musulman) described in chapter 4. During our investigations we also met a few Tablighi, men and women involved in civic or antiracist organizations.

29. Marc Gaboriau, "Transnational Islamic Movements: Tablighi Jamaat in Politics," *ISIM Newsletter* (July 1999).

30. Khaled Abou El Fadl, "Islam and the Theology of Power," *Middle East Report* 221 (Winter 2001).

31. *Le Monde*, September 25, 2001.

32. It should however be noted that many ideologues of national liberation movements in the first half of the century—Bourguiba, Gandhi—also began their struggles in the capitals of the western world.

33. See *Libération*, December 17, 2001.

34. Pnina Werbner and Tariq Modood, *Debating Cultural Hybridity : Multicultural Identities and the Politics of Anti-Racism* (London: Zed Books, 1997). Also Ulf Hannerz, *Cultural Complexity: Studies in the Social Organization of Meaning* (New York: Columbia University Press, 1992).

35. Farhad Khosrokhavar, *Les Nouveaux martyrs D'Allah* (Paris: Flammarion, 2002).

36. André Glucksmann, *Dostoïevski à Manhattan* (Paris: Laffont, 2002). See also Jessica Stern, *Terror in the Name of God, Why Religious Militants Kill* (New York: Ecco, 2003).

37. See André Haynal, Miklos Monar, and Gérard de Puymègue, eds., *Fanaticism, A Historical and Psychoanlytical Study* (New York: Schocken Books, 1983).
38. See Malek Chebel, *Le sujet en Islam* (Paris: Seuil, 2002), 149–150.
39. *Le Nouvel Observateur*, no.1928, October 18, 2001.
40. *Christian Science Monitor*, January 13, 1999
41. See Yotam Felder, "Profils Islamiques radicaux: Londres—Abou Hamza Al Masri," *The Middle East Media & Research Institute*, October 16, 2001. <http://www.desinfos.com/memri/memri_profilsislamiques.html>.
42. *Le Figaro*, April 7, 2003.
43. This radical group was founded in 1953 in Jordanian-controlled Jerusalem by the *qadi* (judge in Islamic law) Taqi al-Din al-Nabhani. The party advocates the creation, by violence if necessary, of an Islamic state throughout the entire Muslim world. It claims members in the Occupied Territories, Lebanon, Syria, Saudi Arabia, and Pakistan, as well as in North Africa, Turkey, Malaysia, and Indonesia. There are also members active in the United States and Europe, particularly in Germany, Austria, and Great Britain. See Suha Taji Farouki, *A Fundamental Quest: Hizb al Tahrir and the Search for the Islamic Caliphate* (London, Grey Seal, 1996).
44. The actual name of the organization is the Islamic Front for Holy War against Jews and Crusaders. See Felder, "Radical Islamist Profiles: Sheik Omar Bakri Mohammad, London," *The Middle East Media & Research Institute*, October 24, 2001.
45. *Birgham Sunday Mercury*, December 12, 2000, quoted in Felder.
46. "Anti-Semitism Worldwide," The Stephen Roth Institute for the Study of Contemporary Antisemitism and Racism, Tel Aviv University, 1997. <www.tau.ac.il/Anti-Semitism/asw97-8/united-kingdom.html>.
47. <www.almuhajirun.com/leaflets/Html/disease/7"%20Sins.htm>.
48. <www.almuhajirun.com/leaflets/Html/Disease/Child%20n%20safe.htm>.
49. <www.almuhajirun.com/leaflets/Html/Disease/Interfaith.htm>.
50. <www.almuhajiroun.com/fatwas/16-09°2001b.php>.

Chapter 6

1. United Nations Development Project (2001), quoted in Gary Bunt, *Islam in the Digital Age, Ejihad, Onlinefatwas and CyberIslamic Environment* (London: Pluto Press, 2003), 9.
2. These terms are taken from Patrick Maxwell, "Virtual Religion in Context," *Religion*, 32, no. 4 (October 2002): 343–355.
3. See especially Gary Bunt, *Virtually Islamic, Computer Mediated Communication and CyberIslamic Environment* (Cardiff: University of Wales Press, 2000).
4. Anastasia Karaflogka, "Religion Discourse and Cyberspace," *Religion*, 32, no. 4 (2002): 279–291.
5. <http://www.stehly.chez.tiscali.fr>.
6. <www.albalagh.net>.
7. See the following works: Jon Anderson, *Arabizing the Internet* (Emirates Occasional Papers, 30, 1998); Jon W. Anderson and Dale F. Eickelmann, eds., *New Media in the Muslim World : The Emerging Public Sphere* (Bloomington: Indiana University Press, 1999); Bunt, *Virtually Islamic*.
8. <http://msanews.mynet.net/MSANEWS.htm>.

9. The site also reprinted an article that first appeared in the October 1, 2001 issue of *Outlook India Magazine*, "Jews Attack the WTC," by Hamid Gul. See http://www.outlookindia.com/full.asp?fname=Cover+Story&fodname=20011001&sid=3.

10. Bunt, *Virtually Islamic*, 51.

11. One message, dated December 9 and said to be written from Kandahar, was an appeal to young Muslims from Osama bin Laden—which, *Newsweek* notes, encouraged the suspicions of American authorities that the site was a front for the instigators of the September 11 attacks. A farewell message, dated November 20, 2002, exhorts "Muslims the world over to give Talibans the maximum possible financial, physical, medical, public relations or moral support." See http://fr.news.yahoo.com/011209/1/2by1y.html.

12. <http://www.isna.net\fiqhaqa>.

13. Muzammil Siddiqui writing on the ISNA website, <www.isna.com>

14. <www.isna.com>.

15. <www. Islam-Online.net/livefatwa/English>.

16. <http://www.islamicity.com/mosque/quran/4.htm>.

17. <www.freeminds.org/women/scarf.htm>.

18. See Richard Falk, *Religion and Human Global Governance* (New York: Palgrave, 2001).

19. See e.g., the English- and Arabic-language website www.muhaddith.org, which offers such services. For other examples, see Bunt, *Virtually Islamic*, 104–131.

20. Such resistance to the appropriation of live ritual practice by the Internet is common to most religions. See Sarah Orsfall, "How Religious Organizations use the Internet: A Preliminary Inquiry," in *Religion on the Internet: Research, Prospects and Promises*, ed. Jeffrey K. Hadden and Douglas E. Cowan (New York: Elsevier, 2000), 153–182.

21. One reason for this mentioned by Gary Bunt is the question of the legitimacy of ritual acts performed via the Internet. For example, if the recitation of prayer is interrupted due to technical malfunction, is the prayer thereby invalidated? Bunt, *Virtually Islamic*, 26.

22. See e.g., the website of the Hazrat Inayat Khan organization: <www.universal-sufism.com>.

23. The founder of this movement is Pir Nureddin Al-Jerrahi (1678–1721), of Istanbul. Muzzafer Ozak, born in 1916, is the nineteenth sheikh.

24. <www.jerrahi.org>.

25. For a definition of this "Perennial Islam," see chapter 2.

26. <www.ashkijerrahi.com>.

27. See e.g., *Radio Al Islam, The Quran, audioKoran.com, Islamcity, Muslim Students Association of Oregon, Qur'an and Hadith Index, The Holy Quran with its Dari and Pashto Translations, Al Islam*, etc.

28. See John B. Thompson, *The Media and Modernity: A Social Theory of Media* (Stanford : Stanford University Press, 1995).

29. See Gregory Starrett, "Muslim Identities and the Great Chain of Buying," in *New Media in the Muslim World: The Emerging Public Sphere*, ed. Dale F. Eickelman and Jon W. Anderson (Bloomington, Indiana University Press, 1999), 577–579.

30. For further details on these and other public intellectuals of Islam, see chapter 9.

31. See <http://www.islam-qa-com/words/how_emily_became_muslim.shtml>.

32. http://www.saphirnet,info/article_839.html.
33. Ahmadiyya was founded in 1889 by Hadharat Mirza Ghulam Ahmad (1835–1908) in the Punjabi village of Qadian. Ahmad claimed to be the *Mahdi*, or Messiah, the reincarnation of the Prophet Mohamed who would come at the end of time. This claim has resulted in Ahmaddiyya's demotion to the status of a sect in the eyes of Sunni and Shiite Muslims (see www.ahmadiyya.com). The movement has managed nonetheless to attract a large number of converts, particularly within the African American community prior to the creation of the Nation of Islam. Yvonne Yazbeck Haddad and Jane Idleman Smith. "The Ahmadiyya Community of North America," in *Mission to America: Five Islamic Sectarian Communities in North America*, ed. Y. Haddad and J. Smith, (Gainesville: University Press of Florida, 1993), 49–78.
34. Gay Egypt <http://www.gayegypt.com>. Quoted in Gary Bunt, "Islam Interactive: Mediterranean Islamic Expression on the World Wide Web," in *Islam and the Current Islamic Reformation*, ed. Barbara Allen Robertson (London: Frank Cass, 2003), 164–186.
35. Bunt, "Islam Interactive," 174.
36. There are, however, many who insist on the possibility that the politicizing of Islam in the context of cultural fragmentation and pluralization will result in a trend toward modernization and democratization. See François Burgat, *L'islamisme en face* (Paris: La Découverte, 1995) . See also John L. Esposito and John O. Voll, *Islam and Democracy* (Oxford: Oxford University Press, 1996); Dale F. Eickelman and James Pescatori, *Muslim Politics* (Princeton: Princeton University Press, 1996).
37. Bryan S. Turner, *Islam, Postmodernism and Globalization* (London: Routledge, 1994).

Chapter 7

1. See Dale F. Eickelman and Jon W. Anderson, *New Media in the Muslim World, the Emerging Public Sphere* (Bloomington: Indiana University Press, 1999). See also Brinkley Messick, *The Caligraphic State: Textual Domination and History in a Muslim Society* (Berkeley and Los Angeles: University of California Press, 1993), 135–151.
2. Mohammed Shahrour, *Dirassat Islamiya Mu'açira Fi ad-Dawla wa al-Mujiama'* (Contemporary Islamic Studies on Government and Society). Damascus: Al-Ahali, 1994. An engineer by training, his Kantian interpretation of the Qu'ran has sold millions of copies in Syria, not to mention the pirated copies circulating throughout the Arab world. See Dale F. Eickelman, "Islamic Liberalism Strikes Back,'" *Middle East Studies Association Bulletin*, 27, 2 (December 1993): 163–168.
3. According to a survey conducted in 2000 by the Ministry of the Interior, almost 90% of all imams in France are foreign-born, of which 40% are Moroccan, 24% Algerian, 15% Turkish, 6% Tunisian, and 6% from sub-Saharan Africa and countries in the Middle East. Being of foreign origin, it should be noted, does not necessarily mean that the imam is affiliated with institutions within the country of origin, although there is no precise data on these kinds of affiliations. Amara Bamba, "La formation des imams, le nouveau défi de l'islam en France," June 12, 2003. <http://www.saphirnet.info/ article_646.html>.

4. Again, no significant data is available on this subject.
5. Interview with the author, November 24, 1999.
6. This council includes more than 90 professors and scholars living in Canada and the United States.
7. Interview with the author, February 2, 2000.
8. There are, of course, exceptions to this rule, such as the aid given by the government of the Netherlands for the construction of mosques during the 1980s (see Chapter 4).
9. Fegang Yang and Helen Rose Ebaugh, "Transformations in New Immigrant Religions and their Global Implications," *American Sociological Review*, 66 (April 2001): 269–288.
10. Interview with the author, October 20, 1999.
11. It should be mentioned that this resistance is found regardless of the nature of the project in question. In every case, the members of the Islamic community have proven amenable regarding details such as the muezzin or the minaret.
12. Khaled Kelkal, a young French-Maghrebi man who was probably involved in these attacks, was shot and killed by the police on September 29, 1995, outside Lyon.
13. Brigitte Maréchal et al., eds., *Muslims in the Enlarged Europe*, 80. According to certain sources, the number Muslim organizations in Great Britain is as large as 1500. See for examlple www.muslimdirectory.co.uk, or the *Daily Times* of August 12, 2003, "Our Mosques Abroad and Our Image." <http://www.dailytimes.com.pk/default.asp?page-story_12-8-2003_pg3_1>.
14. Sean McLoughlin, "Recognising Muslims: Religion, Ethnicity and Identity Politics in Britain," in *Musulmans d'Europe*, ed. Jocelyne Cesari, Cemoti, 2002, no. 33, 43–57.
15. Chantal Saint-Blancat et Ottavia Schmidt di Friedberg, "Moblilizations laïques versus mobilizations religieuses en Italie,"in *Musulmans d'Europe*, Jocelyne Cesari, ed. Cemoti, 2002, no. 33, 91–106.
16. See Xavier Ternisien, "La formation des imams, le nouveau défi de l'islam français." *Le Monde*, July 1, 2003.
17. A highly publicized round-up of Islamic militants in France was ordered by Minister of the Interior Charles Pasqua, following the August 3, 1994 assassination in Algiers, of five French government workers (including three policemen), for which the GIA claimed responsibility.
18. Moussa Khedimellah, "Opposition or Incompatibility between Local and National French Muslim Leaders: The Case of Paris." Presentation at the NOCRIME (Network of Comparative Research on Islam and Muslims in Europe) conference, "Islam, Citizenship and European Integration,'" Paris, Université la Sorbonne, June 23–24, 2002. See http://www.crime.org.
19. See chapter 4 for a description of this Federation.
20. Gerdien Jonker, "The Mevlana Mosque in Kreutzberg-Berlin, An Unsolved Conflict," *Journal of Ethnic and Migration Studies* (forthcoming).
21. Quoted in Dominique Casciani, *Muslims in the UK: Pride and Fear*, BBC news, September 10, 2002.
22. See Mary Lahaj, "The Islamic Center of New England", in Yvonne Yazbeck Haddad and Jane Idleman Smith (eds), Muslim Communities in North America, (New York: State University, 1994), pp. 293–315.

23. According to this report, most imams in France are foreign-born, primarily from Turkey or North Africa, and do not have a good command of the French language.
24. Ihsan Bagby, Paul M. Perl and Bryan T. Froehle, *The Mosque in America: A National Portrait* (Washington D.C.: Council on American-Islamic Relations, 2001).
25. Interview with the author, October 20, 1999.
26. Interviews with the author, April 5 and 12 April, 2000.
27. Ibid.
28. CAIR, "American Muslims One Year After 9/11" (Washington D.C., 2002).
29. *Boston Herald*, October 28–29, 2003.
30. According to Baghby et al., *The Mosque in America: A National Portrait*.
31. See Jonker, "The Mevlana Mosque in Kreutzberg-Berlin, An Unsolved Conflict."

Chapter 8

1. For more on this shift in thinking and action, see Daniel Brown, *Rethinking Tradition in Modern Islamic Thought* (Cambridge: Cambridge University Press, 1996); John Esposito, *Unholy War*. (New York: Oxford University Press, 2002); Giles Kepel, *Jihad: The Trail of Political Islam* (Cambridge: Harvard University Press, 2002); Dilip Hiro, *War Without End: The Rise of Islamist Terrorism and Global Response*. (London: Routledge, 2002).
2. In Egypt, the Brothers began as an activist group, and social action has remained its principal focus despite the criticism of concurrent, more radical groups of the "jihadist" or "Islamic Liberation Party" type.
3. *Reading the Muslim Mind* (Plainfield: American Trust Publication, 1995).
4. The Islamic center is associated with the New Horizons elementary school, which in its curriculum to provide a balance of Islamic and secular education.
5. Dr. Hassen Hathout is one of the founding members of MPAC and a member of nearly every Islamic policy and lobbying organization in the country. (See chapter 3.)
6. This is also the position taken by Sheikh Qaradawi, who has authorized the eating of meat slaughtered by Christians. Youssouf Qardawi, *Le Licite et l'Illicite en islam* (Paris: Al-Qalam, 1992).
7. <www.lailatalqadr.com>.
8. Al Qaradawi, *Islamic Awakening, Between Rejection and Extremism* (London: Zain International, 2nd English edition, 1991).
9. See Jocelyne Cesari, *Musulmans et Républicains: Les jeunes, l'islam et la France* (Bruxelles: Complexe, 1998), 142.
10. The FIOE, created in 1989, brings together twenty-nine national associations from as many European nations. Its headquarters are located in Markfield, Great Britain.
11. Conseil Européen des fatwas et de la recherche, *Recueil de Fatwas*, no.1 (Lyon: Tawhid, 2002), 186.
12. See Alexandre Caiero, "The European Council for Fatwa and Research," *Fourth Mediterranean Social and Political Research Meeting*, European University Institute, Florence, March 19–23, 2003, 28.

13. Sheikh Hanooti was born in Palestine in 1937. A graduate of Al Azhar, he has directed a number of Islamic centers in the United States, and is currently serves as a member of the Fiqh Council of North America.
14. The organization of Warith Deen Mohammed.
15. African Americans who convert to Islam describe it as a "reversion," in that they return to an original Islam that had been taken away from them by Christian whites.
16. <www.masnet.org/askimam_runsess.aspd=8>.
17. A regular contributor to the *Islamic Review of Social Sciences* and the editor of the six-volume *Razis Al Mahsul fi'ilm Usul Al Fiqh*, he has also written numerous articles and publications in both English and Arabic. His titles include: *Outlines of a Cultural Strategy*, IIIT, Occasional Papers Series 1, Herndon, Virginia, 1989; *Crisis in Fiqh and the Methodology of Ijtihad*, IIIT, Occasional Papers Series, Herndon, Virginia, 1993; *The Islamization of Knowledge: Yesterday and Today*, IIIT, Occasional Papers, Herndon, Virginia, 1995; and *Missing Dimensions in Contemporary Islamic Movements*, IIIT, Occasional Papers Series 1, Herndon, Virginia, 1996.
18. The fatwa elicited a good deal of discussion among Muslim decision-makers, not only in the United States but also in the Muslim world. According to an October 30, 2001 editorial in the newspaper *Al-Sharq Al Awsat*, certain religious authorities in the Muslim world that had first given their sanction to the fatwa later rescinded it. See also "US Army Chaplain Questions Duty, Captain Gets Mixed Signals from Foreign Islamic leaders." <http://www.worldnetdaily.com/news/article.asp?ARTICLE_ID=25230>.
19. Text given to the author in 2003 by Dilwar Hussein, director of research at the Islamic Foundation.
20. The vice president of the IIIT, Dr. Jamal Barzingi, was in 2004 under investigation by the FBI for his connections to certain individuals suspected of supporting terrorism and for having received funds from Saudi Arabia. A typical figure within the movement, Dr. Barzinji was born in Syria in 1962. He studied to be a chemical engineer, eventually coming to the United States to write a dissertation at the University of Louisiana.
21. Ziaddin Sardar, ed., *How We Know: Islam and the Revival of Knowledge* (London: Grey Seal, 1989).
22. See the discussion of the work of Seyyed Hosein Nasr, cited below.
23. See Ismael Raji Al Faruqi, chapter 9.
24. These surprising figures were offered by the information service of the American Department of Defense on October 4, 2001. See Jim Garamone, "Islam Growing in America, US Military," *American Forces Services Press*, October 4, 2001. <http://www.defenselink.mil/news/Oct2001.n10042001_200110043.html>.
25. *An Introduction to Islamic Cosmological Doctrines* (Cambridge: Harvard University Press, 1964). *The Encounter of Man and Nature: The Spiritual Crisis of the Modern Man*, London: Allen and Unwin, 1968). *Knowledge and the Sacred, The Gifford Lectures*, Edinburg: Edinburg University Press, 1981). *A Young Muslim's Guide to the Modern World* (Chicago: Kazi Publication, 1993).
26. "Gender Equity in Islam: Basic Concepts and Requirements," "Muslim Woman's Dress According to the Qur'an," and "The Sunna and Islamic Ethics."

27. Conference transcribed on the website of the Al Islam Institute of Pakistan, <http:// members.tripod.com/iaislam/TSOWII.htm>.
28. See <www.jannah.org/sisters/end.html>.
29. Dounia Bouzar. *L'Islam des banlieues: Les prédicateurs musulmans, nouveaux travailleurs sociaux.* (Paris: Syros, 2001.)
30. Exiled from Egypt by Nasser in 1954, he drafted the first charter of the World Islamic League.
31. Paper delivered at the conference: "The Islam We Need" ("L'islam dont on a besoin"). JMF Centre, Le Bourget, June 30, 1997.
32. Method of Interpretation of the Revealed Text.
33. See Xavier Ternisien, *La France des mosquées,* (Paris: Albin Michel, 2004), p.238. In the course of this debate, it was rarely mentioned that Tariq Ramadan had signed declarations condemning anti-Semitism and criticizing those Muslims who fail to draw a distinction between the Israeli-Palestinian conflict and Judaism as a religion.
34. In February 2004, Tariq Ramadan was appointed Professor of Religion, Conflict and Peacebuilding at the University of Notre Dame. A visa of residence and work was originally granted to him. But on July 28, 2004 the Homeland Security Department had decided to revoke this visa. No explanation was given. Source: Genevieve Abdo, "Muslim Scholar has visa revoked", *Chicago Tribune,* August 24, 2004.
35. *New York Times,* October 19, 2001.
36. Sherman Jackson has had some particularly illuminating comments on this subject. See Sherman Jackson, "Islamic Law and its Reception in the West: A Critical Approach," talk given at Harvard University, November 12, 2002.
37. The juridical schools of Sunni Islam were created in the eighth and ninth centuries. Each bears the name of its founder. Abu Hanifa (died 767) founded the Hanafite school; Malik Ibn Anas (died 795) the Malekite school, Shafi'i (died 820), the Shafi'ite school; and Ibn Hanbal (died 855), the Hanbalite school. The founders of these four schools developed a method for interpretation based on clear and systematic principles (Usul Al Fiqh).
38. Interview with the author, February 23, 2000.
39. Margot Badran, "Understanding Islam, Islamism and Islamic Feminism," *Journal of Women's History* 13, Spring 2001, 1, 47–52.
40. Xavier Ternisien, "Un projet du Ministère de l'Intérieur pour former des imams," *Le Monde,* May 11, 2004.
41. Sophie Landrin, "La justice suspend l'expulsion de l'imam de Vénissieux," *Le Monde,* April 24, 2004.

Chapter 9

1. List borrowed from Osman Bakar, " The Intellectual Impact of American Muslim Scholars on the Muslim World," Center for Muslim-Christian Understanding, Edmund Walsh School of Foreign Service, Georgetown University, June 2003, 23p, op.cit. pp. 12–13.
2. Faisal Mawlawi, *Al-usus ash-shari'iyya lil-'alaqât bayna al-muslimîn waghayr al muslimîn* Islamic Laws Governing the Relations between Muslims and non Muslims), (Paris: UOIF, 1987).

3. See the original: "Participation in non Islamic Government," Charles Kurzman, *Liberal Islam: A Source Book* (New York, Oxford: Oxford University Press, 1998), 89–95.

4. Interview with the author, August 13, 2000, recorded in *La Medina*, no. 8, June 2001.

5. Tariq Ramadan, *To Be an European Muslim* (Leicester: Islamic Foundation, 1999), and *Western Muslims and the Future of Islam* (London: Oxford University Press, 2004). We should also mention the work of Tariq Oubrou. Currently imam in the region of Bordeaux, he came to France in the 1970s from Morocco. Associated with the UOIF (Union des Organisations Islamiques de France, discussed in chapter 8), he has worked for many years on a *Shari'a*—not a *fiqh*—specific to the minority condition. The distinction between *Shari'a* and *fiqh* is important here, as Oubrou stresses that his work is more concerned with philosophy than with jurisprudence. His most important article is "Introduction théorique à la chari'a de minorité," published in *Islam de France*, no.2, 1998, 13–27. For an updated version of this article, see "Introduction théorique a la Shari'a de la Minorité," published on the website Oumma.com, 26 May 2000, http://oumma.com/article.php3?id_article=7&var_recherche=Rechercher++Tareq+Oubrou. He recently co-authored a lively debate on freedom, women and Islam with a secular Muslim intellectual, Leila Babès, and Tareq Oubrou, *Loi d'Allah, loi des hommes—liberté, égalité et femmes en islam* (Paris: Albin Michel, 2002).

6. Abu Zayd is an Egyptian scholar who was accused of apostasy by the religious establishment in Egypt due to his liberal interpretations of Islamic law. His marriage was forcibly annulled in 1995 by the Egyptian courts. He is currently living as a refugee in the Netherlands, where he teaches at the University of Leiden.

7. Kurzman, *Liberal Islam*, 210.

8. Khaled Abou El Fadl, *And God Knows The Soldiers, The Authoritative and Authoritarian in Islamic Discourses* (Lanham: University of American Press, 2001), 134.

9. Professor of Islamic Studies at Colgate University, Safi is an Iranian who takes his inspiration from Sufi tradition. Educated in the United States from his childhood, he represents the new generation of critical deconstruction. In 2003, Safi edited the collection *Progressive Muslims, Justice, Gender and Pluralism* Oxford: One World Publication, 2003 which brought him a measure of attention.

10. "Toward a More Comprehensive and Explanatory Paradigm of Secularism," talk delivered at the University of South Florida, Tampa, Spring 1995, quoted by Tamara Sonn in a lecture at Harvard University, October 14, 2003.

11. Mahmoud Sadri and Ahmad Sadri, *Reason, Freedom and Democracy in Islam, Essential Writings of Abdolkarim Soroush* (London: Oxford University Press, 2000), 23–24. See also Valla Vakili, "Abdolkarim Soroush and Critical Discourse in Iran," in *Makers of Contemporary Islam*, ed. John L. Esposito and John O. Voll (London: Oxford University Press, 2001), 150–176.

12. In January 1985, e.g., the Nimeiri regime convicted Mahmud Muhammad Taha of apostasy and decided to publicize both the trial and his subsequent execution by hanging. A still more famous example is the Ayatollah Khomeini's February 1989 call for the murder of author Salman Rushdie.

13. Their argument is that the idea of human rights cannot be treated as a universal paradigm, as it is a product of specific historical conditions. This argument is

also used by many Muslim and African countries as a justification for refusing to ratify certain international treaties. See Jack Donnelly, "Human Rights and Human Dignity: An Analytic Critique of Non Western Conceptions of Human Rights," *American Political Science Review* 76 (1982): 306–313. Also see Adamantia Pollis and Peter Schwab, "Human Rights: A Western Construct With Limited Applicability," in *Human Rights: Cultural and Ideological Perspectives* (New York: Praeger, 1979), 1–18.

14. This term is borrowed from Heiner Bielefeldt, "Muslim Voices in the Human Rights Debate," *Human Rights Quarterly* 17, (1995): 587–617.
15. Abdullahi An-Na'im, "Islam and Human Rights beyond the Universal Debate," 96.
16. His thesis—that the Mekkan *suras* should be considered superior to the *suras* of Medina, which made the message of Islam more restrictive—earned him the hostility of the Islamic government of Sudan and led to his arrest and execution. See the foundational text of his organization, the Republican Brothers, first published in 1967: Abdullahi An-Na'im, *The Second Message of Islam* (Syracuse: Syracuse University Press, 1987).
17. See Abdullahi An-Na'im, *Toward an Islamic Reformation, Civil Liberties, Human Rights, and International Law* (Syracuse: Syracuse University Press,1990); Muhammad Al-Ashmawwy, *L'islamisme contre l'islam* (Paris: La Decouverte, 1989); Subhi Mahmasani, "Adaptation of Islamic Jurisprudence to Modern Special Needs," in *Islam in Transition: Muslim Perspectives*, ed. John J. Donohue and John L. Esposito (Oxford: Oxford University Press, 1982), 183.
18. *Madhab*: schools of jurisprudence.
19. See, e.g., the position of Jamal Badawi, described in chapter 8.
20. Kecia Ali, "Western Muslims and the Gender Issue," Harvard University, December 4, 2003.
21. Ibid.
22. Asma Barlas, *Believing Women in Islam: Unreading Patriarchal Interpretations of the Qur'an* (Austin: University Press of Texas, 2002).
23. Amina Wadud, *Qur'an and Women: Rereading the Sacred Text from a Woman's Perspective* (New York: Oxford University Press, 1999).
24. For example that of Fatima Mernissi; see especially *Sexe, idéologie, islam* (Rabat: Editions maghrébines, 1983) and *Le harem politique: le prophète et les femmes* (Paris: Albin Michel, 1987).
25. The verse in question is sura 4: 34, according to which a husband is allowed to punish his wife if she disobeys him. For commentary and analysis of the sura, see Amina Wadud, 74–75. In particular, she points out that this verse is tied to the historical circumstances of the Qu'ranic revelation, and that it in fact contradicts the essence and universal mission of the Qu'ran and the real message of the Prophet Mohammed. This thesis was also discussed in Wadud's talk "Muslim Women in the West," delivered at Harvard University, December 17, 2002.
26. See *Azizah*, <www.azizahmagazine.com>.
27. Mohammed Shafiq, *Growth of Islamic Thought in North America, Focus on Isma'il Raji al Faruqi* (Brentwood, Maryland: Amana Publications, 1994).
28. Mutazilism was a school of thought created at Basra (in what is now Iraq) during the Ummeyyade caliphate in eighth century by Wasil ibn Ata (died 748). This school was based on the idea of the absolute unity of God (*tawhid*). It maintained that the divine will was unconcerned with human activity; human activity, good and evil, was created by man according to his absolute free will.

Mutazilism was proclaimed the state religion by Caliph Ma'mun in 827, but his successor, al-Muttakawi! (847–861), rejected mutazilism and turned to the Ashrite school. Against the mutazilites the Asharite school denied the free will of human beings: according to its teachings, God has created everything, including the actions of human beings, and then gave human beings responsibility for their acts. See Paul Ballanfat, *le Petit Retz de l'islam.* (Paris: Retz, 1988), 18, 97–98.

29. Ismael Raj al-Faruqi, "Islam and Christianity: Diatribe or Dialogue?" *Journal of Ecumenical Studies* 5, 1 (1968): 45–77. *Historical Atlas of the Religions of the World,* (New York: Macmillan, 1975), 33.
30. John Esposito and John Voll, eds., *The Makers of Contemporary Islam* (Oxford, New York: Oxford University Press, 2001), 36.
31. Fathi Osman, Zalman Schachter, Gerard Sloyan and Dermot Lane, "Jesus in Jewish-Christian-Muslim Dialogue," *Journal of Ecumenical Studies* 14, 3 (Summer 1977): 448–45.
32. Leonard Grob, Riffat Hassan and Haim Gordon, eds., *Women's and Men's Liberation, Testimonies of Spirit* (New York: Greenwood Press, 1991).
33. Abudllahi An-Na'im, "Shari'a and Basic Human Rights," in Charles Kurzman, *Liberal Islam,* (New York and Oxford: Oxford University Press, 1998), 236–237.
34. *Muslim News,* 31 March 1961: 4. See also *Qu'ran, Liberation and Pluralism* (Oxford: One World, 1997).
35. Sherman Jackson, *On the Boundaries of Theological Tolerance in Islam* (Oxford: Oxford University Press, 2002).

Conclusion

1. Cf. Gerard A. Postiglione, *Ethnicity and American Social Theory* (Lanham, New York, London: University Press of America, 1983), 181–182.
2. For a recent study on this topic, see Sean McLoughlin, "Recognising Muslims: Religion, Ethnicity and Identity Politics," in *Musulmans d'Europe,* ed. Jocelyne Cesari, Cemoti, no. 33 (2002): 43–57. See also Irka-Christin Mohr, "Islamic Instruction in Germany and Austria: A Comparison of Principles Founded in Religious Thought," in Cesari, *Musulmans d'Europe,* 149–167.
3. See, e.g., the cases of Islamic mobilization in Belgium and Great Britain described by Ural Manço and Meryem Kenmaz, "De la pathologie au traitement: la gestion municipale de l'islam et des musulmans en Belgique", Sean McLoughlin, 'Recognising Muslims: Religion, Ethnicity and Identity Politics in Britain, in Cesari, J (ed), *Musulmans d'Europe,* 2002, pp. 57–58, and pp. 43–54.
4. See Chantal Saint-Blancat and Ottavia Schmidt di Friedberg in Cesari, *Musulmans d'Europe,* 91–106.
5. Leonard, *Muslims in the United States.*
6. Gabi Sheffer, "Whither the Study of Ethnic Diasporas? Some Theoretical, Definitional, Analytical and Comparative Considerations," in *The Networks of Diasporas,* ed. George Prévélakis (Paris: L'Harmattan, 1996), 37–46. Robin Cohen, *Global Diasporas: An Introduction* (Seattle: University of Washington Press, 1997). See also *La Méditerranée des réseaux,* ed. Jocelyne Cesari (Paris: Maisonneuve Larose, 2003).

7. Peter Mandaville, "Information Technology and the Changing Boundaries of European Islam," in *Paroles d'Islam, Individus, sociétés et discours dans l'islam européen contemporain*, ed. Felice Dassetto (Paris: Maisonneuve et Larose, 2000), 281–297. It would be misleading, however, to consider these electronic versions of Islam as the definitive sign of a democratized public arena. Only the correlation between these forms of discourse and the observation of religious practice in its various other contexts can support the thesis of the democratization of Islamic thought.

8. Interview with the author, January 13, 1999.

Bibliography

Abou El Fadl, K. *And God Knows The Soldiers.* The Authoritaritative and Authoritarian in Islamic Discourses Today. Lanham: University press of America, 2001.
————. "Islam and the Theology of power." *Middle East Report 221*, (Winter 2001): 6.
————. *Conference of the Books, The Search for Beauty in Islam.* New York, Lanham: University Press of America/Rowman and Littlefield, 2001.
————. *Rebellion and Violence in Islamic Law.* Cambridge: Cambridge University Press, 2001.
————. *Speaking in God's Name: Islamic Law, Authority and Women.* Oxford: Oneworld Publications, 2001.
————. ed. *The place of Tolerance in Islam.* Boston: Beacon Press, 2002.
————. ed. *Islam and the Challenge of Democracy.* Princeton: Princeton University Press, 2004.
Abu-Laban, S.M., R.B. Quershi, and E.H. Waugh, eds. *Muslim Families in North America.* Edmonton: The University of Alberta press, 1991.
Al Alwani, Taha. *Outlines of a Cultural Strategy,* IIIT, Occasional Papers Series 1, Herndon, Virginia, 1989.
Crisis in Fiqh and the Methodology of Ijtihad, IIIT, Occasional Papers Series, Herndon, Virginia, 1993.
The Islamization of Knowledge: Yesterday and Today, IIIT, Occasional Papers, Herndon, Virginia, 1995.
Missing Dimensions in Contemporary Islamic Movements, IIIT, Occasional Papers Series 1, Herndon, Virginia, 1996.
Al-Ashmawy, M.S. *L'islamisme contre l'islam.* Paris: La Découverte, 1989.
Al-Hibri, A. "Islamic Law and Muslim Women in America." In *One Nation Under God, Religion and American Culture,* edited by Marjorie Garber and Rebecca L. Walkowitz. New York and London: Routledge, 1999.
Ali, J. "Islamic Revivalism: The Case of Tablighi Jamaat." *Journal of Muslim Minority Affairs,* 23, No. 1 (April 2003), 173–181.
Ali, K. *Western Muslims and the Gender Issue.* Harvard University, December 4, 2003.
Allievi, S. *Les convertis à l'islam.* Paris: L'Harmattan, 1998.
Allievi, S. and J. Nielsen, eds. *Muslim Networks and Transnational Communities in and across Europe.* Leiden, Boston: Brill 2003.
Ally, M.M. *History of Muslims in Britain 1850-1980.* M.A. Thesis, University of Birmingham, 1981.

Al-Massiri, A. "Toward a More Comprehensive and Explanatory Paradigm of Secularism." Delivered at the University of South Florida, Tampa, 1995, quoted by Tamara Sonn in a lecture at Harvard University, October 14, 2003.

AlSayyad, N. and M. Castells, eds. *Muslim Europe or Euro-Islam, Politics, Culture and Citizenship in the Age of Globalization.* Landham, Boulder, New York, Oxford: Lexington Books, 2002.

Amiraux, V. "Expérience de l'altérité religieuse en Allemagne: Islam et Espace public." *Cahiers d'Etudes sur la Méditerranée orientale et le monde turco-iranien*, no. 33, January-June 2002, 128–146.

Anderson, B. *Imagined Communities: Reflections on the Origins and Spread of Nationalism.* New York: Verso, 1983.

Anderson, J.W. *Arabizing the Internet.* Emirates Occasional Papers, 30, 1998.

Anderson, J.W. and D.F. Eickelman, eds. *New Media in the Muslim World: The Emerging Public Sphere.* Bloomington: Indiana University Press, 1999.

An-Na'im, A. *Toward an Islamic Reformation, Civil Liberties, Human Rights, and International Law.* Syracuse: Syracuse University Press, 1990.

———. "Shari'a and Basic Human Rights." In Charles Kurzman, *Liberal Islam.* New York, Oxford: Oxford University Press, 1998, 236-237.

———. "Islam and Human Rights: Beyond the Universal Debate," American Society of International Law, *Proceedings of the 94th Annual Meeting*, (April 5–8, 2000, Washington D.C.).

Appadurai, A. *Modernity at Large: Cultural Dimensions of Globalization.* Minneapolis: University of Minnesota Press, 1996.

Asad, T. *Genealogies of Religion: Discipline and Reasons of Power in Christianity and Islam.* Baltimore: Johns Hopkins University, 1993.

———. *Formation of the Secular, Christianity, Islam and Modernity*, Stanford, Stanford University Press, 2003.

Asward, B. C. and B. Bilgé, eds. *Family and Gender Among American Muslims: Issues Facing Middle Eastern Immigrants and Their Descendants.* Philadelphia: Temple University Press, 1996.

Axford, B. *The Global System: Economics, Politics and Culture.* Cambridge: Polity Press, 1995.

Babès, L. and T. Oubrou. *Loi d'Allah, loi des hommes—liberté, égalité et femmes en islam.* Paris: Albin Michel, 2002.

Badawi, Z. "Muslim Justice in a Secular State." In *God's Law Versus State Law*, edited by Michael King. London: Grey Seal, 1995, 73–80.

Badran, M. "Understanding Islam, Islamism and Islamic Feminism." *Journal of Women's History*, Spring 2001 13, no. 1, 47–52.

Bagby, I. *Report: A Portrait of Detroit Mosques.* Clinton Township: Institute for Social Policy and Understanding, 2004.

Bagby, I., P.M. Perl, and B.T. Froehle. *The Mosque in America : A National Portrait.* Council on American-Islamic Relations, Washington D.C., 2001.

Bakar, O. "The Intellectual Impact of American Muslim Scholars on the Muslim World." Center for Muslim-Christian Understanding, Edmund Walsh School of Foreign Service, Georgetown University, June 2003.

Bakhtiar, L. *Sufi Women of America, Angels in the Making.* Chicago: The Institute of Traditional Psychoethics and Guidance, 1996, 40.

Bakhtin, M.M. *The Dialogic Imagination: Four Essays.* Austin: University Press of Texas, 1981.

Ballanfat, P. *le Petit Retz de l'islam.* Paris: Retz, 1988.

Barlas, A. "Believing Women in Islam: Unreading Patriarchal Interpretations of the Qr'an." Austin: University Press of Texas, 2002.

Bauman, Z. *Globalization: The Human Consequences.* Cambridge: Polity Press, 1998.

Beck, U. *What is Globalization?* Cambridge: Polity Press, 2000.

Betz, H.G. *Radical Right-Wing Populism in Western Europe.* New York: St. Martin's Press, 1994, 94.

Bielefeldt, H. "Muslim Voices in the Human Rights Debate." *Human Rights Quarterly,* 17, no. 4 (1995): 587–617.

Bœnder, W. "Teaching Dutch Ways to Foreign Imams, Between Government Policy and Muslim Initiative." Presentation at the conference, "European Muslims and the Secular State," Paris, La Sorbonne, June 30-July 1, 2003.

Boumedienne, H. "African Muslim Women in France." In *God's Law versus State Law,* edited by Michael King. London: Grey Seal, 1995, 49–61.

Bouzar, D. *L 'Islam des banlieues: Les prédicateurs musulmans, nouveaux travailleurs sociaux,* Paris: Syros, 2001.

Bradford, J. "Muslim Immigrants In the Wake of 9/11: A Case Study in Reactive Identity Formation," HLE-513 Harvard University, September 2003.

Brenner, E. *Les Territoires perdus de la République. Antisémitisme, racisme et sexisme en milieu scolaire.* Paris: Mille et une nuits, 2002.

Brown, D. *Rethinking Tradition in Modern Islamic Thought.* Cambridge: Cambridge University Press, 1996.

Buijs, F.J. and J. Rath. *Muslims in Europe, The State of Research.* New York: Report for the Russel Sage Foundation, 2003.

Bunt, G. *Virtually Islamic: Computer Mediated Communication and CyberIslamic Environment.* Cardiff: University of Wales Press, 2000.

———. *Islam in the Digital Age: Ejihad, Online Fatwas and CyberIslamic Environment.* London: Pluto Press, 2003.

———. Islam Interactive: Mediterranean Islamic Expression on the World Wide Web." In *Islam and the Current Islamic Reformation,* edited by Barbara Allen Robertson. London: Frank Cass, 2003, 164–186.

Burgat, F. *L'islamisme en face.* Paris: La Découverte, 1995.

Caeiro, A. "The European Council for Fatwa and Research." *Fourth Mediterranean Social and Political Research Meeting,* European University Institute, Florence, March 19–23, 2003.

Cesari, J. *Être musulman en France: Mosquees, militants et asociations.* Paris: Karthala, 1994.

——— *L'Islam en Europe.* Paris: La Documentation Française, 1995.

———. *Etre musulman en France.* Paris, Hachette, 1997.

———. *Faut-il avoir peur de l'islam?* Paris: Presses de Science Po, 1997.

———. *Musulmans et Republicains, les jeunes, l'islam et la France.* Brussels: Complexe, 1998.

Cesari, J. "European Islam: A Profile." In *Islam in Europe and in the United States, A Comparative Perspective*, edited by Shireen Hunter. Washington D.C.: Center for Strategic and International Studies, 2002, 11–15.

————, ed. *Musulmans d'Europe, Cahiers d'Etudes de la Méditerranée Orientale et du Monde Turco-Iranien*, no.33. Paris, June 2002.

————, ed. *La Méditerranée des réseaux*. Paris: Maisonneuve Larose, 2003.

————. *"Muslim Women in Western Europe*: 1945 to Present." In *Encyclopedia of Women and Islamic Cultures*, Leiden, Boston: Brill, 2003, 299–303.

————. "Muslim Minorities in the West: The Silent Revolution." In *Modernizing Islam: Religion in the Public Sphere in the Middle East and in Europe*, edited by John Esposito and Francois Burgat. New Brunswick: Rutgers University Press, 2003, 251–269.

————. *Modernisation of Islam or Islamisation of Modernity? Muslim Minorities in Europe and the Issue of Pluralism*, in Jamal *Malik (ed), Muslims in Europe, From the Margin to the Centre*, Frankfurt: Verlag editor, Frankfurt, 2004, pp.93–99.

————. *"Islam in the West: Modernity and Globalization Revisited"*, Birgit Schaebler and Leif Stenberg (ed), *Globalization and the Muslim World, Culture, Religion and Modernity*, Syracuse: Syracuse University Press, in Press, 2004, pp.80–92.

————. "Islamic Minority Rights in Europe and in the USA," in *The Legal Treatment of Islamic Minorities in Europe*, edited by Roberta Allufi B.-P. and Giovanna Zincone. Leuven: Peters, 2004, 11–29.

Chebel, M. *Le sujet en Islam*. Paris: Seuil, 2002.

Cimino, R. "Evangelical Discourse on Islam after 9/11." American Sociology of Religion Congress, Atlanta, August 15–17 2003.

Clarke, P.B., ed. *New Trends and Developments in the World of Islam*. London: Luzac Oriental, 1998.

Cohen, R. *Global Diasporas: An Introduction*. Seattle: University of Washington Press, 1997.

Community Cohesion. *A Report of the Independent Review Team*. Home Office, December 2001.

Conseil Européen de la fatwa et de la recherché. *Recueil de Fatwas*, series no. 1, Lyon: Tawhid, 2002.

Council on American Relations (CAIR). *American Muslims: One Year After 9/11*. Washington D.C., 2002.

————. *Unpatriotic Acts*. Washington D.C., 2004.

Dannin, R. *Black Pilgrimage to Islam*. New York: Oxford University Press, 2002.

Dassetto, F. *La construction de l'islam européen*. Paris: LHarmattan, 1996, 22.

Dassetto, F., B. Maréchal, and J. Nielsen. *Convergences musulmanes: Aspects contemporains de l'islam dans l'Europe élargie*. Louvain-la-Neuve: Bruylant, 2001.

Detalle, R. "L'islam en Allemagne." In *L'islam et les musulmans dans le monde*, edited by M. Arkoun, R. Leveau et B. El Jisr (Beirut: Centre Culturel Hariri), 1993, 291–306, 297.

Dokos, T.P. and D.A. Antoniou. "Islam in Greece." In *Islam, Europe's Second Religion: The New Social, Cultural and Political Landscape*, edited by S.T. Hunter. Westport: Praeger et Center for Strategic and International Studies, 2002.

Donnelly, J. "Human Rights and Human Dignity: An Analytic Critique of Non Western Conceptions of Human Rights." *American Political Science Review*, 76 (1982): 306–313.

Eickelman, D.F. "Islamic Liberalism Strikes Back." *Middle East Studies Association Bulletin*, 27, no. 2 (December 1993): 163–168.

Eickelman, D.F. and J.W. Anderson. *New Media in the Muslim World, the Emerging Public Sphere*. Bloomington: Indiana University Press, 1999.

Eickelman, D.F. and J. Pescatori. *Muslim Politics*. Princeton: Princeton University Press, 1996.

Elkholy, Abdo A. *The Arab Moslems in the United States: Religion and Assimilation*. New Haven: College and University Press, 1966.

Ergun, M. and Caner, Emir. *Unveiling Islam. An Insider Look at Muslim Life and Beliefs*. Grand Rapids: Kregel Publications, 2002.

Esack, F. *Qu'ran, Liberation and Pluralism*. Oxford: One World, 1997.

———. *On Being A Muslim: Finding a Religious Path in the World Today*. Oxford: One World, 1999.

———. *Qu'ran: A Short Introduction*. OXford: One World, 2001.

Esposito, J. *Unholy War*. New York: Oxford University Press, 2002.

Esposito, J. and J.O. Voll, eds. *Islam and Democracy*. Oxford: Oxford University Press, 1996.

———. *The Makers of Contemporary Islam*. Oxford University Press, 2001.

European Monitoring Center on Racism and Xenophobia. *Anti-Islamic Reactions in the EU after the Terrorist Acts against the USA*. Vienna, November 29, 2001.

Falk, R. *Religion and Human Global Governance*. New York: Palgrave, 2001.

Fallaci, O. *La rage et l'orgueil*. Paris: Plon, 2002.

Farouki, S.T. *A Fundamental Quest: Hizb al Tahrir and the Search for the Islamic Caliphate*. London, Grey Seal. 1996.

Faruqi, I. *Historical Atlas of the Religions of the World*. New York: Macmillan, 1958, 33.

———. "Islam and Christianity: Diatribe or Dialogue?" *Journal of Ecumenical Studies*, 5, no. 1 (1975): 45–77.

Fathi, O., Z. Schachter, G. Sloyan, and D. Lane. "Jesus in Jewish-Christian-Muslim Dialogue." *Journal of Ecumenical Studies*, 14, no. 3 (Summer 1977): 448–465.

Foblets, M.C. "Famille, Droit Familial et tribunaux en Europe." In *Convergences musulmanes, Aspects contemporains de l'islam dans l'Europe élargie*, edited by Felice Dassetto, Brigitte Maréchal, and Jorgen Nielsen. Louvain-La-Neuve: Bruylant-Academia, 2000, 77–96.

Freeland, R. "Islamic Personal Law in American Courts." Islamic Legal Studies Program, Harvard University, Fall 2000.

Gaboriau, M. "Transnational Islamic Movements: Tablighi Jamaat in Politics." *ISIM Newsletter*, July 1999.

Geisser, V. *La Nouvelle islamophobie*. Paris: Editions La Découverte, 2003.

Gerholm, T. and Y.G. Lithman, eds. *The New Islamic Presence in Western Europe*. London: Mansell, 1998.

Ghannouchi, R. "Participation in non Islamic Government." In C. Kurzman, *Liberal Islam: A source Book*. New York: Oxford University Press, 1998, 89–95.

Giddens, A. *Modernity and Self-Identity: Self and Society in the Late Modern Age.* Cambridge: Polity Press, 1991.

Glucksmann, A. *Dostoïevski à Manhattan.* Paris: Robert Laffont, 2002.

Goody, J. *Islam in Europe.* Cambridge: Policy Press. 2004.

Grob, L., H. Riffat, and G. Haim, eds. *Women's and Men's Liberation, Testimonies of spirit.* New York: Greenwood Press, 1991.

Haddad, Y.Y., ed. *The Muslims of America.* New York. Oxford: Oxford University Press, 1991.

———, ed. *Muslims in the West: From Sojourners to Citizens.* New York: Oxford University Press, 2002.

Haddad, Y.Y. and J.L. Esposito, eds. *Muslims on the Americanization Path?* New York: Oxford University Press, 2000.

Haddad, Y.Y. and A.T. Lummis, A.T. *Islamic Values in the United States: A Comparative Study.* New York: Oxford University Press, 1987.

Haddad, Y.Y. and J.I. Smith. *Mission to America: Five Islamic Sectarian Communities in North America.* Gainesville: University Press of Florida, 1993.

———, eds. *Muslim Communities in North America.* New York: State University Press, 1994.

———, eds. *Muslim Minorities in the West, Visible and Invisible.* Altamira Press Book. 2002.

Haghighat, C. *L'Amérique urbaine et l'exclusion sociale.* Paris: PUF, 1994.

Hannerz, U. *Cultural Complexity: Studies in the Social Organization of Meaning.* New York: Columbia University Press, 1992.

Haque, A., ed. *Muslims and Islamization in North America: Problems and Prospects,* Beltsville, Md.: A.S. Noordeen, 1999.

Hathout, H. *Reading the Muslim Mind.* Plainfield: American Trust Publications, 1995.

Haynal, A., M. Monar, and G. de Puymègue, eds. *Fanaticism, A Historical and Psychonalytical Study.* New York: Schocken Books, 1983.

Hermansen, M.K. "In the Garden of American Sufi Movements: Hybrids and Perennials." *In New Trends and Developments in the World of Islam,* edited by P.B. Clarke. London: Luzac Oriental Press, 1997, 155-178.

Hervieu-Léger, D. "The Transmission and Formation of Socio-Religious Identities in Modernity." *International Sociology,* 13, no. 2 (June 1998): 213-228

Hiro, D. *War Without End: The Rise of Islamist Terrorism and Global Response.* London: Routledge, 2002.

Hofert, A. and S. Armando, eds. *Between Europe and Islam.* Brussels: P.I.E Peter Lang, 2000.

Hunter, S.T., ed. *Islam: Europe's Second Religion.* Westport, Connecticut, London: Praeger, 2002.

Hussein, D., Mohammed Siddique Seddon, and Nadeem Malik. *British Muslims: Loyalty and Belonging.* Leicester: Islamic Foundation, 2003.

Institute for Jewish Policy Research. *Antisemitism World Report 1997: Germany.* 1997.

Jackson S. "Islamic Law and its Reception in the West: A Critical Approach." Talk given at Harvard University, November 12, 2002.

——. *On the Boundaries of Theological Tolerance in Islam.* Oxford: Oxford University Press, 2002.

Jonker, G. "The Mevlana Mosque in Kreutzberg-Berlin, An Unsolved Conflict." *Journal of Ethnic and Migration Studies* (forthcoming).

Karaflogka, A. "Religion Discourse and Cyberspace." *Religion,* 32, no. 4 (2002): 279–291.

Kepel, G. *Allah in the West: Islamic Movements in America and in Europe.* Stanford: Stanford California Press, 1997.

——. *Jihad: The Trail of Political Islam.* Cambridge: Harvard University Press, 2002.

Khedimellah, M. "Opposition or Incompatibility between Local and National French Muslim Leaders: The Case of Paris." Presentation at the NOCRIME (Network of Comparative Research on Islam and Muslims in Europe) conference, "Islam, Citizenship and European Integration." Paris, Université la Sorbonne, June 23–24, 2002.

Khosrokhavar, F. *Les nouveaux martyrs d'Allah.* Paris: Flammarion, 2002.

Kurzman, C. *Liberal Islam: A Sourcebook.* New York, Oxford: Oxford University Press, 1998.

Lambert, Y. and G. Michelat, eds. *Crépuscule des religions chez les jeunes? Jeunes et Religions en France.* Paris: lHarmattan, 1992.

Leonard, K.I. *The South Asian Americans.* Westport-Connecticut: Greenwood Press, 1997.

——. *Muslims in the United States, The State of Research.* New York: Russel Sage Foundation, 2003.

Lewis, B. and D. Schnapper, eds. *Muslims in Europe.* London: Pinter, 1994.

Lotfi, A. "Creating Muslim Space in the USA: Masajids and Islamic Centers." *Islam and Christian Muslim Relations,* 12, no. 2 (April 2001).

Luke, T.W. "New World Order or Neo World Orders: Power, Politics and Ideologies in Informationalizing Glocalities." In *Global Modernities,* edited by Michael Featherstone et al. London: Sage, 1995, 91-107.

Mahmasani, S. "Adaptation of Islamic Jurisprudence to Modern Special Need," In *Islam in Transition: Muslim Perspectives,* edited by John J. Donohue and John L. Esposito. Oxford: Oxford University Press, 1982.

Malhmann, M. "Religious Tolerance, Pluralist Society and the Neutrality of the State: The Federal Constitutional Court's Decision in the Headscarf Case." *German Law Journal,* 4, no. 11 (2003).

Malik, I.H. *Islam and Modernity: Muslims in Europe and the United States.* London, Sterling, Virginia: Pluto Press, 2004.

Mandaville, P. "Information Technology and the Changing Boundaries of European Islam." *Paroles d'Islam, Individus, sociétés et discours dans l'islam européen contemporain,* edited by Felice Dasetto. Paris: Maisonneuve et Larose, 2000, 281-297.

Marechal, B., S. Allievi, F. Dassetto, and J. Nielsen, eds. *Muslims in the Enlarged Europe*. Boston, Leiden: Brill, 2003.

Martin, D. *A General Theory of Secularization*. Oxford, Basil Blackwell, 1978.

Martinez-Torron, J. "The Legal Status of Islam in Spain." In *Islam and European Legal Systems*, edited by S. Ferrari and A. Bradney. Aldershot: Ashgate, 2000, 47–61.

Mawlawi, F. *Al-usus ash-shari'iyya lil-'alaqât bayna al-muslimîn waghayr al muslimîn* (Islamic Laws Governing the Relations between Muslims and non Muslims). Paris: UOIF, 1987.

Maxwell, P. "Virtual Religion in Context." *Religion*, 32, no. 4 (October 2002): 343–355.

McLoughlin, S. "Recognising Muslims: Religion, Ethnicity and Identity Politics" *Musulmans d'Europe*, edited by in Jocelyne Cesari, Cemoti, no. 33 (2002).

Mernissi, F. *Sexe, idéologie, islam*. Rabat: Editions maghrébines, 1983.

———. *Le harem politique: le prophé'te et les femmes*. Paris: Albin Michel, 1987.

Messick, B. *The Calligraphic State: Textual Domination and History in a Muslim Society*. Berkeley and Los Angeles: University of California Press, 1993, 135–51.

Meyzeaud-Garaud, M.C. "La femme face àla répudiation musulmane: analyse de la jurisprudence franqise." Presentation at the Addawa Mosque, rue de Tanger, Paris, March 6, 2004.

Modood, T. *Church, State and Religious Minorities*. London: Policy Studies Institute, 1996.

Mohr, I.C. "Islamic Instruction in Germany and Austria: A Comparison of Principles Derived from Religious Thought." In *Musulmans d'Europe*, edited by J. Cesari, Cemoti, no. 33 (2002): 149–167.

Nadwi, S.A.H.A. *Hazrat Maulana Muhammad Ilyas Aur Un Ki Dini Dawa't*. Lucknow: Tanwir, 1964.

Nasr, S.H. *An Introduction to Islamic Cosmological Doctrines*. Cambridge: Harvard University Press, 1964.

Nasr, S.H. *The Encounter of Man and Nature: The Spiritual Crisis of the Modern Man*. London: Allen and Unwin, 1968.

———. *Knowledge and the Sacred: The Gifford Lectures*. Edinburg: Edinburg University Press, 1981.

———. *A Young Muslim Guide to the Modern World*. Chicago: Kazi Publication, 1993.

Nielsen, J. *Towards a European Islam*. London: Macmillan Press, 1992.

Nonneman, G., T. Niblock, and B. Szajkowski. *Muslim Communities in the New Europe*, London: Ithaca Press, 1996.

Orsfall, S. "How Religious Organizations use the Internet: A Preliminary Inquiry." In *Religion on the Internet: Research, Prospects and Promises*, edited by J.K. Hadden and D.E. Cowan. New York: Elsevier, 2000, 153–182.

Osman, Fathi. *Concepts of the Qu'ran: A Topical Reading*. Los Angeles: MVI Publications, 1997.

———. *Muslim Women in the Family and the Society*. Kuala Lampur: SIS Forum (Malaysia) Berhad, 1996.

———. *The Children of Adam: An Islamic Perspective on Pluralism*. Washington DC: Center for Muslim and Christian Understanding, 1996.

Panafit, L. *Quand le Droit écrit l'islam, l'intégration juridique de l'islam en Europe*. Brussels: Bruylant, 1999.

Pearl, D. and W. Menski. *Muslim Family Law*. London: Sweet and Maxwell, 1998.

Pollis, A. and P. Schwab. *Human Rights: A Western Construct With Limited Applicability in Human Rights: Cultural and Ideological Perspectives*. New York: Praeger, 1976, 1–18.

Portes, A. and M. Zhou. "The New Second Generation: Segmented Assimilation and its Variants." *The Annals* 530 (November 1993).

Postiglione, G.A. *Ethnicity and American Social Theory*. Lanham, New York, London: University Press of America, 1983, 181–182.

Poulter, S. "Multiculturalism and Human Rights for Muslim Families in English Law." In *God's Law versus State Law*, edited by Michael King. London: Grey Seal, 1995, 83.

Qaradawi, Y. *Islamic Awakening, Between Rejection and Extremism*. London: Zain International, 2nd English edition, 1991.

———. *Le licite et l'illicte dans l'islam*. Paris: Al Qalam, 1992.

Ramadan, T. *To Be an European Muslim*. Leicester: Islamic Foundation, 1999.

———. *Globalisation: Muslim Resistances*. Lyon: Tawhid, 2004.

———. *Western Muslims and the Future of Islam*. Oxford: Oxford University Press, 2004.

Rath, J., and F.J. Buijs. *Muslims in Europe, The state of Research*. Report for the Russel Sage Foundation, New York, 2003.

Rath, J. R. Penninx, K. Groenendijk and A. Meyer, eds. *Western Europe and Its Islam: The Social Reaction to the Institutionalization of a "New" Religion in the Netherlands, Belgium and the United Kingdom*. Leiden, Boston, Tokyo: Brill, 2001.

Reilly, J.E., ed. *American Public Opinion and U.S. Foreign Policy 1995*. Chicago: Chicago Council on Public Relations, 1995.

Reising, R.F. "Unveiling Islam." *Christian News*, March 2003.

Robbers, G. "The Legal Status of Islam in Germany." In *Islam and European Legal Systems*, edited by Silvio Ferrari and Anthony Bradney. Aldershot: Ashgate, 2000, 147–154.

Roy, O. *L'islam mondialisé*. Paris: Seuil, 2002.

———. "Retour illusoire aux origins." *Le Monde Diplomatique*, April 2002.

Rudolph S.H. and J.P. Piscatori, eds. *Transnational Religion and Fading States*. Boulder: Westview Press, 1997.

Runnymede Trust. *Islamophobia: A Challenge for Us All*. London: Runnymede Trust, 1997.

Sadri, M. and A. Sadri. *Reason, Freedom and Democracy in Islam, Essential Writings of 'Abdolkarim Soroush*. Oxford: Oxford University Press, 2000, 23-24.

Safi, O., ed. *Progressive Muslims on Justice, Gender and Pluralism*. Oxford: Oneworld Publication, 2003.

Said, B. *A Fundamental Fear: Eurocentrism and the Emergence of Islamism*. London: Zed Books, 1997.

Saïd, E. *Orientalism*. New York: Pantheon Books, 1978 (1st ed.).

Saint-Blancat, C. and O. Schmidt di Friedberg, O. "Mobilisations laïques versus mobilisations religieuses en Italie." In edited by *Musulmans d'Europe*, Jocelyne Cesari, *Cemoti*, no. 33, (2002): 91–106.

Samad, Y. and J. Eade, eds. *Community Perception of Forced Marriages*. Bradford: Community Liaison Unit, 2002.

Sardar, Z., ed. *How We Know: Islam and the Revival of Knowledge*. London: Grey Seal, 1989.

Seligman, A. "Toleration and Religious Tradition." *Society*, 36, no. 5 (1999): 47–53.

Shadid, W.A.R. and P.S. Van Koningsveld, eds. *The Integration of Islam and Hinduism in Western Europe*. Kampen: The Netherlands, 1991.

———. *Religious Freedom and the Position of Islam in Western Europe*. Kampen: The Netherlands, 1995.

———. *Muslims in the Margin: Political Responses to the Presence of Islam in Western Europe*. Kampen: The Netherlands, 1996.

Shafiq, M. *Growth of Islamic Thought in North America, Focus on Isma'il Raji al Faruqi*. Brentwood. Maryland: Amana Publications, 1994.

Shahrour, M. *Dirassat Islamiya Mu açira Fi ad-Dawla wa al-Mujiama'* (Contemporary Islamic Studies on Government and Society). Damascus: Al-Ahali,, 1994.

Sheffer, G. "Whither the Study of Ethnic Diasporas? Some Theoretical, Definitional, Analytical and Comparative Considerations." In *The Networks of Diasporas*, edited by George Prévélakis. Paris: lHarmattan, 1996, 37–46.

Sikand, Y. "Women and the Tablighi Jamàat." *Islam and Christian-Muslim Relations*, 10, no.1 (1999): 41–52.

Sinno, A. *Deutsche Interessen in Palestina 1841-1898*. Berlin: Baalbeek, 1982.

Smith, J. *Islam in America*. New York: Columbia University Press, 1999.

Smith, T.W. *Estimating The Muslim Population in the United States*. New York: The American Jewish Committee, October 2001.

Starrett, G. "Muslim Identities and the Great Chain of Buying." In *New Media in the Muslim World, The Emerging Public Sphere*, edited by Dale F. Eickelman and Jon W. Anderson. Bloomington: Indiana University Press, 1999, 577–579.

Stern, J. *Terror in the Name of God, Why Religious Militants Kill*. New York: Ecco, 2003.

Taha, M. *The Second Message of Islam*. Syracuse: Syracuse University Press, 1987 (1st ed. 1967).

Ternisien, X. *La France des mosquees*. Paris: Albin Michel, 2002.

Thompson, J.B. *The Media and Modernity: A Social Theory of Media*. Stanford: Stanford University Press, 1995.

Torfs, R. "The Legal Status of Islam in Belgium." In *Islam and European Legal Systems*, edited by Silvio Ferrari and Anthony Bradney. Aldershot: Ashgate, 2000, 73–95.

Bibliography • 257

Tsitselikis, K. "Personal Status of Greece's Muslims: A Legal Anachronism or an Example of Applied Multiculturalism?" Presentation at the colloquium, "The Legal Treatment of Islamic Minorities in Europe and in the United States," Turin. June 19–21, 2003.

Turner, B.S. Islam, Postmodernism and Globalization. London: Routledge, 1994.

Turner, R.B. Islam in the African-American Experience. Indianapolis: Indiana University Press, 1997.

U.S. Department of State Annual Report on International Religious Freedom for 1999: The Netherlands. Washington, D.C.: Bureau for Democracy, Human Rights, and Labor, September 9, 1999.

U.S. Department of State. Germany Country Report on Human Rights Practices. 1998.

Vakili, V. "Abdolkarim Soroush and Critical Discourse in Iran." In Makers of Contemporary Islam, edited by John. L Esposito and John O. Voll. Oxford: Oxford University Press, 2001, 150–176.

Vertovec, S. "Accommodating Religious Pluralism in Britain: South Asian Religions." In Multicultural Policies and the State, A Comparison of Two Europen Societies, edited by Marco Martiniello. Utrecht: Ercomer, 1998, 163–177.

Vertovec, S. and C. Peach, eds. Islam in Europe, The Politics of Religion and Community. Basingstoke: McMillan, 1997.

Vertovec, S. and Rogers, A. eds. Muslim European Youth, Reproducing Ethnicity, Religion, Culture. London: Ashgate, 1998.

Wadud, A. Qur'an and Women: Rereading the Sacred Text from a Woman's Perspective. New York: Oxford University Press, 1999.

———. "Muslim Women in the West." Conference, Harvard University, December 17, 2002.

Weil, P. La France et ses immigrés. Paris: Calmann-Lévy, 1991.

Werbner, P. Imagined Diasporas Among Manchester Muslims: The Public Performance of Pakistani Transnational Identity Politics. Oxford: James Currey; Santa Fe School of American Research Press, 2002.

———. Pilgrims of Love: The Anthropology of a Global Sufi Cult. Bloomington: Indiana University Press, 2003.

Werbner, P. and T. Modood. Debating Cultural Hybridity: Multicultural Identities and the Politics of Anti-Racism. London: Zed Books, 1997.

Wilson, W.J. The Truly Disadvantaged, The Inner City, the Underclass, and Public Policy. Chicago: The University of Chicago Press, 1987

Wolfe, M., ed. Taking Back Islam. Rodale Ince & Belief Net, 2002.

X, Malcolm. "Black Man History." In The End of White World Supremacy: Four Speeches by Malcolm X, edited by Imam Benjamin Karim. New York: Merlin House/Seaver Books, 1971.

Yang, F. and H.R. Ebaugh. "Transformations in New Immigrant Religions and their Global Implications." American Sociological Review, 66 (April 2001): 269–288.

Zoba, W.M. "Islam USA." Christianity Today, 44, no. 4,3 (April 2001): 40–50.

Newspaper and World Wide Web Articles

Abdo,G. "Muslim Scholar has visa revoked", *Chicago Tribune*, August 24, 2004.

"Anti Islam Gen Under Fire", *New York Post*, May 12, 2004. http://www.nypost. com/news/worldnews/20687.htm

"Anti-Semitism Worldwide," *The Stephen Roth Institute for the Study of Contemporary Antisemitism and Racism*, Tel Aviv University, 1997. <www.tau.ac.il/ Anti-Semitism/asw97-8/united-kingdom.html>.

"Antisemitism and Xenophobia Today," 1996. <http://www.axt.org.uk/antisem/ archvel/uk/uk.html>.

Baaz, I. <www.fatwa-online.com/fataawa/innovation/celebrations/cel003/9991018_ 11.htm>.

Bamba A. "La formation des imams, le nouveau défi de lislam en France." June 12, 2003. http://www.Saphirnet.info/article_646.html.

Beliefnet and the Ethics and Public Policy Center. "Evangelical Views of Islam." *Beliefnet*, <www.beliefnet.com/story/124/story_12447.html>.

Bentounes, Cheikh. Interview on http://saphirnet.information/article_649.html, 4 June 2003.

Beucker, P. "Milli Göü, lislamisme loin du Bosphore." *Courier International*, no. 586, January 24, 2002.

Casciani, D. *Muslims in the UK: Pride and Fear, BBC news*, September 10, 2002.

Chaplains for International Students in the Netherlands. *Religion in the Netherlands*. <http://www.geocities.com/Athens/Olympus/8858>.

"Consulate backs down on Passport Photo." *Chicago Tribune*, December 4, 2000.

Dubin, M. "Islam Expert Suddenly in the Spotlight", *Philadelphia Inquirer*, November 29, 2001.

Eggen, D. "Alleged Remarks on Islam Prompt an Ashcroft Reply." *Washington Post*, February 14, 2002.

Felder, Y. "Profils Islamiques radicaux: Londres-Abou Hamza Al-Masri," *The Middle East Media & Research Institute*, October 16, 2001. <http://www.desinfos. com/memri/memri/memri_profilsislamiques.html>.

Galifianikis, N. "U.S. Muslim Population Grows." *Rockland Journal News*, February 10, 1994.

Garamone, J. "Islam Growing in America, US Military," *American Forces Services Press*, 4 October 2001. <http://www.defenselink.mil/news/ Oct2001. nl0042001_ 200110043.html>.

Gautier, A. "Jean-Pierre Raffarin charge le Conseil franqis du culte musulman dùn rłe modérateur auprés des jeunes." *Le Monde*, May 6, 2003.

Ghazali, A.S. "There may not be a Muslim bloc vote this time but..," *American Muslim Perspective*, http://www.amperspective.com/html/there mav_not be.html. August 12, 2004.

Gul, H. "Jews Attack the WTC." *Outlook India Magazine*, 1 October 2001, <http:// www.outlookindia.com/full.asp?fname+Cover+Story&fodname+20011001 &sid+3>.

"How Emily became Muslim", http://www.islam-qa-com/words/how_emily_ became_muslim.shtml>.

"Islamic School Ruled Out." *Oxfordshire*, May 22, 2004.

"Islamic Teachings to be Allowed in German Schools." *IPS*, February 29, 2000.

Jan, A.U. « The Choice Between the Burka and the Bikini," www.allaahuakbar.net/ womens/dioice_between_burqa_and_bikini.htm>.

Kaufman, R.P. "Pipes Helps U.S. Identifies the Enemy", *Insight on the News*, April 15, 2002.

Krishnan, M. "Anti-Muslim Feelings Plague Bradford." *The Rediff Special.* <http://www.rediff.com/news/dec/20brad.htm>.

Landrin, S. "La justice suspend l'expulsion de l'imam de Vénissieux." *Le Monde*, April 24, 2004.

"Learing about Mohammed and the Koran in German." *Deutsche Welle*, August 19, 2003. <http://www.dw-world.de/dwelle/cda/detal>.

Lee, F.R. "A Sketch of Arab-Americans: Survey Touches Off Disputes Over Who Should Study Whom." *New York Times*, 15 November 2003.

"New Scrutiny for Islamic Schools Plan." *Lancashire News*, December 12, 2001.

Oubrou, T. "Introduction théorique a la Sharià de la Minorité." *Oumma.com*, May 26, 2000. <http://oumma.corn/article.php3?id_article = 7&var_recherche = Rechercher + + Tareq+ Oubrou>.

Pipes, D. "What Bush Got Right-and Wrong," *Jerusalem Post*, September 26, 2001.

———. "We're Going to Conquer America", *New York Post*, November 12, 2001.

"Our Mosques Abroad and Our Image." *Daily Times*, August 12, 2003. <http://www.dailytimes.com.pk/default.asp?page-story_12-8—2003_pg3_1>.

"Poll: Muslims voters favors Kerry, Nader", http://www.cair-net.org, June 29, 2004.

Phainikar, S. "Learning about Mohammed and the Koran in German." *Deutsche Welle*, August 19, 2003, <http://www.dw-world.de/dwelle/cda/detail>.

———. "When Faith is More Important than School." *Deutsche Welle*, April 23, 2004, <http://www.dw-world.de/dwelle/cda/detail>.

Shalal-Esa, A. "General who Made Anti-Islam remark tied to Pow case" *Reuters*, May, 11, 2004. http://www.reuters.com/newsArticle.jhtml?type = topNews&storyID = 5109973

Schwartz, P. "The Debate over a Defining German Culture? The Christian Democrats March to the Right." *World Socialist Website*, November 25, 2000, <www.wsws.org/articles/2000/nov2000/cult-n25.shtml>.

Quraishi, A. and N. Syeed-Miller. "No Altars: A Survey of Islamic Family Law in the United States." <http://els4.law.emory.edu/ifl/cases/USA.html>.

Ternisien, X. "Islam: création du Conseil françis du culte musulman." <http://www.premier-ministre.gouv.fr>. February 24, 2003.

———. "4032 délégués dans toute la France." *Le Monde*, April 5, 2003.

———. "Islam de France: dernièe étape des élections du CFCM." <http://www .premier-ministre.gouv>. April 14, 2003.

———. "Défaite de la Mosquée de Paris au scrutin poru le Conseil musulman." *Le Monde*, April 15, 2003.

———. "Le premier Conseil français du culte musulman élit son bureau." *Le Monde*, May 4, 2003.

———. "Un project du Ministère de l'Intérieur pour former des imams." *Le Monde*, May 11, 2004.

———. "Les élites musulmanes à la recherche d'une représentation laïque." *Le Monde*, May 21, 2003.

———. "La formation des imams, le nouveau défi de l'islam français." *Le Monde*, July 1, 2003.

Terry, D. "A Leap of Faith." *Chicago Tribune Magazine*, 20 October 2002.

"US Army Chaplain Questions Duty, Captain Gets Mixed Signals from Foreign Islamic leaders." *Al-Sharq Al Awsat*, October 30, 2001, <http:www.worldnetdaily.com/news/article.asp?ARTICLE_ID = 25230>.

"U.S. General Violated Rules with 'Satan' Speeches." http://www.reuters.com/newsArticle.jhtml?type = topNews&storyID = 6013543, August 19, 2004.

World Wide Web Sites

www.ahmadiyya.com
www.al.fatiha.org
www.albalagh.net
www.askijerrahi.com
www.Assabyle.com
www.azizahmagazine.com
www.cair-net.org
www.familiesonline.co.uk
www.fatwa-online.com
www.freeminds.org/women/scarf.htm
http://www.gayegypt.com
www.ijtihad.org
http://www.islamicity.eom/mosque/quran/4.htm
www.Islam-Online.net/livefatwa/English
www.islam-qa.com
www.islamic-sharia.co.uk/whoitrepresent.html
www.almuhajirun.com/leaflets/Html/disease/7"%20Sins.htm
www.almuhajirun.com/leaflets/Html/Disease/Child%20n%20safe.htm
www.almuhajirun.com/leaflets/Html/Disease/Interfaith.htm
www.almuhajiroun.com/fatwas/16-09 °2001 b.php
www.isna.com
www.jerrahi.org
www.lailatalqadr.com
www.legifrance.gouv.fr

www.masnet.org/askimam_runsess.aspd = 8
www.saudinf.com
www.statistics.gov.uk/census2001
http://fr.groups.yahoo.com/group/suffrage-universel/message/2240
www.universalsufism.com

Index

Printed in the United States
37809LVS00001B/13-105